Hollywood's Film Wars with France

Hollywood's Film Wars with France

Film-Trade Diplomacy

and the Emergence of the French Film Quota Policy

Jens Ulff-Møller

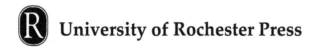 University of Rochester Press

First published 2001
Transferred to digital printing 2017

University of Rochester Press
668 Mt. Hope Avenue, Rochester, NY 14620, USA
www.urpress.com
and Boydell & Brewer Limited
PO Box 9, Woodbridge, Suffolk IP12 3DF, UK
www.boydellandbrewer.com

ISBN: 978-1-58046-086-6

Library of Congress Cataloging-in-Publication Data

Ulff-Møller, Jens
    Hollywood's "film wars" with France: film-trade diplomacy and the
    emergence of the French film quota policy / Jens Ulff-Møller
       p. cm.
    Includes bibliographical references and index.
    ISBN 1-58046-086-0 (alk. paper)
       1. Motion pictures, American—France. 2. Motion picture industry—
    Economic aspects—France. 3. Motion picture industry—Government
    policy—France. I. Title.

    PN1993.5.U6 U15 2001
    384'.83'0973—dc21
                                                            2001017109

A catalogue record for this title is available from the British Library.

Designed and typeset by Gretchen Koessler.
Cover design by Bonnie Coen.
Cover image: Will H. Hays aboard the *Lusitania*, March 1928. Courtesy of the
office of Will H. Hays Jr., Crawfordsville, Indiana.

Contents

Figures

Tables

Illustrations

Abbreviations

CP   Division of Commercial Policy, State Department.

ITP   Division of International Trade Policy, State Department.

MPAA   Motion Picture Association of America, New York and Washington, DC, 1945- . Presidents: Eric Johnston, later Jack Valenti.

MPEAA   Motion Picture Export Association of America (see MPAA).

MPPC   Motion Picture Patents Company.

MPPDA   Motion Picture Producers and Distributors of America. New York, 1922-1945. President, Will H. Hays.

SIMPP   Society of Independent Motion Picture Producers.

USCP   United States, Consulate Paris. Record Group 84, National Archives, College Park, MD.

USDS   United States, Department of State. Record Group 59, National Archives, College Park, MD. See bibliography.

USDC   United States, Department of Commerce. Record Group 151, National Archives, College Park, MD.

USEF   United States, Embassy France. Paris. Record Group 84, National Archives, College Park, MD.

Acknowledgments

My study of Franco-American film diplomacy began in 1993 in the National Archives in Washington. While surveying documents on Danish cinema, I found endless numbers of documents concerning French cinema, containing far more information than could be found in France. This book would not have been possible without the kind assistance of the staff of the textual branch at the National Archives. I would also like to express my gratitude to the following archives and libraries: the Will Hays collection at the Indiana State Archives; Les Archives Nationales, Paris; the Danish Film Archive; the Quigley collections at the Georgetown University Library; and the Herbert Hoover Archive.

I am also grateful to the Brandeis University Library; the library of the Federal Trade Commission; the New York Public Library; the Amherst College Library for giving access to the Will Hays Papers microfilms; the Margaret Herrick Library and the UCLA libraries; the libraries at Harvard University; the Knight Library, University of Oregon; the Library of Congress; la Bibliothèque Nationale and the BiFi in Paris.

I am especially grateful to Will H. Hays, Jr. and Louise Ripple for providing information about Will H. Hays and Fredrick L. Herron; to Richard Maltby and Ruth Vasey, Pierre Sorlin, Jean-Pierre Jeancolas, and Jacques Portes for constructive criticism and friendly discussions, and to Merav Gold, Andrea Kirsch, and Gary Hewitt (LCC) for correcting my text. I also want to thank Søren Stevns, the Media Desk Copenhagen, for constructive discussions of European film policy, and Susan Mango, Michel & Barbara Haggh-Huglo for their hospitality.

I appreciate the positive support of Professor Karsten Fledelius, Institute of Film & Media Studies, the University of Copenhagen, and my dissertation committee, Professors Paul Jankowski, Morton Keller, and Anthony Polonsky, Department of Comparative History, Brandeis University.

Most of all, I am grateful to my wife Susan Boynton, for her unfailing support and assistance, as well as that of my parents-in-law, Alice and Stuart, who have for years constructively read my research.

This research has been supported by grants from Brandeis University, the Danish Forskerakademi, and the Danish Humanistic Research Council.

The author would appreciate to receive comments and questions by e-mail: Ulff@hotmail.com or Ulff@hum.ku.dk

Introduction

Foreign revenues now make up 42% of Hollywood's take....
We are the grand jewel in America's trade crown. We contribute more to the U.S. economy than automotive or aircraft or
apparel or chemicals.
—Jack Valenti, Forbes, December 1, 1997.

It cannot be denied that American films are popular abroad. Indeed, as Jack
Valenti recently noted in *Forbes*, revenues from foreign sales of American
film now account for 42% of Hollywood's total income. He explains the
American global domination of the film industry by simple consumer preference. "The public ought to decide.... We dominate world screens—not
because of armies, bayonets, or nuclear bombs, but because what we are
exhibiting on foreign screens [is what] the people of those countries want to
see."[1] However, this book will show that Hollywood did not rely on the
popularity of its movies to secure its worldwide dominance, but on monopolistic trade practices and the power of the United States government—
primarily through extensive collaboration with the State Department—to
coerce foreign governments into abandoning the effectively similar import
restrictions on Hollywood films that were privately applied to European
films imported into the U.S. There were, to be sure, important factors within
the European film industry that facilitated the imbalance that persists even
today. Nonetheless, as this book will make clear, neither the French view of
cinema as merely the production of art films nor the American concept of
the movie as cultural export commodity subject to "normal" economic laws
of supply and demand can bear close scrutiny as an explanation. Ultimately,
the conclusion that Hollywood's film dominance has been the product of
economic and political maneuvering on a Machiavellian scale is inescapable.

In order to arrive at a more complete understanding of Hollywood's
global film dominance, an appreciation of four major contributing factors is
necessary. To begin with, it is critical to recognize the structural differences
in how monopolistic practices developed in France compared to those in
the U.S. during the late nineteenth and early twentieth centuries. Of particular interest is the way Hollywood was able to skirt United States antitrust laws to set up strong vertically integrated industry organizations which
functioned as an oligarchy. Lack of effective vertical integration in the French
industry, by contrast, provided a serious structural handicap in its attempt
to compete with American film production. A second and hitherto less understood factor involves historical differences in how cinema law was applied more restrictively in France than in the United States.

Third, it must be taken into account that American export trade policy and legislation was much more aggressive in the early post-World War I era. The United States was in a much better position than France and other European countries to take advantage of the new opportunities that the postwar period provided for exports. The politicians took advantage of the chances offered by expanding the diplomatic service of the United States, offering extensive service to exporters—not least to Hollywood. Moreover, following the important passage through Congress of the Webb-Pomerene export trade association act (1918), which gave a legal shield to anticompetitive activity abroad, the Republican administrations of the 1920s identified trade export as their major foreign policy focus in defining relationships with other countries.

The fourth and final essential factor in understanding Hollywood's film hegemony involves differences in U.S. and French diplomacy efforts to support their respective industries. French diplomatic support consisted primarily of introducing protectionist measures, while the U.S. government worked to promote the export of Hollywood films by actively undercutting French foreign film policy as well as serving as a critical intelligence source for the U.S. film industry. In short, the U.S. government acted as a virtual partner in trade negotiations with Hollywood's trade association, the Motion Picture Producers and Distributors of America (MPPDA, which in 1945 was renamed the Motion Picture Association of America, MPAA).

Previous examinations of film history have considered the first three factors in varying degrees of thoroughness. Good analyses of monopolistic trade practices in the film industry and the emergence of Hollywood's dominance have been completed in the last twenty years (Guback 1985, Jeancolas 1992, Portes 1997, Thompson 1985, Jarvie 1992, Higson & Maltby 1999). Moreover, French scholars have looked separately at French cinema law (e.g., Leglise 1970) but did not consider the consequences of the laws on the competitiveness of French cinema in the global film market. The importance of American export trade legislation, in particular the Webb-Pomerene Act, has gone largely unnoticed by most scholars.

Regarding the fourth factor, even less effort has been made to highlight the differences between French and American diplomatic efforts to promote their respective film industries. This missing information is critical for a full understanding of the present global film imbalance, represented by the Franco-American situation. Through an exhaustive examination of previously unutilized government and industry archival documents (see bibliography), this book traces that key diplomatic history between the two countries, while also contextualizing and connecting the more isolated aspects of monopoly, cinema law, and trade legislation as they pertain to the development of the film industry.

Hollywood's worldwide control over the market for movies means that around half of the films shown in the world are American, even though less than 10% of the world's annual production of movies are produced in the United States. American receipts are also larger than those of any other country, reflecting the largest share of global screen time too. The largest European film companies, in fact, are not European, but American.[2] At present, Hollywood holds a market share of around 80% in Europe: for every dollar worth of film Europe exports to the U.S., Hollywood exports fifteen hundred dollars to Europe. By contrast foreign films now represent roughly one quarter of one percent of the American market, down from 10% in the mid 1970s.[3]

The success of American film export is the result of a long development. Hollywood first obtained a dominant position in Europe after World War I (1914–1918) by dumping hundreds of films—whose production costs had already been recouped in the U.S.—at very low prices into the market. Before the war French, Italian, German, English, and Danish film producers dominated the world market for motion pictures. While European film production dwindled as a result of the war, American film production continued uninterrupted by the warfare. As a consequence, American films quickly displaced European films. Hollywood's ascendance thus occurred simultaneously with the emergence of the United States as an international superpower.

In the 1920s the American film industry consolidated into a studio system that may be best described as an oligopoly. Each of the major Hollywood companies arrived at its dominant position by integrating all three aspects of the motion picture business—production, distribution, and exhibition of films. The eight "majors" in the 1920s were Warner Brothers, Paramount Pictures Inc.–Loew's Inc., Twentieth Century-Fox, MGM, RKO, Columbia Pictures Inc., Universal Corporation, and United Artists. The first five of these were fully vertically integrated, as they also distributed and exhibited films, whereas Columbia and Universal engaged only in production and distribution. United Artists was a special case, as it was only a distribution company until 1941.[4] Five large vertically integrated companies, the "Big Five," dominated it: Paramount-Loew's Inc., MGM, Twentieth Century-Fox, Warner Brothers, and RKO. They were the largest producers, but their predominance came first from their control of film distribution and, most importantly, from their control over more than seventy percent of first-run movie houses. They also exhibited the films of the "Little Three": Columbia, Universal, and United Artists.[5]

Although American film companies are often collectively identified as "Hollywood," the decision-making center of the industry remained in New York even after film production moved to the studios in California in the 1910s. The midtown Manhattan[6] corporate offices provided ideal opportunity for collusion while also facilitating collaboration and communication with the federal government through Hollywood's trade association, the Motion Picture Producers and Distributors of America (MPPDA).

It was the MPPDA, in fact, led by its president, Will H. Hays, from 1922 to 1945, rather than the individual companies that handled the industry's foreign policy.[7] The American film companies established their foreign policy in almost daily meetings of export directors in the foreign department, headed by Will Hays's brother-in-law, Frederick L. Herron.[8] The archive of MPPDA's foreign office has never been available to researchers. Only Will Hays's personal archive and a few microfilms are accessible.[9]

The close relationship existing between business and political institutions has never been fully comprehended. It has been a popular misconception that state and industry had a generally antagonistic relationship, since government has had the role of regulating anticompetitive measures within the industry in order to serve the general welfare of consumers. The 1920s has generally been seen as the declining years of laissez-faire capitalism, in which "big business" had its last profligate fling before being reined in by the discipline of the New Deal, which is regarded as a major turning point in government-business relations.[10]

In reality, government regulation has often proved most ineffective, merely serving the corporate economic interests of those businesses that were being regulated. The MPPDA thus maintained close relations with the Department of State and American embassies, cooperation that was important for the expanding interests of these companies. Even when the Justice Department and the Federal Trade Commission examined Hollywood's monopolistic trade practices, the MPPDA received unrestricted support from the State Department and the diplomatic system, including the presidents of the United States. (The personnel of the diplomatic service of the United States and French politicians are presented in appendix C).

Hollywood would have the world believe that its success in exports is quality based. This "explanation" implies that the aesthetic quality of foreign films, reflected by their abysmal market share in the United States of a quarter of a percent, can no longer even pretend to measure up to Hollywood's "high standards"—an absurd notion. Furthermore, we are persuaded to consider the massive diplomatic support to Hollywood inconsequential. In fact, the dominance of American films has very little to do with aesthetics and consumer preference and a great deal to do with politics and greed. That this view is closer to the truth is confirmed by a statement by the current director of the MPAA, Jack Valenti, that anticompetitive measures have been vital for the success of American film exports.[11]

France is the country that, more than any other, has resented the encroachments of American culture. To outsiders, the French preoccupation with its culture may appear unduly nationalistic if not narcissistic. The French sensitivity to Hollywood should, however, be understood as stemming from the persistent pressure of United States diplomacy, forcing France to accept unrestricted importation of Hollywood films, while simultaneously being obliged to accept the American argument for not showing more French films—their alleged inferior quality and unpopularity with American spectators.

In order to counter Hollywood's expansion, France introduced a quota policy in 1928 to limit the number of films imported into France. The Blum-Burnes agreement of 1946 changed the numerical quota into a screen quota, reserving four weeks per quarter of the year for the screening of French films. The French quota policy has been the basis of the current European Union media policy, even though the quota policy has proved to have little effect. The reason is that numerical quotas are deceptive, as they are based on the false assumption that all films have equal attendance. Recent films, such as *ET* and *Titanic*, demonstrate, however, that spectators go to see specific films, with the result that even a single film may have the ability to saturate the market.

This book aims to show how Hollywood has upheld its dominant position in France by using monopolistic trade practices and diplomatic pressure, as well as to show the inefficiency of French quota policies. Hollywood's position must be considered the result of manipulations of the international political economy involving the interplay of economics and politics in the world arena.[12]

---

[1] Testimony by Jack Valenti, President of the Motion Picture Association of America, and Motion Picture Export Association in *International Communications and Information*. Hearings before the Subcommittee on International Operations, Committee on Foreign Relations, United States Senate, 95th Congress, 1st Session, 1977 (Washington, DC: GPO, 1977), pp. 211-12.

[2] Thomas Guback, "Non-Market Factors in the International Distribution of American Films" in Bruce A. Austin, *Current Research in Film* 1 (1985), p: 111; Thomas Guback, "Cultural Identity and Film in the European Economic Community," in *Cinema Journal* 14:1 (Fall, 1974): 3.

[3] David Barsamian, "Monopolies, NPR, & PBS: An interview with Robert McChesney," in *Z Magazine* (Feb. 2000): 41.

[4] Mae D. Huettig, *Economic Control of the Motion Picture Industry* (Philadelphia, 1944), p. 1.

[5] Richard Maltby, "The Political Economy of Hollywood: the Studio System," in Philip Davies and Brian Neve, *Cinema, Politics and Society in America* (Manchester, IL, 1981), p. 43–44; Tino Balio, "A Mature Oligopoly," in *The American Film Industry* (Madison, WI, 1976), p. 213.

[6] The major Hollywood companies had New York addresses around 1930 as follows:
F B O Pictures, 1560 Broadway.
First National Pictures, 383 Madison Ave.
Fox Film Corporation, 850 Tenth Ave.
Metro-Goldwyn-Meyer, 1540 Broadway.
Paramount Famous Lasky, 1501 Broadway.
Pathe Exchange, 35 West 45th St.
United Artists, 729 Seventh Ave.
Universal Pictures, 730 Fifth Ave.
Vitagraph, Warner Bros., 321 West 44th St.
Motion Picture Producers and Distributors of America, 469 Fifth Ave. (26 West 44th St. from 1931).

[7] Will H. Hays was born in Sullivan, Indiana in 1879, and died in 1954. He had a BA from Wabash College and MA from Mount Union College. He was admitted to the bar in 1900, and became city attorney in Sullivan, 1910–13. His political career in the Republican party led him to the chairmanship of the Republican National Committee (1918–1921) and Postmaster General in Harding's cabinet (1921–22). As president of the MPPDA (1922–45) Hays has become known for the "Hays Code," which outlawed offensive topics from American films, even though his main role was to promote the American film industry in general. In retirement Hays served as special adviser to the MPAA, using his considerable influence in support of the anti-Communist investigations in the 1950s. Liz-Anne Bawden (ed.), *The Oxford Companion to Film* (Oxford, 1976), p. 324, 481; Will Hays's curriculum vitae from 1927 in *Will Hays Papers* (see n.9 below).

[8] Herron and Hays became friends at Wabash College, Crawfordsville, Indiana. Will Hays married Herron's sister Jessie Stutesman on Thanksgiving 1930 in Washington, DC, in the home of her brother, General Charles D. Herron (he was the commander of Pearl Harbor, Hawaii, and was relieved shortly before the Japanese attack). Source of information: personal communication with Herron's niece, Louise Ripple.

[9] This book makes use of MPPDA materials from the Will Hays president's archive published by Douglas Gomery on seventy-eight microfilms with an introduction, *The Will Hays Papers: a Guide to the Microfilm Edition of the Will Hays Papers* (Frederick, MD, 1986); and the photographs and newspaper clippings of the Will Hays collection, Indiana State Archive. The few microfilms the MPPDA has donated to Richard Maltby and the Margaret Herrick Library, Los Angeles.

[10] Butler Shaffer, *In Restraint of Trade: The Business Campaign Against Competition, 1918–1938* (Lewisburg, PA, 1997), p. 13–15. See also: Ellis W. Hawley, *The New Deal and the Problem of Monopoly* (New York, 1966, 1995).

[11] Jack Valenti, "Webb-Pomerene: The Great U.S. Ally in the Battle for World Trade: Delivered before the First National Conference on Export Trading Companies, Sponsored by U.S. Chamber of Commerce, Washington, DC, September 30, 1980," in *Vital Speeches of the Day*, vol. 47, no. 1 (October 15, 1980), p. 26–28.

[12] Jeffry A. Frieden and David A. Lake, *International Political Economy* (New York, 1995), p. 1.

Part One

Structural Differences

1

Development of Monopolies and
Monopolistic Trade Practices

The hegemonic position of American film industry has been significantly determined by structural differences between the French and the American markets that emerged very early in the development of the film industry. Whereas the history of the movie deals with art, the history of the film industry is one of monopoly. Integration and monopolization is an intricate part of the film industry. The French film historian Georges Sadoul explains the American hegemony as a result of film exhibition being much more developed in the United States, which had powerful associations of producers, distributors, and exhibitors. The failure of European attempts at monopolization was a result of essential structural differences between the European and American markets.[1] This section aims at examining how those structural differences emerged.

Like most other commercial sectors, the film industry has a tripartite structure, being subdivided into production, distribution, and exhibition. Producers have a strong incentive to create vertical integration of the three parts, absorbing distribution companies and establishing cinema chains in order to eliminate competition. American film manufacturing should be regarded as industrial production in a modern, highly developed capitalist society in which large, vertically integrated, monopolistic companies dominate production. In contrast, European production is petty industry, with little vertical integration.

The legislature has often prohibited monopolization stemming from both vertical and horizontal integration through antitrust laws, such as the Sherman Antitrust Law, but these laws were rarely enforced against the American movie industry.

Cinema as Commerce: Background Principles and History

The commercial laws that govern business in general also apply to the film industry. Films are in themselves typical examples of a mass-produced commodity, fully accommodating the principles within modern business. The distribution of films—from the producer to the consumer—does not in principle differ from the distribution of other commodities. Production of cameras, raw film, and other technical equipment falls outside this definition of the movie industry.

Vertical integration in the film industry has been enhanced by monopolistic qualities inherent in the movie product. Even though motion pictures are commercial products like any other, they differ from other kinds of commodities in having inherent artistic and monopolistic qualities. The movie commodity is peculiar because what is sold is an artistic and intangible "product." Spectators buy an "experience," not a product. In this respect movies do not differ from other artistic areas. There are entrance fees to concerts, theater performances, and exhibits, and books have a monetary as well as an artistic value. The movie product differs from these artistic areas in being a mass-produced commodity which, as a movie performance, can be repeated an endless number of times. As a consequence, the film industry is more prone to the establishment of cartels and trusts than other industries.

The commercial aspect is, however, much more predominant within the film industry than within other art forms, primarily because film production is extremely costly and demands investors willing to take a high risk to produce a film. A film director is able to produce his film only if he can find a producer willing to invest capital in the project. Consequently, the producer is in control of what the final product will look like. A publisher or a theater director does not have the same power over an author's product that a film producer has over the product of a film director.

Another peculiarity of films is that initial production costs are extremely high, while it is inexpensive to make copies. Therefore, a producer who controls a huge market has a strong competitive advantage. Because the initial high costs can be divided among a larger number of customers, prices can then be lowered, stifling competition. While film producers can create an unlimited number of films, cinemas can show only a very limited number. As a result, film producers have strong incentives to create vertical integration by obtaining control over movie houses and their programming.

Owning film exchanges and movie houses is not the only way a producer may control the marketing of the company's films. American film companies with many films in rental could reduce the economic risk of film production by forcing independent exhibitors to rent several films simultaneously through the introduction of "block-booking" and "blind selling" film rental contracts as a standard distribution method. Films were not rented individually but in blocks, as contracts would cover an exhibitor's need for films for six months to a year. "Blind selling" meant that the exhibitor was also required to book unseen films, often because they had not yet been made. In order to uphold block-booking, it was necessary for a producer to be able to cover the total demand for films over an extended period of time.

The American company Famous Players-Lasky (Paramount) systematized block-booking by producing a few "blockbusters" (attractive films produced at great expense, the "A-films"), which exhibitors could only rent together with a large number of less attractive, cheaply produced "B-films." The purpose of the B-films was to fill out the screen time of the movie houses so that competitors would not be able to get their films shown. The *Motion Picture Herald* explained in 1939 that "The big pictures are utilized to sell the B's. Without the A's to bolster their sales, there would be little if any profit in the 'program' pictures."[2]

Block-booking was a monopolistic trade practice that distorted competition, and it became illegal in the 1950s with the Paramount verdict, which declared that block-booking was a restraint of trade in violation of the Sherman Antitrust Act. With the growth of American exports, block-booking was transferred to Europe, and became a widely used principle in film rental in France. The introduction of block-booking meant that it became difficult to show domestic productions in movie houses that also showed American films. The English Cinematograph Films Act and the Danish cinema laws from the 1920s prohibited exhibitors from entering block-booking contracts. Not until 1934 did France prohibit blind booking.

Of more direct relevance is how the "independents" industrialized film production in Hollywood in reaction to Thomas Edison's successful film trust, the Motion Pictures Patent Company (MPPC). In order to fight the trust, the independent company Paramount developed the monopolistic trade practices of block-booking and blind selling. These tactics, along with legal challenges, effectively crippled the MPPC by 1913, and the trust itself was finally declared illegal in 1917. When block-booking was subsequently employed in France, it prevented the French film industry from having many of its films shown on the domestic market, especially in provincial cinemas.

There are other legal limitations on the free proliferation of movies as well. Patent rights protected the "hardware" side of films, as both films and equipment were patented. The inventors of the film technique in both France and the United States had an advantage. For example, Edison's film trust, the MPPC, was established to exploit patent rights optimally by controlling exhibition from 1908 to 1914. With the introduction of sound film, the German and the American industries also entered patent agreements in 1929–30. However, the patent contentions themselves had no direct effect on the ability of the Hollywood film companies to dominate the French film market.

There are also restrictions attached to the use of films in relation to the "software" side of films, which is copyrighted. The producer, the director, the actors, and the scriptwriter own the copyright of a film. The United States refused to enter the international conventions on copyright in the 1920s; American producers could therefore plagiarize the films of other companies without the threat of being sued. This was especially detrimental to the French producer George Méliès, as it was a contributing factor to his bankruptcy, but copyright problems alone do not explain the emergence of the dominant position of American films.

Another essential piece of background information involves a brief history of U.S. governmental response to the threat posed by monopolistic practices of large businesses. The Sherman Antitrust Act of 1890, supplemented in 1914 by the Clayton Antitrust Act, was the most important government action for controlling such behavior, but antitrust action declined in the 1920s as the American film hegemony was being consolidated. On the other hand, the United States encouraged the formation of trusts for the purpose of promoting exports with the Webb-Pomerene Act of 1918. The American film industry has subsequently been the major benefactor of this law, partly through the substantial diplomatic support obtained from the State Department and the American embassy in France. The support of the Department of Commerce was less significant, and took the form of providing information. (For a more complete explanation of the American policies toward big business, the reader is referred to appendix A).

Cartel practices were predominantly the province of the major companies' New York-based offices. These companies acted in official concert through the MPPDA. The MPPDA functioned as an instrument of cartelization under the guise of "business self-regulation" in the United States, and also handled the foreign affairs of the major film companies. The cartel behavior of the major companies was even more outspoken in foreign sales, which in the late 1930s provided approximately thirty-five percent of total industry income. The Foreign Department of the MPPDA had the twofold duty of trying to keep foreign distribution channels open for U.S. films, and of informing Hollywood about the idiosyncrasies of foreign censors. This represented a tremendous responsibility in dealing with other governments on matters pertaining to quotas, tariffs, and exchange restrictions, and therefore the Foreign Department necessarily collaborated with the Department of State, even maintaining a Washington office. Occasionally members of the organization also went abroad to assist the official diplomacy efforts; for that reason the MPPDA also operated its own office in Paris, headed since the spring of 1928 by the former diplomat at the Paris embassy, Harold L. Smith.[3]

The Emergence of Monopolies, 1895–1914

French film companies dominated the world market for feature films before World War I, and there were no obvious signs that American films would obtain a dominant position after the war. French, English, and Danish film companies such as Pathé Frères, Gaumont, Éclair, Hepworth, and Nordisk Films Compagni dominated the tiny world market for motion pictures; the war reversed this scenario in Hollywood's favor.

French entrepreneurs were the first to combine the many inventions necessary for establishing the first motion picture performances. In order to exploit the new medium, it was necessary to develop technical equipment, the quality of the film material, and the film aesthetics. French film pioneers such as the brothers Auguste and Louis Lumière and Georges Méliès were the first to develop these aspects.

The first projection of films on a white screen for a paying public was first accomplished by the Lumière brothers, on December 28, 1895, a date that is considered the birth of the moving picture. They were the first to produce a workable cinema projector system, the "Cinématographe." It was both a camera and a projector. They entered into the production of projectors, cameras, and raw film; motion picture production itself was only an extension of their technical activities. Their films had a documentary character, illustrating the everyday life of the French middle class. The first film show included topics such as workers leaving Lumière's factory, a train arriving at the station, and feeding the baby.[4]

The production in Georges Méliès's Star Film company between 1896 and 1905 also remained artisanal. His company obtained an international dominant position by developing a dramatic film style and using trick films, even though he used a static stage-bound camera. His staging introduced decor and historical reconstruction, while also employing theatrical styles such as drama, comedy, or opera.[5] The films became more interesting as they began to incorporate a dramatic action. Méliès's *The Voyage to the Moon* (1902) and Edwin S. Porter's *The Great Train Robbery* (1903) were some of the earliest films that clearly demonstrated that the movie had dramatic abilities.

It was, however, businessmen such as Charles Pathé and Léon Gaumont who industrialized film production and established the commercial business practices that included monopolization. The industrialization of film production started after 1896, when Léon Gaumont and Charles Pathé established the film companies Pathé Frères and Gaumont Films. Film production, artisanal before 1903, became industrialized with the expansion of Pathé's activities, and from 1907 until World War I the company was the largest film producer in the world.

The establishment of permanent movie houses after 1902/03 resulted in the emergence of the three-part division of the film industry into production, distribution, and exhibition. With the improvement of the film product in the beginning of the twentieth century it became possible to operate permanent movie theaters. At first, movie houses had been short-lived because films could not retain public interest; the programs lasted only twenty minutes to half an hour. Films were instead shown in itinerant cinemas at markets or meeting halls. The same films were shown repeatedly, but the location changed.

The improvements of the film product made it possible to operate permanent movie theaters, which gradually supplanted the mobile cinemas which had dominated exhibition in the earlier years. The transition from ambulant to stationary movie houses took place in the larger industrial cities of Europe in 1904/05, and in the United States by 1902/03.[6] As the location became fixed, movies had to be changed regularly. At first exhibitors bought film copies directly from the film producer, but then the cinema owners began to exchange films, with the result that film distribution gradually emerged as a separate line of trade. The establishment of film rental resulted in a boom in all sectors of the film business.

Between 1909 and 1914 business relations underwent radical changes when Pathé Frères attempted to monopolize the film business. Power struggles to control the international film trade emerged in the United States and in Europe. In the United States the rivalry led to the establishment of the Edison trust, the MPPC, in January 1909. The aim of the trust was to monopolize the American market, as well as to keep out European competitors. When the "independents" headed by William Fox filed an antitrust suit against the MPPC in 1913 for violating the Sherman Antitrust Act, the trust gradually became inoperative, even before it was declared illegal in 1917.

European film producers tried to create a trust similar to the MPPC at a conference which Sadoul has called the "congrès des dupes." The conference was a meeting of the directors of the most prominent European film companies held in Paris in February 1909. But the powerful European exhibitors succeeded in preventing the establishment of production monopolization. The failed attempt at monopolization led to a clash between Pathé Frères and all other film producers, eventually causing Pathé to lose its dominant international position.

Pathé Frères

Georges Sadoul[7] has called the period 1903 to 1909 the golden age of Pathé, and Charles Pathé "the Napoleon of the cinema." The control he exercised over the vast industrial company provided Pathé with dictatorial power over the French and international markets in the period before World War I.

Charles Pathé was originally a retailer of equipment who began to produce projectors and films. The company Pathé Frères was founded on September 30, 1896, with the purpose of selling phonographs, film projectors, and motion pictures. Pathé incorporated on December 11, 1897, under the name "Compagnie Générale de Phonographes, Cinematographes et Appareils de Précision." Behind the establishment of the association were the investors Claude Grivolas and Jean Neyret, the latter having connections to Crédit Lyonnais.[8] It was the good connections to French banks that gave Pathé Frères its strength and dominant position.

Pathé's attempts at monopolizing the film industry in its entirety had an ominous influence on the development of international business relations. At first, in the period 1901 to 1907, Charles Pathé expanded his film production into a so-called horizontal trust, by constructing studios, film-copying institutions, and factories for the manufacture of equipment and installation and financing of affiliates abroad. Pathé opened offices for the distribution of its films everywhere in the world. In 1904 Pathé opened offices in London, New York, Moscow, Brussels, Berlin, and St. Petersburg; in 1906, Amsterdam, Barcelona, and Milan; in 1907, Rostov on the Don, Kiev, Budapest, Warsaw, Calcutta, and Singapore; and in 1909, Copenhagen. By 1914 Pathé operated forty-one affiliates all over the world.[9]

In 1907, Pathé began to monopolize the film industry by introducing rental films to licensed movie houses. Up to 1907 the film industry resembled any other industry, by selling the film product to the retailers at a certain price per meter of film. The buyers passed the films on to their colleagues after they had finished using them. But when film distribution developed in the period 1905–1907, with distribution companies carrying the films of several film producers, Pathé started his attempt to monopolize film rental and exhibition of his own films. The new policy was heralded in an article by Pathé's proponent, Edmund Benoît-Levy in *Ciné-Gazette* in 1905, published under the name Francis Mair: "What is a film? Is it an ordinary commercial commodity, which the buyer can use as he likes? ...no, a film has artist and author rights. In order to show them it is necessary to pay a fee. The present debate concerns the establishment of this right, which will lead to the suppression of the film distributors, because in the future one will only see producers who rent their own films."[10]

To implement the ideas brought forward by Benoît-Levy, the Pathé trust expanded vertically by creating film distribution and cinema companies intended to show the company's own films. In July 1907 Pathé advertised the cessation of film sales. Pathé's aim was to eliminate independent film trade and distribution by booking his own films directly to the cinemas. Instead, Charles Pathé created a complicated structure of distribution companies, consisting of a holding company, the "Compagnie Générale," and five regional affiliates that obtained a monopoly on showing Pathé films for twenty years.[11] Pathé then prohibited the exhibition of Pathé films produced before August 15, 1907, by any companies other than the concessioned cinemas.

Historians have not described the bitterness French cinema owners must have felt over Pathé's attempts to force them out of business, attempts not soon forgotten. In the summer of 1907, in order to drain the market and destroy the earnings of his competitors Pathé sent twenty-four mobile cinemas on tours around France to show films a week or two before markets started. Pathé probably did not succeed at monopolizing the cinema exploitation in France to the full extent he had planned, largely because Crédit Lyonnais and Jean Neyret seem to have been unwilling to invest the enormous capital that would have been necessary. To finance the production of phonographs and films, it had been sufficient to borrow two or three million francs, but to construct movie houses everywhere in France would have required an investment of several million more.[12]

The introduction of Pathé's new rental system signaled the beginning of a new period in the history of cinema in the years 1908 and 1909, which were characterized by vicious competition and attempts at monopolization. In the United States, the transition came in connection with the establishment of the MPPC in January 1909, in which the Edison consortium and Pathé Frères had a decisive influence. The MPPC was of direct importance to the development of the situation in Europe.

It is a popular belief that if any film company has produced a good movie, it will have the same opportunity to have the film shown as any other company. However, such democratic conditions existed only in the infancy of the motion picture industry. They ended in 1909 when trusts and monopolies began to dominate film business.

The Motion Picture Patent Company, 1909–1914

In the United States the years 1908 to 1914 were also a time of feverish activity, with ruthless struggles over the control of the motion picture world. Two events affected the course of history—first, the establishment of the MPPC trust, which dominated all motion picture activities for four years, and second, the introduction of the long "feature" film which soon became firmly established and revolutionized the movie business.

The growth in the demand for movies produced a bitter and widening competition. The number of manufacturers, importers, and distributors rose to between fifty and a hundred, and nickelodeons expanded into the thousands. Film production was an open field for producers who had a legal right to the patents of any of the three companies, Edison, Biograph, and Vitagraph. With the spread of lawsuits, the situation became critical.

In order to provide some increased stability and to forestall further unsettling competition, nine leading manufacturers and the major distributors of foreign films banded together and on January 1, 1909, announced the formation of the MPPC. The company comprised seven domestic manufacturers—Edison, Biograph, Vitagraph, Essanay, Selig, Lubin, and Kalem—along with two French companies Méliès's and Pathé—and the distributor George Kleine. All pooled their patent claims, and each received a license to manufacture motion pictures. Lewis Jacobs[13] has established that the parties all agreed at that time that no additional licenses would be issued. Movie making was to be restricted to these initial nine companies, and Edison, acknowledged as the owner of the basic patents, would receive royalties for the use of cameras and films. To strengthen their plan to control and monopolize the production of motion pictures, the MPPC contracted with the Eastman Kodak Company to supply only the licensed members of the pool with raw film.

To regulate exhibition and production, the MPPC set up a system of patent fees. Exhibitors were charged two dollars a week for the right to use projectors and to rent films from the licensed members of the trust. Around ten thousand exhibitors signed contracts with the MPPC, but not surprisingly, the trust met bitter opposition from manufacturers and distributors who were outside the pool. Jacobs explains that as the independents began to bootleg films and projectors, an underground business between independents and exhibitors flourished. Many companies openly fought the trust; most important among these were Carl Laemmle's Motion Picture Distributing and Sales Company and William Fox's New York Film Rental Company.[14]

In 1910, the MPPC established a national film exchange, the General Film Company, and to secure its monopoly control swallowed up all licensed exchanges. By January 1, 1912, fifty-seven out of fifty-eight principal exchanges had been bought out. The only company that did not succumb was William Fox's Greater New York Film Rental Company, whose power came from the ownership of many movie houses in New York. Fox headed the opposition to the trust, and instituted a lawsuit against the MPPC as an unlawful conspiracy in restraint of trade in violation of the Sherman Antitrust Act. The lawsuit resulted in the MPPC's dissolution in 1917. Even though the trust was no longer functioning by 1914, the Department of Justice continued to monitor monopolization without taking serious action.[15]

The independent competitors, in their struggle to survive, focused attention on improving the quality of their films. They also discovered and established Hollywood as their base for production, which was located in a place with good weather conditions, and where they could escape attacks from the trust. They developed the "star system" as a method to increase profits, and they greatly expanded publicity for their films. They lured away many of the trust's foremost filmmakers by offering higher wages. By 1913 Hollywood was so well developed that it became its own municipality.[16]

The change in the international business relations that occurred in 1909 changed film business for good. The international power struggles over control of the motion picture industry that emerged simultaneously in Europe and in the United States led to monopolization. After having defeated the MPPC, the independents, in their turn, created their own monopoly. After 1909, trusts and cartels dominated the motion picture industry.

Monopolization in European Cinema, 1909–1914

Pathé's attempts at monopolization of European film distribution were also a threat to the distribution of films by other producers, who organized to defend themselves against Pathé. The first film producers' conference took place in Paris on March 9, 1908, as a joint British-French initiative. Léon Gaumont had just created a cinema section under "la Chambre Syndicale Française du Phonographe." The result was that most French film producers and representatives of foreign companies joined, except Charles Pathé. This organization arranged the subsequent congress.[17]

There was a certain common interest among film producers in favor of film rental. The disadvantage of Pathé Frères' new film rental practice was that it aimed at eliminating independent film distribution in order to monopolize the distribution of the company's own films, thereby controlling the cinemas. But film rental itself was in general an advantage for all of the film producers, who until then had sold the copies of their films, and thereby lost control over their exploitation. The purpose of the conference, which Georges Sadoul has labeled "le congrès des dupes'" [18] was first to decide how films could be exploited better and ultimately to create a European film trust.

Congrès des Dupes

In 1908, the European film companies obtained their largest profit from the United States, and it was therefore a great shock to them to find that Edison had established a film trust in February 1908. The trust accepted several American film producers, but of the European companies only Pathé Frères and Georges Méliès's Star Film were invited to enter the trust. All other film producers were excluded from the American market. In March 1908 Gaumont, Urban Trading, and Cinès asked through Méliès to be included in Edison's trust, but their request was turned down because Pathé objected to their membership.[19]

The proposal of the British film producers' organization to arrange a conference to discuss the film situation was universally accepted by French and other foreign film producers, with the exception of Pathé. Charles Pathé, the "monopolizer" of European cinema, vehemently opposed the planned congress; to him the crisis was welcome, because it would eliminate competitors. When Méliès transmitted the congress invitation from Vitagraph-Nordisk to Pathé he replied arrogantly that he was bound by agreements, and that the situation could only be solved by inevitable bankruptcies. The congress organizers abandoned the idea of having Pathé join the conference.

The French film producers' organization, the "Chambre Syndicale Française du Phonographe," arranged the congress, which opened on March 9, 1908. The president and founder of the association was Léon Gaumont, and Marcel Vandal from Éclair served as vice president. They discussed the advantages to the film producers of establishing their own film distribution, which was an attack on Pathé but not against the Edison trust. Nordisk Films Company and Stuart Blackton from Vitagraph suggested holding another international congress in Paris to explore how they could fight the trust. An initiative committee elected Méliès as organizer, even though his Star Film company was in great economic difficulties, and survived only due to its agency in New York.[20]

The European producers saw the planned new congress as a means of evading the crisis with George Eastman's help. The congress was therefore postponed to December 10, 1908, the day Eastman was supposed to arrive in Paris. But Eastman delayed his departure from America until after the formation of the MPPC, thus forcing a further postponement for the congress.

Meanwhile, Pathé thought he would benefit personally from monopolizing the American market. He spent the summer of 1908 in New York trying to establish his own film rental agencies similar to those he had created in France. But Edison would not allow him to infringe on his own arrangements with the distributors and thereby allow his foreign rival to gain strength. Charles Pathé left the United States in September 1908 without having established his agencies.

Georges Sadoul has established that when Eastman came to Paris in January 1909, he went directly to discuss the establishment of the MPPC with Pathé in Vincennes before the congress opened. The leaders of the company—Pathé, Iwatts, and Prévost—argued that the most important reason to establish a different license method was to be able to eliminate European competitors. Eastman concluded that they would not succeed. To Eastman, the European producers' conference was of only secondary importance compared to the establishment of the American trust. The Edison trust would collapse if it did not obtain an arrangement with the leading European film producers because the association of European film producers was more powerful than the American. To prevent them from uniting, it was necessary to provide access to the American market for a few of the most important companies—Gaumont, Urban, Cinés, and Nordisk Films Compagni. Pathé accepted the deal made two weeks earlier which created the MPPC. Eastman also made Pathé accept the establishment of a European film producers' association.[21]

Thus, despite his earlier opposition, Pathé was present when the congress opened on February 2, 1909, presided over by Georges Méliès and in the presence of Eastman and thirty of Europe's leading film producers (the directors of Cinès, Urban, Gaumont, William Paul, Hepworth, Nordisk, Messter, and Duske). Charles Pathé was the architect behind the initial success of the conference to create a trust similar to the Edison trust.

The congress decided that exhibitors should be obliged to return films after four months, without exception. Films were not to be sold but rented at 1,75 francs per meter for the four months, of which 50 centimes would be refunded. A minimum film rental fee was imposed on the movie houses. The producers also agreed to demand that Eastman-Kodak should monopolize the providing of raw film for the trust, just as he had agreed to do for the MPPC. In compensation, the trust obliged itself to buy film only from Eastman.[22]

After the conference, the film producers realized that the trust devastated the film distributors and exhibitors, and that it would be advantageous only to film producers who were also distributors—in other words, Pathé Frères. If distributors ceased to exist, the exhibitor would have to turn to the producer-distributor, and if they were unable to pay 1,25 francs per meter for films they would have to go out of business.

In order to challenge the trust, exhibitors and distributors organized When the distributors at a meeting on March 15 recommended a boycott o films from the trust, it began to fall apart. Disagreements had already emerged on March 5, when Méliès unsuccessfully negotiated the film rental agreement, because the new companies Éclair and Lux were unwilling to offend their customers. At a meeting on March 15, Charles Pathé suddenly rescinded his agreement to destroy films after four months and also rejected the fixed price system. Shortly thereafter George Eastman resigned. The subsequent problems relating to the supply of raw film led to the final destruction the trust. It could not exist without Pathé and Eastman. Éclair resumed the free sale of films and gave up renting, and the English companies Williamson and Walturdaw followed suit.[23]

On the basis of his Marxist outlook, Georges Sadoul has explained the failure of the trust and the conditions it sought to impose, in comparison with the MPPC, as a result of essential structural differences between the European and American markets. In essence, he notes that film exhibition was much more developed in the United States, which also had powerful associations of distributors, while in Europe small trade had remained important, and film distribution was not yet developed. The congress had failed, he remarked, as a result of too large a gap between the interests.[24]

Sadoul did not examine whether the greater stagnancy of internal structures within film exhibition in Europe resulted from the enforcement of antiquated license systems for cinemas, which made investment in movie houses risky. With increases of the amusement taxes during the 1910s and 1920s, investment in exhibition certainly became less profitable.

The description of "le congrès des dupes" is followed by a lacuna in Georges Sadoul's film history.[25] A Danish film journal[26] reports that because of resistance from distributors and exhibitors, another conference held in Paris in April reestablished the free film trade. All producers accepted the new convention except Pathé, who would not give up renting films directly to the cinemas. Thereby Pathé entered into a new conflict with other film producers, and a combat against Pathé began which led to a total boycott of the company all over the Continent. The original decree that films had to be returned was rejected by the producers, but prices were fixed by a convention until April 1, 1910. All participants except Charles Pathé and some English companies signed the protocol. The Danish journal claimed that Charles Pathé had said "the distributors have too high a profit; they have to be struck down—then the theaters would have to 'dance to the producer's pipe'." It also claimed that Pathé's intention was not only to eliminate film distribution, but also to create a vertical cartel in control of film production, distribution, and exhibition—a serious threat to the existence of other film companies.

The convention was a declaration of war between the European film distributors and the Pathé Company, which was excluded from the continental market. Everywhere in Europe they established coalitions with exhibitors in order to halt Pathé's strategy of monopolization. A congress in Berlin on April 29, 1909, decided to create a united organization, which had its constituting assembly on May 13. This assembly passed a resolution to exclude Pathé Frères from Germany.[27] Everywhere unions of distributors and exhibitors were created. In Austria, a common film rental company was created which excluded rental of Pathé films from the market. Pathé was eventually forced to resume delivery to film distributors and had to give up direct rental to the exhibitors.

Pathé seems to have been successful temporarily in distributing his own films in France, Britain, Denmark, and Sweden, but the evidence is at present too sparse to conclude how successful he was in monopolizing the distribution of his own films. In 1913 the war against Pathé resumed in Britain and Sweden. By January 1914, the Pathé Company had weakened to the extent that even the Danish distributors, by creating a "trust," could force the company to terminate its film rental in Copenhagen.[28] The Swedish distributors imitated the Danes by also creating a "trust," but the conflict continued in 1915, and by 1917 Pathé rented films to only a few movie houses, which consequently were excluded from renting films from other distributors.[29] The results of the conflicts in other European countries are unknown, but it seems likely that Pathé Frères must have been forced to drop film distribution.

With the European film trust in ruins, only one film trust came into existence: the American. The American trust succeeded at monopolizing the American film market to an extent only dreamed of by Pathé.

---

[1] Georges Sadoul, *Histoire générale du cinéma, II: Les Pionniers du cinéma* (Paris, 1947), p. 512.

[2] *Motion Picture Herald*, November 18, 1939. Cited in Peter Bächlin, *Der Film als Ware* (Basel, 1978), p. 108.

[3] "The Hays Office," *Fortune*, vol. 18 (December 1938). Reprinted in Tino Balio (ed.), *The American Film Industry* (Madison, WI, 1976), pp. 311–12.

[4] Lumière's first programs consisted of the films: *La Sortie des Usines (the Lumière factory), Le Déjeuner de Bébé, La Sortie du Port, La Démolition d'un Mur, L'Arrivée du Train en Gare, La Partie d'Écarté.*

[5] David A. Cook, *A History of Narrative Film* (New York, 1981), pp. 46–47.

Georges Sadoul, *French Film* (London, 1953), p. 4.

[6] Peter Bächlin, *Der Film als Ware* (Basel, 1947), p. 18.

[7] Georges Sadoul, *French Film* (London, 1953), p. 7.

[8] Jean-Jacques Meusy, *Cinquante ans d'industrie cinématographique* (Aubenas d'Ardèche, 1996), pp. 14, 121ff.

[9] Sadoul, *Histoire générale du cinéma, II*, p. 248. Cited in: Kristin Thompson, *Exporting Entertainment: America in the World Film Market 1907–1934* (London, 1985), p. 5.

[10] "Qu'est-ce qu'un film? Est-ce une marchandise ordinaire dont l'acheteur peut faire l'emploi qui lui convient?... Non, un film est une *propriété littéraire et artistique*. Pour le représenter, il faut payer un droit. C'est sur l'établissement de ce droit que le débat portera un jour, et ce sera la suppression des loueurs, car on ne verra plus que des fabricants louant eux-mêmes." Cited in G.-Michel Coissac, *Histoire du cinématographe* (Paris, 1925), p. 348; also cited in Paul Leglise, *Histoire de la politique du cinéma français*, p. 35.

[11] Pathé divided France among the five affiliates; see Sadoul, *Histoire générale du cinéma, II*, p. 250–52.

[12] Ibid., p. 251.

[13] Lewis Jacobs, *The Rise of the American Film* (New York, 1939), p. 82.

[14] Ibid., p. 83.

[15] Ibid., p. 84, and U.S. Department of Justice, RG.60, National Archives.

[16] Ibid., p. 88.

[17] Sadoul, *Histoire générale du cinéma, II*, pp. 509–10.

[18] Ibid., p. 509ff.

[19] Ibid., p. 509ff. This contains the most detailed description of the film conferences of the years 1908–1909.

[20] Article in *Argus Phono-Ciné* (March 1908), cited in Sadoul, *Histoire generale du cinéma, II*, pp. 509–10.

[21] Sadoul, *Histoire générale du cinéma, II*, pp. 513–14.

[22] Ibid., p. 517ff.

[23] Ibid., pp. 524–26.

[24] Ibid., p. 512.

[25] The later conferences in April are not mentioned by Sadoul, and he has not described the conflicts between Pathé and the European film industries abroad in the years 1909 to 1914, which crippled the French film hegemony.

[26] "Blade af Krigen mod Pathé Frères," *Nordisk Biograf-Tidende*, 1. årg., nr. 3 (Copenhagen, November 1909), pp. 41, 43.

[27] Ibid., pp. 43–44. Pathé's regeneration of films is mentioned by Sadoul, *Histoire générale du cinéma, II*, p. 526.

[28] Jens Ulff-Møller, "Da Filmen kom til Danmark...," *Sekvens 1989* (Copenhagen, 1990): 45–46.

[29] "Filmkrig i Sverrig," *Filmen* 3. årg., nr. 13 (Copenhagen, April 15, 1915): 110. And, from "The Film Trust," Report to the Secretary of State from the American Consulate General, Stockholm (September 7, 1917):

> The formation of a film trust in Sweden has caused much dissatisfaction. The Trust, following the example of Denmark, has boycotted Pathé Frères films.... In Sollefteå a theatre had a contract with Pathé Frères to show a certain number of their films, and a high fine was to be paid if the contract was broken. The trust, however, would not let any other films be supplied to the theatre as long as it showed Pathé films, and so it had to choose between paying the heavy fine for breach of contract or closing up.

2

The Emergence of Hollywood's Hegemony, 1914–1921

When war broke out in August 1914, Pathé Frères' international power had already been broken, and the power of the MPPC also succumbed to the restraint of trade suit against the trust launched by the distributor William Fox in 1913. By the end of 1914, the companies second in line, the "independents," were free to assume power, and it became their turn to establish a monopolistic position. The intense conspiratorial rivalry of the MPPC trust, however, had forced the independents to move production to California, while maintaining their corporate offices in New York in order to be in closer contact with Wall Street and Washington. All important administrative and policy decisions continued to be made in the New York offices.

The move to Hollywood meant that activities were split between the East and the West Coasts. The previously small independent East Coast producers—Carl Laemmle, William Fox, Adolph Zukor, Jesse Lasky, Lewis J. Selznick, Marcus Loew, Joseph Schenck, Samuel Goldwyn, Louis B. Mayer, Harry, Abe, Sam, and Jack L. Warner—suddenly directors of giant industrial corporations—chose either Hollywood or New York as their principal base. For example, Adolph Zukor, the president of Paramount (Famous Players-Lasky) was in New York, whereas Jesse Lasky headed production in Hollywood. Marcus Loew, who owned a theater chain and bought the Metro production, was the New York president of Metro-Goldwyn-Mayer, while Louis B. Mayer became the studio head of MGM in Hollywood.

A crucial factor in the takeover by the independents was the emergence of the feature film, the "star" system, and a new block-booking film rental system in 1914, which triumphed over the short films and the sales methods of the MPPC companies to the extent that they were completely wiped out in a very short time. Also, the termination of World War I restrictions on movie import and export meant that the independents could expand film distribution overseas.

Through mergers based on incorporation law, the independent film companies obtained a monopolistic control of the American market. The most powerful of the new companies was Adolph Zukor's Famous Players-Lasky Corporation, a merger of the Famous Players Film Company and the Jesse L. Lasky Feature Play Company, Inc. Both companies successfully produced three to four feature films per week and distributed their films through

Paramount Pictures Corporation. In December 1917 Famous Players-Lasky merged eight subsidiaries into one corporation. The Paramount Company was itself a consortium of five independent regional distributors organized in 1914 by W.W. Hodkinson. He lost control of Paramount in 1916, and within a year the company was in Adolph Zukor's hands. In 1927 the conglomerate took the name Paramount Pictures Inc. Through mergers, the Famous Players-Lasky Corporation acquired theater companies everywhere in America, such as the Stanley Company of America, which operated a chain of theaters in the Delaware region.[1] The feature film, film stars, and block-booking first emerged in Europe, but it was Zukor who first systematically applied the new inventions to monopolize the market.

Zukor's Block-Booking and Blind Selling

When promoting the sale of its films the Famous Players-Lasky Corporation did not rely exclusively on the popularity of its film stars and the appeal of its films. The company came to dominate the industry by using the distribution practices of block-booking and blind selling, which forced exhibitors to enter long-term film rental contracts. Zukor elaborated block-booking into a system. In order to rent the few films produced at great expense, the "blockbusters," the exhibitor was obliged to rent a large number of mediocre releases produced at low cost. Zukor planned to produce around thirty films a year, but he did not intend to produce all equally well; therefore, he divided the production up into Class A films, consisting of "famous" plays in which "famous" stage actors appeared, and Class B, in which only "known" actors appeared. The high budget A films would draw the interest of an exhibitor to enter a block-booking contract, whereas the low budget films saturated the movie house bookings, excluding would-be competitors.[2] The all-or-nothing distribution policy favored the producer, who both obtained a stable outlet for his films regardless of their quality, and at the same time prevented competitors from having his films shown. Soon all film production companies adopted the effective block-booking distribution method.[3]

The problem with block-booking contracts was that they excluded competitors from having their films shown, which might violate Federal antitrust legislation. A block-booking contract would usually involve the delivery of films to be shown for six months to one year in one big block. Clearly, cinemas only have a limited capacity for showing feature films, compared to the great number of films produced. In order to be able to enforce block-booking, a film producer would have to produce a large number of films, which would enable the company to supply the exhibitors with all the films they needed. In one year a movie house would show fifty films or more, and around 1918, Zukor distributed about 220 feature films. Block-booking contracts were first used extensively by Famous Players-Lasky beginning in 1916, and thereafter all other American film companies followed.[4]

Block-booking inevitably became a legal problem. Legal scholars have defined block-booking as the simultaneous leasing of groups of films at a fixed total price, based on the condition that all the films in the block are taken. In practice it meant that an unaffiliated exhibitor would have to rent all the films in the block offered, or none at all.[5] Almost everybody took a position for or against block-booking. Film distributors defended the practice by stating that block-booking was wholesaling, comparable to discounts for quantity purchases in other lines of business. Howard T. Lewis agreed with this line of questionable reasoning—provided that a discount was actually offered. Good trade practice would, however, normally dictate that films in a group should be of uniform quality. Even though it would be impossible for all films to have a consistent quality, he nonetheless refused to condemn block-booking practices.[6]

Independent exhibitors insisted that the resemblance between block-booking and wholesaling was purely coincidental, because of the forced application of the trade method. The exhibitors were alarmed, not only because the film rentals increased, but also because they disliked being pressed to buy unwanted films in order to secure the better movies, and most of all they dreaded the all-or-none policy that formed the basis of Zukor's business method. Ralph Cassaday Jr. supported their view by maintaining that block-booking is in effect a "tying" agreement. If, for example, a film producer plans sixty films, he knows that perhaps only ten will be successful. These ten are generally films that are particularly in demand because special stars play in them. The fifty mediocre movies must be taken with the desirable ten, in an all-or-none agreement.[7] The arrangement was further extended to films that had not yet been made, the so called "blind selling."

In 1915 the Mutual company began to rent films based on an "open booking" system, which meant that the cinema owners could book films freely at a higher price per film. At the same time the film producers began to sell the rights to the distribution companies only for a certain time and within a certain area, which was the basis of the so-called monopoly film.[8] Before 1920, several methods of renting films were used, but block-booking became the most prominent in the 1920s.

The Struggles between Famous Players-Lasky and First National

In order to counter Zukor's selling methods the exhibitors created their own integration based on ownership of movie houses. The first organization of exhibitors to appear in 1917 was the First National Exhibitors Circuit, the purchasing agent for twenty-six of the largest first-run exhibitors, which in the beginning of the 1920s controlled about three thousand theaters throughout the United States. The group constituted the largest purchasing power of the film industry, and its national distribution network rivaled the size of Zukor's Paramount exchange. When the corporation established First National Pictures, Inc. in 1919, the exhibitors also entered film production and distribution.

Both parties in the conflict recognized that whoever controlled distribution controlled the industry. First National was able to eliminate block-booking temporarily by 1918. In retaliation, Paramount Pictures entered the theater business itself, and bought up first-run houses and exhibition circuits all over the country. By 1921 Zukor's ruthless campaign to acquire movie houses had resulted in Paramount owning 303 theaters, compared to First National's 639. The race for control of distribution and exhibition extended into the 1920s, when Fox, Goldwyn, and Universal joined Zukor's race for theater acquisition. The race to acquire movie houses required huge capital, which was provided by Wall Street banking houses, and as a result trained financiers obtained managerial positions within the film industry to protect their investments. Within less than a decade, the cinema had become a large industry.

When Zukor entered the business of owning movie theaters in 1919, his activities began to conflict with American antitrust legislation. His plan, described democratically as "selling the product direct to the people," meant in reality that he would become the largest exhibitor in America as well as the leading producer and distributor. The planned circuit of key theaters would enable the corporation to dominate the motion picture industry and at the same time increase its percentage of profits. Zukor's business policy exhibited a pronounced tendency towards creating a monopoly. The Federal Trade Commission stated in 1921:

> Because of the dominant position of Famous Players-Lasky Corporation in the motion picture industry, its methods of competition, policy and practice are necessarily followed, adopted and maintained by all competitors of Famous Players-Lasky that are strong enough to acquire and operate first-class, first-run theatres to exploit their most meritori-

ous pictures... [t]herefore, it is made difficult for small and independent producers or distributors of films to enter into or remain in the moving picture industry or market, or to lease individual pictures on merit.... By said methods, Famous Players-Lasky Corporation has unduly hindered, and is unduly hindering competitors, lessening competition, and restraining trade in the motion picture industry, with a dangerous tendency toward the creation of a monopoly therein in the several parts of the United States.[9]

Famous Players-Lasky Corporation simply ignored the orders of the Federal Trade Commission to discontinue block-booking trade practices and not to dominate exhibition, and soon block-booking became the only trade method used throughout the film industry. The interwar period saw several attempts to make block-booking illegal, but the practice was never effectively countered in the United States until 1948, when the Paramount decree had some success in separating production and exhibition interests.

Block-booking made it impossible for other independent producers and foreign film companies to have their films shown in the United States unless the films were bought by one of the major American film-producing companies. During the 1920s, the president of MPPDA, Will Hays, repeatedly claimed that the motion picture industry was in a healthy condition, thereby denying that the American film industry exercised any form of monopoly, or that the MPPDA was operating as a cartel preventing foreign films from being shown in the United States. In Europe, the Americans claimed that their success resulted from the better quality of their films; if only the quality of French films were to improve, they would also succeed domestically as well as in their exports to the U.S. According to Will Hays, "a really good motion picture, no matter by whom it might have been made, is bound to have proper distribution and exhibition."[10]

Will Hays' propagandistic optimism was, however, not shared by Carl Laemmle, the director of Universal Film, who himself had been frozen out of large parts of the American market by monopolistic trade practices. He wrote angrily to Will Hays:

...I do not believe the industry "is in splendid condition with sound business methods prevailing." I do not believe it was ever in a more unsound condition nor that poorer business methods ever prevailed than those of this very day. I do not know of any business or any art that could suffer more from monopoly than this business, and yet, as sure as Fate, monopoly is coming to this business with giant strides....A limited group of companies is trying this very minute to dominate the field.

And most certainly a really good picture is <u>not</u> bound to have proper distribution regardless of who makes it....The people who support the movies ought to know that quality has less to do with what pictures they see than the fact that certain theaters are controlled by certain producers.[11]

The developments in the American market in the 1910s led to a situation where a small group of so-called independent producers formed an oligopoly that controlled the American market through vertical integration. The quality of the films became less important to their success than control over their distribution to movie houses. A production company would not benefit from producing the best film possible if other companies were able to prevent its exhibition by monopolizing all available cinemas. By the 1920s, the American film industry had, in fact, achieved just such a monopoly in film distribution and exhibition in the United States and become dominant in France as well.

Hollywood's International Expansion during World War I

When the American film industry gained a foothold in the European market, it was partly the result of real improvements in the quality of American films. Already in 1914, a Danish film magazine noted that the previously jerking American films had improved technically and the stories had become more interesting. American films had caught on all over the world, in large part because their technique had become clearer and more consistent, and because they did not experiment with strange lighting effects, instead using sharp daylight with deep shadows and heavily lit faces. The subjects reflected a wholesome and unsophisticated life. The plots were brief and the tempo exaggerated. The directors brought excitement into the films using fast cutting, which emphasized the actor's speed and gripped the spectators. Cowboy films especially attracted the public.

The Americans have found their specialty, they do not try to imitate the European art films. They don't have an Asta Nielsen, no Max Linder, but an ample crew of dash fellows, who look great in sunshine, and who are firmly seated in their saddle on a horse in run. American films have a flight, speed and initiative, light, intensity, and cheerfulness— and those movies have a great mission around the world, and undoubtedly have just as large a public.[12]

The author of the article could not, of course, foresee that the American film industry would soon remedy this deficiency by acquiring leading European actors and directors, such as Charlie Chaplin, Marlene Dietrich, Greta Garbo, Pola Negri, Maurice Chevalier, Victor Sjöström, Mauritz Stiller, and Benjamin Christensen, just to mention a few of the Hollywood emigrants.

Another article from 1917 commented that the success of American films was the result of freedom from an outdated cultural elitism. There was no conflict between the cinema and the theater in the United States, where nobody looked down on the cinema. The article described the expansion of the American film exports as a military conquest. Triangle Films, which carried the films of D.W. Griffith, headed the "battle," and the Americans had great "victories" due to the World War. European film production was handicapped, since both Pathé and Gaumont had almost ceased producing films due to the war. Furthermore, in the "film war," the Americans had the advantage that the battle would always take place in the land of the "enemy." According to the article, it was hopeless for the European film industry to "invade" the United States, because here all theaters were owned by the large film companies, which would allow only individual foreign films to enter, and never the whole or even half the production of a film company. The American home market was so enormous that all expenses and some profits could be earned domestically, with the result that American producers could supply films to Europe at a very low price. This imbalance would threaten European film production, which depended on the home market to recuperate costs. As a result the European film situation looked rather gloomy. The author of the article predicted that when the war ended, a "film war," severe and protracted, would follow, during which the European film producers would try to unite, because unity offers strength.[13]

The American film producers must also have realized that the world war would be followed by a film war, and therefore they organized, sought alliances with the government of the United States, and introduced tactics to thwart collaboration among European film companies.

An important factor in the implementation of the strategy of the American film industry was the establishment of good contacts with the government of the United States, which first began during World War I. The first contacts were made soon after the American film industry organized into the National Association of the Motion Picture Industry (NAMPI, a precursor to the MPPDA) in 1916. The industry had already mobilized the foreign service to collect economic intelligence for it and had fed back tips as to what sort of information would be most helpful.[14] The information gathered by the embassies provided the basis of statistics about the film trade and competition in foreign markets, later becoming the source of publications such as the *Film Year-Book*. Other invaluable information on film politics, such as the names of cinema owners who had shown American films, was sent directly to the American film industry.

The Beginning of the American Film Hegemony

It is difficult to document precisely how the American film industry acquired its dominant position during World War I because of the scarcity of information. The MPPDA representative Oscar Solbert stated that "Our companies never made an effort to obtain this foreign trade. It was thrust upon them through the fortuitous circumstances of the war."[15] Hollywood's dominance at first glance appears to have been established without much resistance, but the position was not acquired without the efforts and diplomatic assistance of the government of the United States.

The American expansion seems to have developed through certain stages in which the government became involved, mainly because it wanted to ensure that the films were not re-exported to Germany. At first, American film companies gave concessions to local companies, such as Gaumont or Pathé, or they sent a competent agent to Paris who appointed subagents in the provinces.[16] Foreign agencies were eager to acquire American films for distribution, as they were cheap and in high demand and, consequently, extremely profitable.

The American film industry seems to have acquired a foothold in the European market by using dumping practices, as huge quantities of films were sold at very low prices.[17] Ian Jarvie is incorrect to argue that the American film industry was successful in its exports initially as a result of block-booking. Block-booking could not have been used in the establishment phase, but only later, once the American industry had become better situated in foreign markets and it was necessary to defend the position industry had obtained abroad. Block-booking could not have been a method that itself established the American film hegemony.[18]

It is also difficult to determine exactly when the American film industry became dominant, both because the definition of a position of strength is elusive (it differs according to the criteria used) and because the statistical information is incomplete (the statistics are presented in appendix B). Kristin Thompson[19] has concluded on the basis of American export statistics relating to the U.K. and the British Empire that the American films became dominant around 1916. Her estimate of 1916 in Norway seems to be too early, and in continental Europe, Hollywood's move toward hegemony more likely occurred in the wake of World War I. The turning point seems to have been in 1917 in France and Italy, but it cannot be documented firmly. Certainly the American dominance may have been apparent, since at the same time Pathé was successful with the series *Le Main qui étreint* (*The Clutching Hand*) and *Tillie's Punctured Romance*, but in order to fulfill their contracts with the theaters, Pathé had to distribute American films.[20]

In any event it is clear that by the end of World War I American companies were successfully operating directly in European markets through affiliates, thereby establishing a control which European producers found difficult to erode during the 1920s. Clearly, the achievement of Hollywood's film hegemony during and after the war relied heavily on the ability of the U.S. film industry to take advantage of structural differences between American and European economies.

However, in reaching a more complete understanding of U.S. film dominance it is important not to overlook the impeding effect of European cinema legislation, exemplified by the history of French cinema law, on the development of the French film industry.

---

[1] The Will Hays Papers: A Guide to the Microfilm Edition of the Will Hays Papers, ed. Douglas Gomercy (Frederick, MD, 1986), roll 6, frame 325–29. Robert H. Stanley, The Celluloid Empire (New York, 1978), p. 23–25.

[2] W. M. Seabury, *The Public and the Motion Picture Industry* (New York, 1926), p. 18, cited in Mae D. Huettig, *Economic Control of the Motion Picture Industry* (Philadelphia, 1944), p. 32.

[3] David A. Cook, *A History of Narrative Film* (New York, 1981), p. 44–45.

[4] Huettig, *Economic Control of the Motion Picture Industry*, p. 32.

[5] Ibid., p. 116.

[6] Howard T. Lewis, *The Motion Picture Industry* (New York, 1933), p. 154.

[7] Ralph Cassaday, "Some Economic Aspects of Motion Picture Production and Marketing," *Journal of Business* (April, 1933):120.

[8] Knud Rønn Sørensen, *Den danske filmindustri (prod., distr., konsumption) indtil tonefilmens Gennembrud* (Copenhagen, 1976), p. 79.

[9] *Federal Trade Commission v. Famous Players-Lasky, et al.* Complaint No. 835, p. 961. Cited in Huettig, *Economic Control*, p. 36.

[10] According to the press release Will Hays deployed his masterful rhetoric in a speech at the Inland Press Association Convention, West Baden, Indiana: "The motion picture industry is in splendid condition, with sound business methods prevailing, complete harmony in the ranks of his [Hays'] association, and ever-increasing artistry in the pictures themselves.... A really good motion picture, no matter by whom it might have been made is bound to have proper distribution and exhibition....There are never too many good pictures, and producer, distributor and theatre owner all welcome thought and productions by whomsoever made that are up to the continually rising standards." Press release, May 26, 1925, *Will Hays Papers*, roll 22, frames 439–40.

[11] Response to Will Hays's talk in West Baden; letter from Carl Laemmle, June 1, 1925. *Will Hays Papers*, roll 22, frames 761–63.

[12] E. M., "Den amerikanske Film. Et Par Betragtninger," *Filmen* 2, no. 11 (Copenhagen, March 15., 1914):171–72.

[13] "De amerikanske Films," *Filmen* 5. årg., nr. 16 (Copenhagen, June 1, 1917): 165–66.

[14] Ian Jarvie, *Hollywood's Overseas Campaign* (Cambridge, 1992), p. 276.

[15] Oscar Solbert, Confidential report to Will Hays. Bruxelles, July 2–4, 1925. *The Will Hays Papers*, roll 22, frame 980.

[16] Vice Consul Paul H. Cram, "Motion-Picture Trade in Southern France," *Commerce Reports* no. 255 (Washington, October 30, 1916): 393.

[17] American trade practices are not commonly discussed in the diplomatic correspondence, but that American film companies had been guilty of dumping practices, later discontinued, is mentioned in a "Memorandum to Mr. Reagan," dated June 19, 1929 in the Archive of the American Embassy in Paris.

[18] Jarvie bases his argument on a statement by Kristin Thompson that the American success in international trade in motion pictures was founded upon innovation in supply, particularly distribution, and on a letter from Clarence J. North, from February 11, 1927. North was the first chief of the Motion Picture Division, within the Bureau of Foreign and Domestic Commerce, in the USDC.   Jarvie, *Hollywood's Overseas Campaign*, p. 277.

[19] Kristin Thompson, *Exporting Entertainment* (London, 1985), p. 63–74.

[20] Ibid., p. 89–90.

Part Two

Cinema Law

3

The Effect of Cinema Law

Another reason why the American film industry could dominate the European market was that public authorities in Europe hindered the free development of the national film industry by introducing serious limitations on film exhibition. These obstacles derived from older regulations for theaters and public amusements, including operating licenses for theaters, censorship of films and performances, and exorbitant amusement taxes. U.S. legislators did not introduce similar restrictive cinema laws. Unlike modern European film legislation, which acknowledges the artistic qualities of motion pictures by supporting their production economically, the aim of public legislation before the 1960s was to restrict and tax the showing of films in movie houses.

One reason for introducing restrictive cinema regulations at the turn of the century was that the authorities and the public thought that films had detrimental effects on the spectators and the larger society as well. Another reason was that the authorities were suspicious of the power of the moving image, and therefore they sought to maintain strict control of movie houses through regulations that had survived virtually unchanged since the days of absolutism. The laws were not created specifically for the cinema, but were derived from old regulations for theaters and public amusements already in existence before the first showing of motion pictures in France in 1895.

The Theatrical Prejudice

The reason for the restrictive state regulation of theaters and mass media had a historical explanation. Since antiquity, Western civilization has been suspicious of the theater and of actors. Vigilant censorship has been based on the belief that theater has extreme powers of persuasion. Furthermore, a characteristic feature of modern European thought has been the belief that culture should contribute to the amelioration of social conditions and to the mental and moral improvement of the citizenry. Seen in that perspective, theater and amusements have had only corrupting influences on the character of the people. The ancient Greeks thought that theatrical entertainment might infect a healthy mind, just as a body could become ill from exposure to disease. The idea that spectacle could have a cathartic effect, as claimed by Aristotle, was ignored for centuries.

Plato excluded poets and writers of fiction from his ideal state in *The Republic* because of their harmful influence on citizens. He believed that poets should be supervised and prohibited from representing the licentious, the illiberal, the graceless, because evils accumulate in the soul. Since people imitate what they see, they should see only harmony and beauty.[1] Plato also dismissed tragedy and comedy as well as painting because he regarded them as imitative arts. The leaders of the ideal state, the guardians, ought not to imitate anything else; if they imitate at all, they should imitate good and suitable characters, such as the courageous, and they should certainly not depict baseness.

The Platonic idea that poetry and theater were harmful to the citizen was taken over by the Church fathers. Tertullian took the position that theatrical spectacles of all types promoted the sins of the world, offended God, and should be renounced by all good Christians. He condemned theatrical pleasures as a form of lust.[2] In *De Civitate Dei* Augustine argued that there was an intimate connection between all kinds of scenic games and pagan worship.[3] He asserted that by attending plays the spectator not only sullied Christ, but also adopted the vices shown in the theater. The audience was not aware of the danger that "through eyes and ears vices pass as through open windows on their way to the human heart." The Church fathers repudiated the theater for moral reasons, because of its indecency, atrocities, and vanity—not to speak of theater's affinity to paganism.[4]

In the eighteenth century dramatic censorship became firmly established in Europe. With increased secularization in the seventeenth and eighteenth centuries, French moralists began to discuss the psychological effects of the theater on the individual rather than using religious arguments. They argued that spectators re-enacted in actuality what they experienced in a play; the spectators thus had to be protected because they were unable to judge what they saw and to make the right moral choices.[5] Jean-Jacques Rousseau (1712–1778) thought that, rather than having a civilizing effect, theater would instead degrade man.[6] The public identified with what was produced in a show, and therefore the theater would only affirm morals; it neither had a cathartic effect nor was able to correct established morals. Rousseau feared that the libertinism of actors would disseminate among the youth. Conversely, he did suggest that theaters might have a positive effect on people living in decadent cities (i.e., Paris). It might be possible, in his opinion, to remedy some of the problems by instituting severe laws concerning the conduct of actors.[7]

Rousseau argued against the key figures of the Enlightenment—Voltaire, Racine, and Boileau—who maintained that plays had a cathartic effect. They proposed that by arousing passions and showing consequences of acts arising from irrational behavior, theater could actually lead to some form of emotional self control.

In a non-democratic society the theater was the foremost public place to express opinion, but with the excesses of the French Revolution, philosophers became suspicious of the psychology of the crowd and mass movements. In the mid-nineteenth century, theater riots occurred frequently in France as a means of expressing discontent with society. Gustave le Bon continued the tradition of Rousseau in his *Psychologie des Foules*, arguing that the spectator loses his individuality and even descends several rungs on "the ladder of civilization."

In *The Theory of the Theatre* (1910), Clayton Hamilton also expressed fear of the effects of crowd psychology on spectators. Behind the psychological reservations were the threatening theories of "mass man" and "mass society." Middle-class reformers feared the growing working class and thought the cinema could seduce it. The psychological justification for this theatrical prejudice lost importance with the development of experimental psychology in the 1920s, long after the laws and regulations had been established.

With the growing secularization and economic progress in the late eighteenth and nineteenth centuries, the theatrical prejudice became economically justified. Philosophers such as John Stuart Mill began to distinguish between productive and unproductive labor, regarding theater as unproductive and futile leisure. Society, Mill argued, gained nothing from the work of the actor or the theater workers, who only promoted pleasure:

All labour is, in the language of political economy, unproductive, which ends in immediate enjoyment, without any increase of the accumulated stock or permanent means of enjoyment. And all labour, according to our present definition, must be classed as unproductive, which terminates in a permanent benefit, however important, provided that an increase of material products forms no part of that benefit. ... When a tailor makes a coat and sells it, there is a transfer of the price from the customer to the tailor, and a coat besides which did not previously exist; but what is gained by an actor is a mere transfer from the spectator's funds to his, leaving no article of wealth for the spectator's indemnification. Thus the community gains nothing by the actor's labour; and it loses of his receipts, all that portion which he consumes, retaining only that which he lays by. [8]

With the invention of the cinema, the new medium grew up in this atmosphere of suspicion, and it had to develop a style of its own before it might be acceptable to its critics. Older media—painting, sculpture, dance, drama, and opera—had developed their special sophistication and elaboration of styles over a long period. The motion picture had to strike roots and develop its own form of artistic style at around the turn of the century, when realism held sway in literature, theater, and art, depicting the living conditions of poor people in the metropolis, in industry, and in agriculture. These themes were accepted in painting and literature because of the idea of freedom of expression and freedom of the arts.

But the cinema and theater, due to the greater audience impact of the image in combination with the spoken word, did not partake in such freedom of expression. The result was that social problems, though described in literature, were censored out of the films, often because the showing of provocative topics might result in public disturbances. Most people preferred to see exotic places, royal people, and high life, and not to be presented with the well-known ills of society. Realistic themes were banned also because lifelike films had the power to shock. Themes of morality, sexuality, and crime were unmentionable in "good society" and were not to be shown to the public, which to a significant extent consisted of children.

With the development of the dramatic film in the beginning of the twentieth century, descriptions of social problems and crime became more frequent, usually as the background of detective films. So when films took up subjects such as crime, murder, suicide, execution, or sexuality,[9] they conflicted with moral standards and shocked the middle classes, which began to demand stricter censorship of the movies even though they tolerated similar descriptions in literature.[10] Censorship aimed particularly at protecting children against moral corruption, on the untested assumption that children's morality would be better protected by ignorance than by knowledge of the dangers of life. There was also general anxiety that moving pictures promoted political subversion. These fears of subversion were a crucial element both in justifying stricter control and censorship with movie houses after World War I, and in creating state-controlled broadcast systems.

In the beginning of the twentieth century, the theatrical prejudice became incorporated in the "progressive" ideology, which was based on the idea that continuous social progress was thought to evolve from an evolution of the morals of the citizens rather than from economic progress. Movies were considered harmful not only to the spectators, and especially to youth, but to social progress itself. The "progressive" ideology had proponents on both sides of the Atlantic.[11]

The legislation of cinemas was partly a form of discrimination that placed them under a more rigorous system of taxation than other kinds of amusements. In accordance with Mill's thoughts, theatrical shows and especially the cinema were regarded as unnecessary luxuries like cigarettes and alcohol that could be taxed heavily without harming society. As a consequence, the taxation of French cinemas increased excessively when society needed extra funds during and after World War I.

French Cinema Legislation

In accordance with the old prejudice against entertainment, the French State upheld "feudal" regulations for cinemas. The privileges granted by the absolute monarchs to theaters continued almost unchanged in modern legislation for entertainment. Traditional religious hostility towards entertainment had nonetheless yielded to a "progressive" political ideology, as described above, which considered movies pernicious to public morality and social development.

The public aspect of the cinema also caused the authorities to take an interest in controlling film exhibition, like theater and other amusements, by means of licensing, censorship, and taxation. Film shares with publishing and the theater the ability to communicate to a mass public, but exceeds them both in effective penetration.[12] The reason the authorities wanted to control film exhibition was to be able to obstruct undesirable communication to the audiences. Furthermore, in both the United States and Europe the public adhered to a progressive ideology which opposed commercialization of the cultural sphere. In America a few states introduced film censorship, but the federal administration did not interfere with the development of film business. In comparison, several European states introduced strict control of the ownership of movie houses and censorship of performances, which occasionally functioned as a ban on films already produced.

Whereas the production and exhibition of films in the U.S. has been regarded as free enterprise and free from public control, the exhibition of films in France was regulated by antiquated state rules for theaters and other forms of public amusements. Since the French state chose to apply the regulations for temporary public entertainment to permanent movie houses, the rules were especially harmful to film exhibition.

These rules demanded, as mentioned previously, that owners be licensed, and the license could be revoked at any time. The police censored the shows, which nevertheless could be closed down at will. As compensation for the theatrical "privilege," the licensees were obliged to pay extraordinary amusement taxes. On the other hand, film exhibition was distinguished from film production, which was came under the law of free enterprise.

Licensing

The aim of the theatrical license system was to enable public authorities to control performances. The issuance of licenses was a royal prerogative. The license system emerged in 1699 when the Comédie Française obtained a monopoly on dramatic performances in Paris by offering to pay a larger percentage of its profit in amusement taxes to the Church. When the "Second Théâtres" emerged, they were only permitted to carry a light entertaining repertoire in the vaudeville style in order not to infringe on the monopoly of the Comédie Française.[13] The French Revolution abolished theatrical monopolies in 1791, but they were reinstated five years later, freedom of the theater being suppressed until 1864.

A decree of 1864 liberated permanent theaters, which became free enterprises, but maintained a license obligation for temporary amusements such as horse races, market fairs, and festivals, and the authorities defined cinemas as being a temporary or "minor" amusement. To operate a cinema in France it was necessary to obtain a license from the mayor, which required renewal every year and could be withdrawn at any time. The local police could still close a show at will.[14] The license system made it unattractive to invest large sums in movie houses, and the French cinema developed more weakly than in Germany or Great Britain.

The Edouard Herriot decree of February 18, 1928, assimilated the regulations of the cinema to those of the theater, which implied that the decree revoked the obligation to obtain a license from the mayor to operate a movie house.[15]

Censorship

French film censorship had its roots in the theater censorship of the absolute monarchy. The decree of 1864 upheld the principle of advance censorship on theatrical performances. The regulations determined that dramatic censorship of plays would fall under the jurisdiction of the Ministry of Fine Arts. The control of the performance was the domain of local authorities, that is the mayors and the police prefects. The police established the general rules and gave permission to perform a play. The mayor had authority to prevent individual shows according to a law of 1790 if he believed they might cause public disorder. The local police had limited power over theaters, whereas they had extensive power over the "spectacles de curiosité," which included movie houses.[16]

The dramatic censorship at the Ministry of Fine Arts disappeared in 1906 when parliament refused to allocate funds for the censorship institution.[17] But, since the Ministry of Justice thought that juvenile delinquency increased during World War I because of the influence of such films as *Mystères de New York*, film censorship was reintroduced by decree on July

25, 1919. This decree also established a central film commission. Yet even approval by the censors did not guarantee that a film could be shown anywhere in France, since local authorities could still prohibit its showing.

The film commission played a central role in French film policy. In 1928 Edouard Herriot gave the commission authority to negotiate film quotas with the American film industry.

Taxation

France upheld no fewer than three different amusement taxes during the interwar period. The oldest amusement tax, the "droit des pauvres," originated in King Charles VI's decree of 1407, which fixed the payment at ten percent of the box office revenues. He justified the tax on the grounds that shows distracted people from religious services and diminished the alms.[18] A decree from 1875 changed the tax to become a payment to public poverty relief. A law from 1920 converted the municipal tax into a state tax, thereby rendering it an entirely secular tax, shed of its original religious justification.[19]

During World War I, the government introduced a state and a municipal tax on public entertainment. Although initially intended as temporary, these amusement taxes continued after the war and became an integrated part of French fiscal policy. In 1928 the tax for Parisian movie houses was 7.2% for the lowest tariff group, but 30% for the highest tariff group; the tariff for provincial movie houses was half that of their Parisian counterparts.[20]

In justifying the upholding of the excessive tax, the Minister of Finance, Louis Klotz, stated in 1920 that "the cinema can bear the tax more easily than anybody else."[21] A year earlier, industry representatives had warned the government of the commercial and political dangers that would result from a cultural colonization of the screen by American films, if French films were to come uncompetitive. But since the American films were not yet solidly established at that time, these fears seemed unjustified.[22]

The government did not consider that the excessive amusement taxes might be detrimental to the development of the French film industry. There can be no denying, however, that the taxes drained the resources needed for improving the movie houses and film production. As a result of the license system, French movie houses had no legal status similar to that in other lines of business, making investment in them a hazardous gamble. The cinema legislation was a factor that contributed to the downfall of the French film industry from its leading international position prior to the first world war.

The Effect of Cinema Laws on the French Industry

The decision of the Ministry of Fine Arts to uphold antiquated regulations on cinemas was detrimental not only to French film exhibitors but to the French production industry as well. The cinema law had two serious drawbacks for the development of the French film industry. First, the laws made it difficult for producers to establish large-scale vertical integration, which in turn would have enabled producers to control exhibition, which might have led to the exclusion of Hollywood films. Second, entertainment taxes drained the French film industry of funds needed to produce high-quality movies that might challenge American competition. The French government did finally act in support of French film production, raising tariffs in 1921 and introducing the film quota system in 1928, but the measures had little effect on reducing American movie exports because profits were taxed away from the film industry.

The antiquated legislation and the excessive taxation also made it risky and costly to operate movie houses, and caused a peculiar structure to come into existence in French exhibition, which consisted mainly of two groups: A large number of inferior provincial movie houses, and a relatively small number of large, prosperous movie houses in the major cities. Harold L. Smith[23] described the French film industry in 1928 as consisting of a few dominant companies, several dozen minor producers, and fifty distributing houses. There existed around 4,000 cinemas, of which no more than forty percent operated daily and only 500 could pay "good" film rentals. Of the 3,500 to 4,000 movie houses in France, two-thirds of them—or roughly 2,500—were small, impoverished provincial movie houses which opened only on the weekends. The owners operated them as secondary occupations,[24] renting only the cheapest films, which were three-to-five-year-old, low-budget films, at an average rental of 200–600 francs per week. Fifty percent of the receipts were derived from cinemas that paid the lowest state tariff (3.6% or 7.2%) in amusement tax. These small movie houses were the typical customers of the American film distributors.[25] The American film hegemony seems to have depended less on the quality of the films than on low rental prices.

Because of the Americans' prevalent use of block-booking, many of the small provincial cinemas would probably book only American films for a half or whole year at a time, and would rarely, if ever, show a French film.[26] As described in chapter three, block-booking was used extensively in the United States from 1916 on, especially by Paramount, and was expanded into a system with deliberate production of high- and low-budget films. In order to book the lavishly produced block-busters, cinema owners were compelled to book a large number of mediocre, low-budget movies, squeezing out the exhibition of competitors' films. For example, Abel Gance's *Napoleon*, distributed by MGM, was used for the block-booking of ten to fifteen American films.[27] The practice continued to be legal in France late into the 1930s.[28]

In the mid 1930s Harold L. Smith thought that the total amount of American block-booking had been greatly reduced because more pictures were available and the blocks of pictures the Americans were able to sell were not very large; the average block had been brought down to around eight films whereas previously—in the heyday of block-booking—it was as high as forty pictures. Blind selling and block-booking were mainly to the advantage of French producers, he claimed, since the principal exhibitors desired to see the American pictures before booking, which automatically eliminated block-booking for the more important houses.

Still, Smith thought that the Americans should opt for retaining blind selling and block-booking for "future advantages," because if it became illegal to block-book, American selling costs would be greatly increased. The MPAA companies still were block-booking in many secondary towns, and a lot of small exhibitors bought American films in blocks of pictures. If the Americans were hindered in entering into block-booking contracts, the exhibitor would take full advantage of his rights, and the Hollywood would be unable to force him to take certain pictures he did not wish to take, and he would show only what he considered the best American pictures. The pictures he did not rent from the Americans would result in a loss in the number of play-dates, and the films with which the exhibitor filled his program would not necessarily be of a quality superior to those he refused to take from Hollywood. Smith added, "In other words, any commercial advantage that we would have in a lucky year with one or more very fine pictures would be automatically lost because we could not be authorized to oblige an exhibitor to take several other pictures which he did not think were so good!"[29]

The other distinctive group in French exhibition consisted of 85 to 250 cinemas with the largest receipts, which was chiefly controlled by large French and American film production companies. The Parisian theaters in this group paid a 30% amusement tax, whereas the largest provincial movie houses paid only 15%. While the receipts from this group of cinemas accounted for only around 15% of the total incomes of French cinemas, the cinemas paying according to the highest tariff (30%) represented around 38% of the total amusement taxes. As this group of movie houses would be more inclined to show French movies, the amusement tax would consequently hit the French film industry disproportionately harder than the American.

The hardships inflicted by the governmental regulations incited a deep antagonism between the small group of French film producers and the exhibitors. To protect their interests, the exhibitors united in several organizations, of which La Fédération Générale des Associations de Directeurs de Spectacles de Province, whose journal *La cinématographie française* was the most articulate in its vehement opposition to all restrictions on the import of American films.

The cinema owners estimated that in 1933 the total box office was around 900 million francs and the fees levied by public authorities around 180 million, whereas only 97 million francs were returned to the French film producers. A similar sum was paid to the Americans for renting their films, even though they carried a much larger number of films.[30] The problem of French film production was that it had lost to the Americans the provincial cinemas and the substantial profit they represented.

The Ministère de l'Instruction Publique et des Beaux Arts, which had general jurisdiction over French cinema, was caught in the conflict of interest between film producers and cinema owners. The ministry tried to promote French film production by restricting the import of American films, but not so severely as to oust American interests. The fact is, the French state had become dependent on the income from the excessive amusement taxes, which to a large extent was derived from showing American films.

As a result of overtaxation, the French industry was unable to generate sufficient profits from its domestic market,[31] and the export of French films also failed to provide the necessary funds. Even though the cost of producing films grew over time, the government was not inclined to lower the taxes. In its annual report, the MPPDA commented on the French situation: "Production increased from 55 films in 1926 to 74 in 1927, but excessive cinema taxation prevented exhibitors from paying rentals which would better enable producers to amortize production costs in the French market."[32] In 1934, industry leaders complained—in vain—that the cinema had become the milk cow of the state.[33]

---

[1] Plato, *The Republic* Book II-III, *The Dialogues of Plato*, translated by B. Jowet. Third Edition (New York, 1892).

[2] Tertullian, *Apology, De Spectaculis*, with an English translation by T.R. Glover (Cambridge, MA, 1953), pp. 230–301.

[3] Elbert N. S. Thompson, *The Controversy between the Puritans and the Stage* (1903) (New York, 1966), p. 18.

[4] Werner Weismann, *Kirche und Schauspiele: die Schauspiele im Urteil der lateinischen Kirchenvater unter besonderer Berucksichtigung von Augustin* (Würzburg, 1972), p. 94–99, 197.

5 Henry Phillips, *The Theatre and Its Critics in Seventeenth-Century France* (Oxford, 1980), pp. 245–46, 250–51.

6 Hilde Haider-Pregler, *Des sittlichen Bürgers Abendschule* (Wien, 1980), pp. 32–33.

7 J.-J. Rousseau, *Politics and the arts, letter to M. d'Alembert on the theatre* (New York, 1960), pp. 4–5.

8 John Stuart Mill, *Principles of Political Economy* (New York, 1883) vol. I, pp. 77–78.

9 Certain films elicited responses in favor of censorship, such as: *The Execution* (1903), *Crime, Sherlock Holmes, Nick Carter* (Eclair, 1908), *The Kiss* (1910), *The White Slave Trade* (1912), *From the Depths of a Great City, Opium Dream, The Great Bank Robbery, The New York Mysteries, The Clutching Hand.*

10 H. Andersen, *Filmen i social og økonomisk Belysning* (Copenhagen, 1924), p. 79.

11 Ellis Hawley, "Three Facets of Hooverian Associationalism: Lumber, Aviation, and Movies, 1921–1930," in *Regulation in Perspective: Historical Essays*, ed. Thomas K. McCraw (Cambridge, MA, 1981), p. 95 ff.

12 Wilbur Schramm, *Mass Communications* (Urbana, Ill. 1949), p. 23 ff.

13 Lisbet Jørgensen, *Teatermonopolet og bruddet på det. Speciale på overbygning ved Teatervidenskabelig Institut om det københavnske teatermonopol, sekondteatrene og Johan Ludvig Heiberg* (Copenhagen, 1990), p. 13, gives an explanation of French theater law: "The privileged theatres had the monopoly to plays with dialogue. The privileges forced comedians to use songs to known melodies, and characters were distinguished by their different leitmotifs, which was a vital element in the success of the genre." The thesis implies that the development of the genre was caused by this circumvention of the privileges. The theatres Théâtre du Vaudeville, Théâtre des Variétés, Théâtre du Gymnase Dramatique specialized in the genre.

14 E. Meignen, *Le code du cinéma* (Paris, 1921), pp. 134–36.

15 Paul Leglise, *Histoire de la politique du cinéma Français: Le cinéma et la IIIe République* (Paris, 1970), p. 69–70. Leglise does not clarify how the cinema was assimilated to the theater; I assume it meant that the license obligation was revoked for movie houses.

16 Marcel Nussy, *Le cinématographe et la censure* (Montpellier, 1929), pp. 30–34

17 Leglise, *Histoire de la politique du cinéma français*, p.27.

18 Meignen, *Le code du cinéma*, p. 154: "que, par le spectacle, le peuple était distrait du service divin, ce qui diminuait les aumônes".

19 Georges Billecocq, *Le régime fiscal de l'industrie cinématographique en France* (Paris, 1925), pp. 74–81.

20 "Produit de la taxe d'état sur le cinéma," *La cinématographie française* (Dec. 9, 1933):10. Further information in: Billecocq, *Le régime fiscal de l'industrie cinématographique en France.*

21 "En raison de la vogue dont il jouit, le cinématographe peut plus facilement que tout autre supporter le poids de la taxe." Billecocq, *Le régime fiscal de l'industrie cinématographique en France*, p. 136, and cited by Leglise, *Histoire de la politique du cinéma français*, p. 55.

22 "In 1919, the redoubtable commercial and political danger liable to result from a colonization of our screen was signaled to the French Government by producers, authors, composers and moving picture actors. In 1917, Mr. Klotz, then Minister of Finance, had already received the same complaints. The American film, our sole serious competitor at that time, not having been installed so solidly in our country eight years ago, our fears seemed chimerical." Translation by consul A. Gaulin of an article in the Dec. 31, 1927, issue of *La Cinématographie française*. Appendix to despatch, USEF, Jan. 9, 1928.

23 Ibid.

24 Very little information can be found concerning the cinemas of *all* of France. This discussion is based on statistical information in *La cinématographie française*, 453, July 9, 1927; Dec. 9, 1933; May 20, 1933.

25 A report from Harold L. Smith, MPPDA's Paris representative, confirms that less than 40% of French cinemas operated daily, and only 500 paid "good" film rentals. Confidential report to Will Hays, May 1, 1928, *Will Hays Papers.*

26 My summary of an unidentified article: If a cinema in the big cities wanted to rent an exceptional film, in the style of *Ben-Hur*, the American distributor often imposes the obligation to enter a contract for forty other films. It is impossible for the French industry to compete with the low film rental offered by American companies..."Il y a des cinémas nombreux qui passent 35 à 40 programmes américains par an contre 8 à 10 français. Il y a un nombre de petites salles où jamais on ne projette un film français!" "Note sur l'action en France de certains films américains," USEF, June 17, 1929.

[27] From an article in *Le Journal*, cited in *Le Courrier Cinématographique* (Nov. 5, 1927). Translation by consul A. Gaulin in appendix to a letter to Herron, USEF, Nov. 14, 1927.

[28] "Interdiction du Blocage de Films," *Le Courrier cinématographique* (Dec. 15, 1934): 6.

[29] "Extracts for Mr. Williamson," undated and unsigned memo, obviously written by Harold L. Smith in Paris in the fall of 1934 to Harold L. Williamson, Second Secretary, USEF.

[30] Pamphlet from an unnamed cinema organization , USEF, 1933.

[31] "A large French production can not be profitable if limited to the home market."*Film Yearbook* (New York, 1926), p. 394.

[32] Annual report 1927–1928, Foreign Department, MPPDA, p. 11. *Will Hays Papers*, roll 39, frame 769.

[33] "Sur toutes les sommes encaissées par une salle de spectacles cinématographiques, il est prélevé 10% pour le droit des pauvres, d'une part, et de 2,5 a 25% au titre de la taxe d'Etat, d'autre part. Connait-on une seule industrie au monde qui soit capable de supporter un prélèvement de 35% sur son chiffre d'affaires?" Charles Delac, "Les taxes des spectacles seraient allégées," in *Le Courrier cinématographique* (Dec. 15, 1934): 6.

Part Three

Export Trade Legislation and Administration

4

The Emergence of The French-American Conflict, 1920–1926

The business of America is business.
—*Calvin Coolidge*, 1925

The third factor that promoted Hollywood's international dominant position was the introduction of expansionist American foreign trade policies. Adhering to the "Open Door" principle, the United States demanded equal access for all businessmen to conduct trade in foreign markets. The U.S. Congress ensured, however, that an Open Door policy would play to the advantage of American exporters by first introducing a tariff policy disadvantageous to importation and then passing the Webb-Pomerene Act (1918), which permitted anticompetitive activity in exports. U.S. foreign trade policy was a negation of the traditional European concept of foreign policy, which was based on balance of power and spheres of influence, the American version calling instead for peaceful economic expansion as a substitute for political and military confrontations between rival powers.

In contrast, French foreign trade policy was based on the principle of self-sufficiency, reducing imports by quota restrictions and import substitution. American diplomacy was able to break French quota policy measures by strengthening and reorganizing the United States foreign service in the 1920s to serve the export industries. Hollywood's position as the major movie exporter was significantly enhanced by the new developments in U.S. diplomacy. With the growth of Hollywood's film export to Europe, the movie industry entered the minefield of international trade policy. By the early 1920s international political relations were still far from recovering from the disturbances that World War I had wrought on the economic order, further exacerbated by the resulting limitations on international trade and increased tariffs each country required to protect its crippled economy. Import restrictions increased, but they seem not to have impeded the export of Hollywood films.

While World War I brought economic and political chaos to most European nations reconstructing their societies after the war, the American economy was healthy, the United States having become the world's largest creditor nation. In contrast, economic growth in Europe was uneven in the decade following World War I. After a period of economic crisis in 1919–21, when rampant inflation was followed by rampant deflation, the European economy had recovered to a greater extent by 1925. The years before the Great Depression of the 1930s were relatively prosperous, even though international trade became increasingly impeded by tariff barriers and limited by import prohibitions.

U.S. foreign trade policy ignored the impact of the heavy losses the war had wrought on Europe. The material and economic losses in the war were unprecedented. Most of the fighting had taken place in France and Belgium, which had suffered more than any other nation from the war. The recovery from World War I was impeded in Europe by the loss of the cream of its youth. French war casualties totaled 1.35 million killed and almost 3.5 million maimed, and German losses amounted to 1.6 million.[1] With the heavy toll in lives and infrastructure, people became disenchanted with the old politicians. The quest for new political solutions led to revolutions in Germany and Russia and a highly unstable political situation in France.

Reconstruction of the international economic system was further undermined by the lack of international solidarity during the interwar period. The international order was threatened by an unwillingness to collaborate, which emerged when Germany was unable to fulfill the payment of reparations to France stipulated in the Versailles treaty, and France was consequently unable to repay war debts to the United States that American politicians insisted upon. As a consequence, the United States withdrew from international organizations that would have helped stabilize the international political system. Instead the American government focused on promoting exports and limiting imports by increasing tariffs, which worked to further handicap the weak European economies. The United States government worked especially hard on promoting motion picture exports.

The war had dealt a deadly blow to the liberal economic order, and most aspects of economic life had become subject to controls and intervention on the part of the State. Many politicians began to regard the war economy, which became heavily state-managed, as a new model for solving the economic problems in society by encouraging a new corporatist partnership among the state, industry, and labor, which was called managerial capitalism or state capitalism. Much of the war organization had been temporary, illegal, and unconstitutional, but it had succeeded in winning the war.

The Trade Policy of the United States

The foreign economic policy of the U.S. at large had the effect of maintaining Hollywood exports. To American legislators and administrators the most important trade issue was the tariffs, and trade legislation was the paradise of pressure groups. International conferences throughout the 1920s advised against the imposition of higher tariffs, but to no avail. In the 1920s the strong pressure to increase tariffs throughout the world led to the depression of the 1930s. In order to counter the depression by stimulating growth and international trade the New Deal foreign economic policy aimed at reducing tariffs through bilateral trade agreements. The United States entered such an agreement with France in 1936, providing substantial support to Hollywood's film export to France in compensation for which France obtained a substantial reduction in tariffs for a wide range of export products, most substantially for wine and alcohol.

The Democratic president Woodrow Wilson strongly opposed the growing post-World War I demand for increasing tariffs, vetoing a tariff bill that would have raised tariff rates in 1921. His party lost the election in 1920, however, and almost immediately, new and more cynical economic policies were substituted for the idealistic "progressive" moral policies of Wilson. With the inauguration of the Republican president Warren G. Harding in 1921, the aim of the economic policy of the United States became the promotion of exports. Will Hays was involved in the new Republican policy from its inception, having headed Harding's presidential campaign. For this he was rewarded with the directorship of the postal service, before becoming director of the MPPDA.

The Republican administration favored isolationism in foreign political relations, rejecting Wilson's international policy of promoting international understanding through the League of Nations. In contrast to the isolationism in foreign policy, in international economic policies the United States was extremely vigilant.[2] Herbert Hoover was the major architect of the new policy; as secretary of commerce, he promoted close cooperation between private business and public administration. Hoover served as secretary of commerce from 1921 to 1928 and as president from 1929 to 1933, when Franklin D. Roosevelt defeated him, by which time, following the onset of the Great Depression, Hoover's policies lay in ruins.

In contrast to its foreign relations policies, the Republican administration's economic policies were far from isolationist. In reality, the American government vigorously promoted exports by increasing diplomatic efforts to gather information about foreign markets both through the Department of Commerce and by diplomatic support through the State Department and American embassies. Hoover endeavored to increase the efficiency of American exporters so that the American market share in foreign markets would increase. Because of the unilateral promotion of American exports, combined with the lack of international solidarity, Hoover's policy has been labeled a "beggar thy neighbor policy," since he did not consider effects on either foreign societies or the international economic system. The American trade policy was in essence economic "warfare," derived from the military mentality of World War I. Both the United States and France promoted strictly nationalist policies that aimed at protecting the home market and relying economically and politically on national resources as far as possible.

The tariff policy of the United States followed a different principle from that of France. Historically, the United States had high tariff protection until the Underwood Act of 1913, which moderately reduced the duty rates. The law also endorsed the principle of reciprocal tariff reductions. After World War I, the United States raised its duties moderately with the Fordney-McCumber Act of 1922, which also introduced a more active trade strategy based on the unconditional most-favored-nation principle. The export policy of the United States was to accept foreign tariffs unless they discriminated against American producers.

French trade policy presented the greatest threat to the new American commercial policy. France also sought new foreign markets but had adopted a commercial policy based on reciprocity and protection. The reciprocity principle was designed to secure better treatment of French exports by high-tariff nations like the United States, and thus represented a direct threat. Simply put, as a State Department officer in fact suggested, if the American policy was to prevail, that of France had to be overthrown. The American commercial policy was firmly fixed by 1923, and France had emerged as the leading antagonist.[3]

The Republican administrations in the 1920s twice increased United States tariffs. In 1922, the Fordney-McCumber tariff was enacted, and the Smoot-Hawley Tariff of 1929 subsequently represented the high-water mark of protectionism for the United States, raising average tariffs to fifty-nine percent. The predictable result was that European countries also raised their tariffs, and the entire western world moved closer to economic collapse.

A lasting solution to the international economic and political problems might have been found by means of the League of Nations, to which France made considerable contributions. Similarly, a solution to the export problem could have been reached at the International Conference for the Abolition of Import and Export Prohibitions and Restrictions, held in Geneva in 1927. However, the clauses were not binding, and the United States and other countries withdrew from the treaty. The feeling of the necessity for national self-reliance and protectionism could have been dissipated only by collective action.[4]

Its global economic effects notwithstanding, the "New Era" economic policy coined by the Republicans in 1920 was especially advantageous to the American film industry. Hoover's ideas might be seen as a continuation of the wartime policies to promote exports; the flagship of these policies was the "Webb-Pomerene Act" of 1918, which exempted export corporations from the Sherman Antitrust Act.

The Webb-Pomerene Act of 1918

In the postwar period the political pro-business stance in Washington was extremely important for the promotion of American film exports, aided by the introduction of federal export legislation. In 1918 Congress adopted a policy to promote the foreign trade of the United States by passing the Export Trade Act, popularly called the Webb-Pomerene Act, which is still in force in an amended version under the title of the Export Trading Company Act of 1982. The purpose of the law was to enable exporters to fight foreign, and especially German, cartels by permitting them to cooperate in exports which the Sherman Antitrust Act would have made illegal. The Sherman law continued to prohibit cartels in domestic trade. But the Webb-Pomerene Act, in contrast, allowed American film companies to collaborate in exports under the leadership of the MPPDA and the State Department. The collaboration ensured that American film companies would not compete with each other in export markets. The legalization of American export cartels enabled the American government to give the export cartels full diplomatic support in conflicts with foreign governments.

The law made it possible for the American film industry to operate an export cartel throughout the interwar period. Although the intention of the law was to help small companies launch combined export campaigns, in reality big business associations benefited the most from the law. In fact, the film industry has been the major beneficiary of the Webb-Pomerene Act, which essentially gave it the right, if not the directive, to use monopolistic practices in foreign markets that had been expressly outlawed for domestic trade.

The present director of the MPAA, Jack Valenti, has expressly stated that the Webb-Pomerene Act has been vital to the success of American film exports. In a speech in 1980 he stated that

> without the embrace of the Webb-Pomerene, the U.S. film and television industry would have been seriously, perhaps fatally, crippled in its efforts to win the admiration and the patronage of foreign audiences....We face daily a panoply of obstructions designed to shrink the American share of the cinema and television world market. As Tarzan said to Jane: "There's a jungle out there." The American film industry is peculiarly vulnerable to unfavorable action by foreign governments and by combinations of foreign private interests, by industry cartels, and by an ava-

lanche of non-tariff trade barriers that are both endless and ingenious....[R]ampant anti-Americanism…lies like a fungus across the marketing landscape, and…without the canopy of Webb-Pomerene, under which we operate, we would be powerless to counter these restrictions and aimless in our attempts to increase our trade….We face, in some countries, exhibitor monopolies or combinations, where theaters are municipally or government-owned or otherwise bound together in a tightly controlled entity, sealed against intrusion. Webb-Pomerene provides us legally the ability to jointly negotiate and take action where necessary. Without this congressional authority we would stand no chance at all to survive.[5]

The irony aside, Valenti's statement confirms that without the Webb-Pomerene Act, the American film industry would not in 1980 have been able to secure an $800 million surplus balance in the export trade—a sum which made the film industry the largest single beneficiary of the Webb-Pomerene export company law. All told, the film industry has benefited the most of all sectors of commerce from the Webb-Pomerene Act, as more than eighty percent of the film export was supported by the law in 1962; the film companies provided around forty-seven percent of all Webb-Pomerene supported export trade earnings reported by the thirty-six Webb-Pomerene associations in existence in the late 1960s.[6]

Apparently lost in the perspective of the American lawmakers is the fact that the Webb-Pomerene Act conflicts fundamentally with the American concept of freedom, whereby (as Charles R. Whittlesey puts it)

entrepreneurs are free to act, free to enter new markets, and free to expand— without being hindered by any public or private power. The democratic ideal implies an aversion to anything that wields power, whether it be the state or private organizations, domestic or foreign. Nor is private economic power allowed to upset the workings of the free market [by] acquiring too great [an] influence in economic life."[7]

Nonetheless, the development of foreign cartels was a large factor behind the enactment of the Webb-Pomerene Act. The high degree of cartelization of German industry especially influenced American legislators to favor anti-competitive measures in exports.

The Webb-Pomerene Act, however, permitted monopolistic and cartel practices by American export businesses only if these practices were limited to trade outside of the United States, and did not result in restraints or domestic trade and competition.[8] The Federal Trade Commission was given authority to investigate the practices of such associations.

American export law was thus of fundamental importance to Hollywood's success in overseas markets. The American film companies were first registered under the law after World War II, but MPPDA's foreign office was already functioning as a Webb-Pomerene association by the mid-1920s without formally registering under the law.[9]

During the 1920s, the Supreme Court came to approve the position of large enterprise almost without regard for how large a proportion of the business sector it controlled. The judicial interpretation of the antitrust laws had the effect of legalizing almost any degree of concentration of economic power if certain legal formalities were observed. Consent decrees rather than convictions became the favored antitrust device. Hollywood's monopoly in the home market was not questioned. Although the United States Senate has several times investigated the trade practices in the movie industry (for example, patterns of control in the motion picture industry were examined in 1941[10]), the business-friendly stance in the federal administration has repeatedly protected the monopolistic tendencies within the film industry from too thorough a scrutiny.

Economic Diplomacy

The active support of the diplomatic services of the United States, which were expanded in the 1920s, was of crucial importance for the success of American movie exporters in their dealings with the intricacies of import restrictions in foreign markets. The State Department controlled the diplomatic system that handled the problems of the MPPDA when dealing with foreign governments. The prewar State Department was fundamentally different from the organization it became in the postwar period, being closer to its nineteenth-century predecessor both in what it did and in how the work was done, explains former Secretary of State Dean Acheson.[11]

The State Department then was preoccupied with commercial treaties, while the general run of business involved helping American businessmen to engage in commercial ventures from which other countries wished to exclude them. As a result, State Department policies arose from specific incidents or problems which then evolved into policies, rather than beginning as matters of broad decision making that resulted in specific action.

The basic departmental divisions of jurisdiction dealing with incidents formed the basic instrument not only for the formulation of policy, but also for its execution. Bureaucratic power rested at first with geographic division chiefs, but jurisdiction became blurred after World War I with the introduction of functional divisions dealing with political, legal, and economic matters. To the traditional four geographic divisions—America, Europe,

Near East, Far East—came the functional divisions, Office of the Legal Adviser and the Passport and Visa divisions, which had almost absolute power to decide who might enter and leave the country. In the 1920s Henry Stimson created the position of Economic Adviser, and in the 1930s Cordell Hull established the Commercial Treaties and Agreements Division and the Division of Special Research, the latter concerning itself with world organization for peace.

Authority of decision fell to the person who had the power to handle the matter. The heads of all these divisions, like barons in a feudal system, were constantly at odds, as their jurisdiction was vague and overlapping. Obscurity in lines of command permitted the division chiefs to circumvent the line of command at will and go directly to the Secretary of State or the Under Secretary.

Hoover took the lead as Secretary of Commerce in intensifying the U.S. trade competition with the Europeans. By sending out a corps of commercial attachés from the Department of Commerce, he complemented the diplomatic and consular service of the Department of State. The job of Hoover's attachés was to return information about the opportunities for American businesses, look for foreign firms which might like to trade with the U.S., and spot changing markets where the Americans could introduce new products. Almost as soon as the first commercial attachés took up their posts in 1921, Hoover received complaints both from foreign competitors and from the Department of State. Europeans resented being hustled out of overseas opportunities, while the professional State Department diplomats saw their privilege to direct foreign policy slip away.

Career Foreign Service officers of the diplomatic and consular corps bitterly resented having to share their authority with Hoover's new corps. Led by the chief of the consular bureau, Wilbur J. Carr, and the undersecretary of state, Joseph C. Grew of the diplomatic branch, the diplomats and the consuls headed off the Commerce Department's attempt to direct the foreign economic policy of the government by complaining to Secretary of State Hughes. In 1923, Hoover agreed that all business conducted overseas would be channeled through the ambassador who reported to the secretary of state. In July 1924, career Foreign Service officers won another more important battle in the war to capture control over foreign policy when Congress passed the Rogers Act, combining the diplomatic and consular branches into a single foreign service. Over the next five years Grew, as undersecretary of state, outmaneuvered Carr and successfully promoted the diplomatic branch at the expense of its consular cousin.[12]

The emergence of commercial attachés was a part of Herbert Hoover's "new era" economic policies to promote exports by enabling the state to work hand in glove with private business. Therefore, it was important that all sectors of commerce organize trade associations, with permanent contacts with the government, in order to be able to disseminate information and promote an efficient trade policy. Daniel Verdier argues that Herbert Hoover's ideas were never taken seriously and were opposed by other parts of the administration, with the result that the program did not work as intended. The divisions in the Department of Commerce functioned only as fact-finding agencies and not as a part of any decision-making process.[13]

The information gathered was invaluable for the export sectors, as it was all-encompassing, providing background materials for decision-making. The information gave American businessmen crucial advantages in the foreign markets. Verdier minimizes the importance of obtaining detailed information about foreign markets and he does not realize that there existed a division of labor between different agencies which collaborated closely with each other and with private business to promote exports.

Since foreign governments were more attentive to démarches presented by a diplomat than by the attaché, it was expedient that State Department diplomats handle the export policy of the United States. The division of labor functioned in such a way that the State Department officers and top diplomats at the embassies handled policymaking, whereas the main task of the Department of Commerce staff and the American consuls was to gather information useful for the diplomatic decision making and for expansion of exports for private business.

The United States Embassy in France and the MPPDA

The American commercial film policy was especially well organized in France, since the main office of the American film industry in Europe was in Paris. The MPPDA enjoyed government support at the highest executive level. The support it received from the State Department and the American Embassy in Paris had the approval of Presidents Harding, Coolidge, Hoover, and Roosevelt. The diplomatic effort intensified after 1926, when Congress appropriated special funds to operate a Motion Picture Section in the Department of Commerce specifically to collect and publish information concerning the motion picture situation abroad.[14] To this end, the Bureau of Foreign and Domestic Commerce appointed George R. Canty trade commissioner at Paris in 1926, with the exclusive charge of studying the European motion picture situation.[15]

American diplomats followed the French film situation carefully throughout the 1920s and 1930s. In May 1928, the American embassy consisted of thirteen diplomats, eight of whom were actively involved in film policy (an overview of embassy personnel is found in appendix C). They were the ambassador, Myron T. Herrick, Embassy Counselor Norman T. Armour, and the First Secretaries of the Embassy, George A. Gordon and Edwin C. Wilson. All embassy diplomats in the commercial attaché's Office took part in film policy, namely Commercial Attaché Henry C. MacLean and Assistant Commercial Attaché Daniel J. Reagan. George R. Canty was to gather political and statistical information for the Commerce Department's Motion Picture Division. In the U.S. Consulate, Consul General Alphonse Gaulin was also actively involved in reporting, often directly to the MPPDA. Will Hays convinced Vice Consul Harold L. Smith to manage MPPDA's local office in Paris in April 1928.[16]

Diplomatic and political information was, however, officially confidential, and the officers of the MPPDA were the only outsiders to have access to it. Even though the MPPDA had a wide range of important functions, it is generally known only for the motion picture censorship, the "Hays Code" (ca. 1930). The code conscientiously attempted, partly on the basis of diplomatic information about what foreign censors would accept, to mold the Hollywood product into a totally inoffensive form of family entertainment that would be exportable throughout the world. Joe Breen administered the code in Hollywood.[17]

In the mid-1920s the MPPDA also created its Foreign Department, headed by Major Fredrick L. Herron, a school friend and brother-in-law of Will Hays. Herron directed the film policy of the MPPDA towards France through almost daily consultations with the State Department and the embassy of the United States in Paris. The Foreign Department of the MPPDA was already operating as a de facto Webb-Pomerene organization in the beginning of the 1920s, even though the film industry did not register under the law until after the World War II.

It was only when Oscar Solbert provided more practical details about how the law functioned that it was brought to the attention of the MPPDA. Solbert explained that the law permitted cooperative association in exports, whereby the film industry would be able to "present a solid front in any country to its government or combined producers or exhibitors."[18] Solbert wrote that the film industry should organize on the same lines as other large export trades, like steel, copper, or textiles. The Foreign Department in the MPPDA was to gather, correlate, and disseminate accurate information to the producer members. Furthermore, it was to have agents in strategic points abroad who would gather information on film business and foreign film industries, as well as on the activities of foreign governments. The home office, in turn, was to communicate with all departments of the federal government that might be of assistance to the motion picture trade.

Solbert saw that the strength of the export association was in its greatly improved ability to reach agreements on price fixing and uniform contract arrangements, as well as on agreements regarding the percentages of total production to be exported to any country in order not to flood the market, which would depress prices and thereby spoil the market for American films themselves.[19]

The MPPDA first sent Colonel Edward G. Lowry to negotiate trade arrangements with France involving intimate contact with the embassy, whereas Oscar Solbert was merely charged with studying the European film market situation. But with the growth of diplomatic problems around American film export, the MPPDA opened a permanent Paris office in 1928 headed by Harold L. Smith, a former diplomat at the Paris embassy.[20] Smith was in almost daily contact with the embassy beginning in 1928 and throughout the 1930s. Although all major American film companies operated local offices in Paris, the individual representatives were consulted in policy matters but were not directly involved in film policy-making, This task was left to the MPPDA representatives and American diplomats to carry out.

All American agencies—the State Department, the Department of Commerce, the American embassies, and the MPPDA—were united in promoting American movie exports, and it was to prove virtually impossible for the French to break this combined American business strategy.

The Trade Policy of France

While all American energy was united around promoting the export of Hollywood movies, the French government was forced to follow an ambivalent film policy because there existed a fundamental split in the French film industry. On one hand, French film producers demanded protection for their industry, but on the other the cinema owners demanded free access to the American films for exhibition. The policy of the French film producers was carried out by the "Chambre Syndicale de la Cinématographie Française." The director of the Pathé-Cinéromans company, Jean Sapène, was the main promoter of restrictions on the import of American films, while the French provincial exhibitors, in particular those organized in "La Fédération Générale des Associations de Directeurs de Spectacles de Province," demanded free access to American films. With the establishment of Hollywood's dominant position in France, severe conflicts arose between the American film industry and the French when the latter tried to recapture their home market. In this conflict both parties sought governmental support. The American film industry had the full backing of its government, whereas the French Ministry of Fine Arts, which had jurisdiction over the film industry, had to balance its policy in accordance with the wishes of the two groups with opposing interests within the French film industry.

The French political and governmental system was also in crisis. The parliamentary groups did not represent true parties. There were two coalition groups, the "Cartel des Gauches" comprising in the Senate the group of the Democratic Left, and in the Chamber the Radicals and Radical Socialists, Socialists, Republican Socialists, and French Socialists, but excluding the Communists. The other group was the National Block (Bloc National) comprised in the Senate of the Republican Union, the Republican Left, and the Democratic and Radical Union, and in the Chamber of the Republican-Democratic Union, the Republican-Democratic Left, the Democrats, the Left Republicans, the Independent Left, and some radicals.

The Radical and Radical Socialist Party was the largest party in France and usually formed the interwar period governments. (Interested readers can refer to the table of French presidents, prime ministers, and ministers of public instruction and fine arts in appendix C). It was intermediary between the conservative parties who wanted to uphold the present order of society, and the socialist parties, who sought to establish a new economic and social order. The radicals represented mainly small farmers, retail merchants, and officials of all degrees. The leaders of the party were Daladier, de Monzie, Jouvenel, Klotz, Lamoureux, and, most significantly, Edouard Herriot, who was Minister of Fine Arts from July 1926 to November 1928. Being members of a middle-class party, the politicians would be generally inclined to support the stance of exhibitors rather than the film-producing industry. Besides, with the constant change of governments, the French state was at best an unpredictable ally for the film industry.

Nonetheless, the French state was certainly not against protecting the national industries against foreign competition during the interwar period. Protective policies had emerged during the war, when the government limited the economic liberties of the citizens as the state extended its powers into the private-economic sphere by maintaining centralized control of commerce, transport, and prices. Many business people saw in the economic controls of wartime a new regulatory role to help avoid economic crises which the state could perform in peacetime as well, and therefore they were willing to reject the laissez-faire principles of classical liberalism.[21]

After the war, France at first favored in principle a return to the prewar system of free enterprise, but as in other countries, the controls over trade and industry could not be entirely abandoned, and new forms of regulation emerged. The Méline tariff of 1892 continued to underlie French commercial policy.[22] However, the tariff system had changed during World War I when the state resumed complete control over foreign trade through export and import prohibitions. A law of May 6, 1916, gave the government discretionary powers until its abrogation in 1923. The French government obtained a free hand to mold new customs policies with a decree of April 23, 1918, which denounced almost all most-favored-nation agreements. Most of the prohibitions were removed in 1919, but some continued until 1927. France returned to the normal tariff regime in the beginning of the 1920s, but the tariff levels were higher than in 1913.

In the absence of international cooperation in the 1920s, France was forced to rely on its own resources in the economic and political fields. As Frank Arnold Haight put it, "the commercial policy became directed toward the reduction of foreign imports to an absolute minimum and the complete mastery of tariffs. Having become disillusioned with the prospect of political and industrial security based on international cooperation, France retained and intensified its protectionist regime in industrial and trade matters. It was a policy of self-sufficiency, which was in keeping with the tendencies of the time."[23]

The major device used in French economic policy to reduce imports was to increase tariffs and to introduce import quotas. The quota arrangements were not introduced as a system, but as a few isolated measures intended to deal with a temporary emergency that affected only a limited number of commodities—including motion pictures.

The French film quotas introduced in 1928 can be seen as a precursor to the general employment of the quota principle by the second half of 1931. Import quotas were by nature more efficient than custom duties in restricting imports, which in some cases, such as the import of American motion pictures, had little or no effect. Furthermore, quotas did not liberate exporters from the payment of customs charges. When the quota was exhausted, importation was closed until the beginning of a new quota period. Haight characterized the quota policy as a halfway measure between complete prohibition and a customs duty.[24]

Import quotas could also be expanded into a "reciprocity" quota, in which the severity of restrictions would depend on the exchange of goods with another nation. The bargaining of quotas would be a clear violation of the most-favored-nation policy maintained by the U.S.[25] Originally, the French film industry opted for a "reciprocity" quota, which would have forced the American film industry to buy a large number of French films. But the French government did not consider the French film export so important as to insist on this principle. Therefore, the Herriot-Hays agreement in 1928 was merely an import quota arrangement to reduce the number of imported films, and did not demand that the Americans buy French films as compensation.

The French government was very slow to realize that American films had become dominant in French cinemas. What finally provoked the French government to interfere in support of the French film industry was a discussion in the American Congress about raising the tariffs on imports to the United States with the Fordney Bill in 1921.

The organization of the French film industry

The French film policy was inconsistent from the beginning of the interwar period as a result of the many different interests it had to serve. The deep split and polarization between film producers and exhibitors described above principally characterized the French film industry. There were a couple of dozen film production companies and between thirty-five hundred and four-thousand movie houses in France. On a variety of occasions, American film diplomacy was able to use this split very effectively to dismantle proposed measures to protect the French film producers.

To better promote film industry interests, the French film producers organized in the Chambre Syndicale Française de la Cinématographie et des Industries qui s'y Rattachent. At first this organization represented both producers and exhibitors, but in 1926 the producers began to dominate the organization when Jean Sapène joined it as an honorary member. (Sapène had initially refused to join because he was trying to reach an independent agreement with American firms to finance his productions and to distribute his films in the United States). [26] In the mid-1920s the producers Jean Sapène and Louis Aubert, who carried out the film quota project, ran the organization. In 1928 the president was Louis Aubert, and later, Charles Delac.

Pathé-Cinéromans and Jean Sapène

The American film policy-makers regarded Jean Sapène, the director of the Pathé-Cinéromans Company, as the most important figure in French film policy and the greatest potential danger to the continuation of American domination of the French film market. The gray eminence of French cinema and father of the French film quota legislation, Sapène, was also the general director of services of the newspaper le Matin. Today the name Sapène hardly rings a bell, but in the 1920s, it was on everybody's lips.

Jean Sapène was born in 1867 in the Pyrenees. Henri Fescourt[27] describes him as calm and heavy, broad shouldered as a wrestler, sure of his force and self-assertive, being a former sergeant of artillery and awarded Legion d'Honneur in 1921. He had a belief in the unfailing value of his projects, which he found to be excellent. Therefore, he let it be known that the French cinema was a healthy and fortified industry that radiated its beneficial light on the world. He declared: "The small chapels have never interested me; I want to construct a cathedral."

Sapène's interest in cinema probably started in the 1910s, when his newspaper *Le Matin* published the screenplay of the film serial *Les Mystères de New-York*.[28] In 1919, Sapène started the Cinéromans company. By 1922 he had become the most influential director of French film industry when he assumed the de facto leadership of the Pathé Consortium, formed from a merger of the old company Pathé Frères, which was close to bankruptcy, with Cinéromans, Films de France, and Lutetia.[29] In the 1920s, the Pathé consortium, owner of the largest and best studios in France, produced a dozen films a year, operated some twenty cinemas, and controlled the booking for several hundred other cinemas.

Sapène had gained control over the Pathé Company by being an influential stockholder in a younger group of Pathé companies. When the Pathé company, like other French companies, failed to earn profits after World War I, Jean Sapène and a few of his associates put fresh capital into the company, assuming virtual control of it. And Sapène's right-wing newspaper *Le Matin* was on friendly terms with the government.[30]

Edward G. Lowry from the MPPDA was also impressed with Sapène's powerful personality; he was shrewd, direct, as full of driving energy as anybody in downtown New York, and "a person to be reckoned with in everything done in France, both on the political and the business side."[31] Sapène's weak point was his wife, the "café-chanteuse" Claudia Victrix, whom he tried to elevate to stardom in the films *Princesse Marsha* and *L'Occident,* much as William Randolph Hearst promoted Marion Davies, and with as little success.[32]

Due to his influential position in French politics, Sapène immediately became the main target of an American strategy to undermine French measures to protect its film industry. The American strategy was based on the idea that if American film companies imported a token few of Sapène's films they would be able to secure his good will and positive influence on French politicians and thus prevent anti-American measures. As Jean Sapène was the only visible defender of the French film industry against Hollywood films in the early 1920s, the Americans assumed he was the key figure in French film politics. In fact, while Edouard Herriot was minister of culture he relied greatly on Sapène's support.

The aim of Sapène's policy towards the American film companies was not so much to restrict their operations in France as to open the monopolized American market for French film. In 1922, the Pathé Company even led a cartoon campaign in the United States against the Fordney Tariff Bill and the Republican Party. B. Lockwood, the secretary of the Republican National Committee, reported that on armistice day in 1921, the Pathé company had shown an animated cartoon, "presenting a lot of sob stuff about Mr. Wilson and his league of nations. There was soft music supposed to be accompanied by showers of tears over the vacant chair at the council table of the League [of Nations]."[33] Their apparent attempts to appease Sapène notwithstanding, the MPPDA member companies were determined to squeeze the Pathé Company out of the American market, in the process buying single French films only if it would promote their strategy in France.

Jean Sapène's policy towards the American film industry was, in essence, extremely pragmatic and self-interested. He seems to have had very little interest in improving the position of the entire French cinema industry, occupying himself mainly with the expansion of his own film sales, especially since the Pathé Company was on the verge of bankruptcy throughout the 1920s. Harold L. Smith, who became Paris representative of the MPPDA in April 1928, stated that Sapène had also tried to reach an agreement with various American firms for financing his production and distributing his films in the United States.[34]

Aubert and Gaumont—GFFA

Harold Smith also observed that the second most important French film company after Pathé-Cinéromans was Gaumont, which, after its contract with MGM expired in 1928, merged with the Établissements Louis Aubert and Franco-Films (GFFA). The company controlled twenty cinemas and produced six-to-eight films per year. Louis Aubert had mainly distributed French and German films and shown American films in his first-run movie houses, whereas the Gaumont company produced films only on a small scale during the 1920s, and until 1928 was mainly the local subsidiary of MGM. Louis Aubert also headed the "Chambre Syndicale" at that period. Aubert and Sapène were the promoters of the contingent project to reduce the number of American films entering France, which met stiff opposition from the cinema owners.[35]

Will Hays argued that the reason why Americans did not buy more French films was their inferior quality. It should be noted that French high-budget avant-garde films produced by directors such as René Clair, Jean Renoir, Abel Gance, and Marcel l'Herbier were of the highest aesthetic quality of the time, easily rivaling and even surpassing the best American blockbusters. However, French popular films, such as those produced by Jean Sapène, were in deep trouble both artistically and economically.[36]

The Emergence of French Tariff Measures, 1922

The first confrontations between the United States and France occurred in 1921, when France increased the tariff on imported American films. This measure was introduced in response to the Fordney Tariff Bill and not specifically for protection of the film industry. The French cabinet raised the tariffs to 20% "ad valorem" by decree of October 26, 1921,[37] but only the Pathé and Gaumont companies were authorized to estimate the value of the films, assigning them high values. It soon became apparent, however, that protective tariffs were ineffective because American films could "jump" over any tariff "wall" since the production costs had already been redeemed on the home market.[38]

The confrontations between the United States and France began when the Inter-Ocean Film Corporation (IOFC) on March 20, 1922 complained to the Department of Commerce about the new tariffs, and the MPPDA sent a similar complaint to the State Department, arguing that the French appraising experts were overestimating the value of the films they examined.[39] The law specified that the value of the films should be estimated on the basis of how much it would cost to produce the film in France. Not knowing the cost of film production, the customs officers called in experts from Pathé and Gaumont. The IOFC maintained that the method used for estimating these valuations increased the duty to almost 100% of the royalties it would receive, and that it had become unfeasible to do business in France.

The tariff had the unintended effect of creating unemployment in the French film industry.[40] American film companies had sent negatives to France to make positive prints and texts in different languages, but the tariff increase made it more advantageous to have the post-production work done in Germany at a lower price. It was also advantageous to export the completed movies from Germany to France because the French duty on positives had been raised only slightly. The French film industry had to dismiss thousands of workers. Since tariff increases did not have the desired effect of decreasing the import of American films, another policy solution had to be found, one which incorporated the use of quotas.

The resulting French quota system proved a thorn in the side of American foreign trade policy, ultimately culminating in the reciprocal trade agreements program, enacted in 1934. With the New Dealers in power in 1933, Franklin D. Roosevelt's secretary of state, Cordell Hull, became responsible for the execution of the new trade arrangements. The new bilateral trade agreements marked a significant turning point in the management of United States foreign economic policy.[41] The New Dealers recognized a high degree of international economic interdependence that made the prosperity of all nations a prerequisite for the prosperity of each. This international mechanism required intricate adjustments that could not be accomplished as long as the tariff structure remained in the hands of the legislature. When the executive achieved authority over tariff-making, tariff policy became embedded in the foreign policy of the United States.

The reciprocal trade program meant negotiations of bilateral tariff reductions in which the United States was able to pressure France to soften restrictions on Hollywood imports in compensation for tariff reductions for wine and alcohol, as well as for other important French export products. In other words, France sold out the interests of the French film industry, as it was obliged to compromise its quota policy as a result of the reciprocity-based Franco-American trade agreement.

---

[1] Marc Ferro, *The Great War 1914–1918* (London, 1991), p. 227.

[2] Daniel Verdier, *Democracy and International Trade: Britain, France, and the United States, 1860–1990* (Princeton, NJ, 1994), p. 190.

[3] Melvyn P. Leffler, *The Elusive Quest* (Chapel Hill, NC, 1979), p. 51–53.

[4] Frank Arnold Haight, *A History of French Commercial Policies* (New York, 1941), p. 104ff.

[5] Jack Valenti, "Webb-Pomerene: The Great U.S. Ally in the Battle for World Trade: Delivered before the First National Conference on Export Trading Companies, Sponsored by U.S. Chamber of Commerce, Washington, D.C. September 30, 1980," in *Vital Speeches of the Day*, 47:1 (Oct. 15, 1980): 26–28.

[6] Federal Trade Commission, *Webb-Pomerene Associations: A 50-Year Review* (Washington, DC, 1967).

[7] Charles R. Whittlesey, *National Interest and International Cartels* (New York, 1946), p. 15ff.

[8] "[N]othing contained in the Act entitled 'An Act to protect trade and commerce against unlawful restraints and monopolies,' approved July 2, 1890 (the Sherman Antitrust Act) shall be construed as declaring to be illegal association entered into for the sole purpose of engaging in export trade and actually engaged solely in such export trade, or an agreement made or act done in the course of export trade by such association, provided such association, agreement, or act is not in restraint of the export trade of any domestic competitor of such association." Section 2 of the Act, cited in Adolph Charles Hugin, *Private International Trade: Regulatory Arrangements and the Antittrust Law* (Washington, DC, 1949) p. 128–29.

[9] FTC, *Webb-Pomerene Associations: A 50 Year Review*, p. 53.

[10] United States Temporary National Economic Committee, *The Motion Picture Industry—a Pattern of Control*, (Washington, DC, 1941).

[11] Dean Acheson, *Present at the Creation: My Years in the State Department* (New York, 1969), p. 15–16.

[12] Robert D. Schulzinger, *U.S. Diplomacy since 1900* (Oxford, 1998), p. 126–27.

[13] Verdier, *Democracy and International Trade*, p. 190.

[14] U.S. Department of Commerce, *Motion Pictures Abroad* (Washington, DC, 1926). "At the last session of Congress (1925–26) a special fund of $15,000 was appropriated for the creation of a Motion Picture Section in the Bureau of Foreign and Domestic Commerce." C. J. North was the chief of the section, and George R. Canty became trade commissioner, investigating the motion picture markets in Europe. *Film Year Book* (New York, 1927), p. 925.

[15] George Romuald Canty was a naturalized Irishman born in Cork on February 7. 1889. He went to business school at Northeastern College, Georgetown University, and Washington School of Accountancy. He was in the U.S. navy 1918–19, and entered the bureau of Foreign and Domestic Commerce on July 7, 1924. He was appointed trade commissioner at Paris August 16, 1926, and he was delegate at the International Conference for the Protection of Literary and Artistic Works, Rome 1928. On January 16, 1932 he was appointed trade commissioner at Berlin. During World War II he was a member of the Interdivisional Commission on Motion Pictures in the State Department (1943–44), and he was appointed assistant chief of Telecommunications Division, August 12, 1944. He ended his diplomatic career as First Secretary and Consul at the Embassy in Bern, appointed on December 5, 1947. *Biographic Register of the Department of State* (Washington, DC, April 1, 1949), p. 73.

[16] Harold L. Smith's first assignment as head of the MPPDA's Paris office seems to have been to prepare the "Memorandum for Mr. Will H. Hays," p. 52. Paris, May 1, 1928, *Will Hays Papers*.

[17] Joseph Breen's Production Code Administration is described by Ruth Vasey, *The World According to Hollywood* (Exeter Press, 1997).

[18] Oscar Solbert, "When I say that the producers must collectively organize..." An undated report, apparently from the summer of 1925. Will Hays erroneously dated it 1927. *Will Hays Papers*.

[19] Ibid.

[20] Harold L. Smith was born in Pennsylvania. He studied at Swarthmore College, and became lieutenant during World War I. After the war he became American consul in Antwerpen, Gibraltar, and then in Paris. From 1927 he was the head of the American film industry in France, and he became commander of the Parisian section of the American Legion in 1933. *La cinématographie Francaise* (Oct. 21, 1933): 11.

[21] Haight, *History of French Commercial Policies*, p. 101ff.

[22] Verdier, *Democracy and International Trade*, p. 160.

[23] Haight, *History of French Commercial Policies*, p. 104–5.

[24] Ibid., p. 162ff.

[25] Ibid., p. 172ff.

[26] Report from Harold Smith (May 1, 1928), p. 10. *Will Hays Papers*.

[27] Henri Fescourt, *La Foi et les Montagnes*. (Paris, 1959), p. 356–63.

[28] Title page reproduced in Jacques Kermabon, *Pathé: Premier Empire du Cinéma* (Paris, 1994), p. 96. *Les Mystères de New-York* prompted an investigation by the Ministry of Justice on the effects of the cinema on crime, which resulted in the introduction of film censorship in 1918, and thereby the general interest in regulation of the cinema.

[29] Sapène's position in the Pathé company is described by Richard Abel, "Survivre à un nouvel ordre mondial," in Kermabon, *Pathé*, p. 158–89.

[30] Vice Consul Alfred D. Cameron, Paris, "Motion Picture Situation." Despatch no. 281, from USEF, Paris, January 19, 1926, USDS.

[31] Edward G. Lowry, July 1926. *Will Hays Papers*.

[32] "...Sapène, qui rêvait de devenir le W. Randolph Hearst français. Ce *Citizen Kane* au petit pied essaya d'imposer vainement au public sa Suzanne Alexander, l'actrice Claudia Victrix." Georges Sadoul, *Le Cinéma français (1890–1962)* (Paris, 1962), p 44.

[33] Pathé's cartoon campaign against the Republican Party was the topic of Lockwood's article "Movies and Partisan Propaganda," in *National Republican*, July 3, 1922. Will Hays wrote to the secretary of the Republican National Committee, George B. Lockwood, stating that Pathé was not a member of the MPPDA. *Will Hays Papers*.

[34] "Memorandum for Mr. Will H. Hays," Report from Harold Smith, Paris, May 1, 1928, p. 10. *Will Hays Papers*.

[35] Ibid.

[36] Abel, "Survivre à un nouvel ordre mondial," p. 158–89.

[37] Extract of the "Hearing of the Minister of Finance in the Parliament at the Séance, January 20, 1923," *Journal Officiel*, USEF, Jan. 21, 1923. USDS.

[38] "... l'Amerique peut, chaque année, introduire une quantité formidable de négatifs qui, complètement amortis et deja bénéficiaires chez elle, pénétrèrent en France sans représenter pour la succursale ou l'agence installée dans ce pays, une valeur quelconque, il est clair qu'aucun producteur français ne pourra, si les Americains le veulent, lutter contre un tel état de choses et que ce "dumping", formellement interdit dans tous les pays, conduira surement et rapidement le producteur français à la disparition." "Pour la Cinématographie française. Du contingentement," *Le Matin* (Nov. 27, 1925). USEF.

[39] Letter from Paul H. Cromelin, Inter-Ocean Film Corporation, to Herbert Hoover, Secretary of Commerce, New York, Mar. 30, 1922 and later, USDC.

[40] "Une note parue dans un grand quotidien proteste contre l'élévation des droits de douane qui frappent, à leur entrée en France, tous les négatifs étrangers. Elle signale aussi que, pour échapper au paiement des tarifs douaniers, les importateurs introduiront désormais non pas le négatif des films, mais les copies tirées en Allemagne à des prix très bas: les droits d'éntrée sur les positifs étant peu élevés. Elle conclut que la généralisation de ce procédé amènera dans un avenir très prochain un chômage presque total des ouvriers d'usines cinématographiques." Mercure Prudhomme, "Les Droits de Douane et candeur," *La Semaine Cinématographique* (April 7, 1922). USDC.

[41] Arthur W. Schatz, "Cordell Hull and the Struggle for the Reciprocal Trade Agreements Program, 1932–1940," Ph.D. Dissertation, University of Oregon, 1958), p. 1, 28–30.

Part Four

Franco-American Film Diplomacy

5

Diplomacy 1924-1928

We are at a critical time in the European market. Austria, Czecko-Slovakia, France and England are all calling on their governments and pointing to the success of the German contingent system as the only means of keeping out the American pictures to give their own production a chance.

—Oscar Solbert[1]

Federal foreign economic policy-makers have been particularly attentive to the interests of Hollywood, even when Hollywood's monopolistic trade practices were closely scrutinized by the Justice Department or the Federal Trade Commission. Hollywood has been able to maintain its international dominant position through an intimate collaboration between the State Department, the American diplomatic system, and the MPPDA. The Department of Commerce also assisted Hollywood by gathering extensive information about the film situation abroad. Government documents reveal a much more intimate relationship between the American government and film industry than previously assumed. This extensive state support confirms what as we have already seen—that Hollywood's hegemonic position in the world markets rests on something other than film aesthetics and the working of free-market principles. It would not have been possible for Hollywood to sustain its dominant position in Europe without the unconditional diplomatic assistance that the state provided the industry beginning in the early 1920s.

The Emergence of the Quota Policy, 1924–29

Already in 1924 Jean Sapène had begun to agitate for the introduction of a quota system in his newspaper *Le Matin*. Neither the tariff protection nor his safety film initiative had any visible effect on the worsening economic situation of French film production, as they did not succeed in diminishing Hollywood's dominant position. Sapène proposed the introduction of a quota policy that aimed at reducing the number of American films imported to France while simultaneously increasing the export of French films to the United States. It was of vital importance for French producers to augment film export to the United States, because they could not recuperate the cost of the films produced in the home market. Sapène thought he could not succeed unless the flooding of the French market by American films was stopped.

A quota policy had, however, three important drawbacks. First, the producers lost control over the film policy, which was taken over by unappreciative civil servants and politicians whose objectives differed from those of the film producers. The film businessmen certainly must have been appalled at the thought of entrusting the film policy to the minister of fine arts, whose major charge was to censor films and inspect national monuments and buildings. Consequently, it was outside the competency of the ministry to head an industrial conflict with Hollywood and the State Department. Second, the film quota policy was bound to become a factor in international economic diplomacy. In trade negotiations, France would trade off the demands of the film industry in order to promote the interests of more profitable export industries such as wine and alcohol exports. The United States as well as other countries might retaliate against French exports, thereby reducing the advantages of the quota arrangement. Finally, it was impossible to uphold the quota policy because French exhibitors protested any measure aimed at reducing the import of Hollywood films. In order to fight the film quota, Hollywood threatened to boycott the French market. A boycott would endanger the livelihood of French exhibitors, whose existence depended on showing American films.

In order to sell as many films as possible, American film diplomats followed a policy of maintaining the status quo by trying to delay the introduction of sanctions, since they considered a conflict with foreign film industries and governments to be inevitable. With the introduction of the film quota laws, and the exchange of visas between countries, the European film policy began to look like retaliation against American producers. Section 404 of the Tariff Law obliged the United States to retaliate against countries that discriminated against American products. Therefore, the State Department investigated carefully whether the film quota policies were discriminatory or constituted a violation of any trade agreement, in which case the protest would be prompt. In this matter, American film exporters had the full backing of their government through the MPPDA.

Rather than carry out a traditional trade policy based on profit maximization, the American model was instead one of economic warfare, based on a zero-sum strategy. Collaboration would provide no mutual advantage. What a competitor gained, Hollywood would lose, and vice versa. The policy was a continuation of World War I with economic weapons. This policy did not emerge within the industry, which left the international film diplomacy in the hands of the MPPDA. The staff of the MPPDA had been high ranking army officers in the U.S. Army in Europe during the war. Their military outlook was reflected even in the way they addressed each other by their military rank, for example General Hays (even though he did not serve in the war), Major Herron, Major Solbert, and Colonel Lowry. Herron even resumed his military career when the United States entered World War II.

A German invention

The French film quota system was inspired by the German contingent system (essentially, a two-for-one quota), which gave Hollywood the most serious resistance to its international expansion. After World War I, Germany supplanted the wartime embargo on importation of movies with import limitations. In September 1920 the imports were limited to fifteen percent of the 1918 production of German films.[2] Germany permitted the import of only 600,000 feet of films annually, and the quota was divided among German production companies existing before January 1, 1919, and dealers established before January 1, 1917.[3]

With such import restrictions the American film industry was unable to market its films in Germany, but when the restrictions were lifted with the stabilization of the mark, the German market was flooded with American films. The introduction of the contingent system in 1925 saved the position of the German film industry, whereas the French, Italian, English, and Scandinavian film industries were up against the wall. With the development of the expressionist film style, and the successful production of such movies as *The Last Laugh*, *The Cabinet of Dr. Caligari*, *Dr. Mabuse*, *The Niebelungen*, and *Metropolis*, the German film industry became a serious international competitor.[4]

The Americans observed with anxiety the developing German quota system. According to a report drawn up by Douglas Miller, U.S. trade commissioner in Berlin, and Oscar Solbert, representing the MPPDA,[5] plans for a German quota system came into being at a Leipzig exhibitors' convention in the fall of 1924, which aimed at obstructing the import of American films. American films were imported under government licenses. In order to promote the national production of motion pictures, the German union of exhibitors, distributors, and producers, the so-called "Spitzenorganisation," demanded that the government impose a quota on the importation of foreign films beginning on January 1, 1925, in the proportion of one foreign film for each German film produced. The suggestion was to let the foreign films pass censorship in equal numbers with German films, and allowing only German distributors, who had handled new German films in the period from January 1924 to December 31, 1925, to apply for censorship permits.

The report characterized the German film industry as the largest in Europe, but it was in sharp decline in 1924, chiefly as a result of increased film imports from the United States.[6] At the same time German film export to the United States was also in decline. German film exporters talked about an American boycott of European films, but they did not find any deliberate attempts to keep European films out. Douglas Miller was led to believe that the real reason for the decline was that German films did not appeal to the tastes of the American audiences. He was unaware that block-booking and monopolization in American exhibition prevented both foreign and domestic competitors to the MPPDA companies from showing their films.

Just as in other European countries, the introduction of high amusement taxes and an increase in film rentals created a general business depression that struck German movie houses in 1924 when the industry was already in its worst crisis due to the competition from Hollywood. The tax was a burden not only to theater owners and the public, but also to producers, who lost profit. Will Hays thought that a reduction of the amusement taxation would benefit both exhibitors and producers.[7] Germany had the largest number of movie houses in Europe—roughly 3,000 all over Germany and 350 in Berlin alone. The amusement tax exacerbated economic problems because it reduced the number of people who could afford to attend the cinema. During the summer of 1924 only ten percent of the seats were occupied in mid-week, the only satisfactory business being on weekends.

The MPPDA tried to stop the German quota bill with diplomatic pressure. On November 10, 1924, Will Hays and two other staff members appeared before Undersecretary of State Joseph C. Grew to inform him that the German quota bill, if enacted, would be detrimental to American film exports, as it permitted only one foreign film to enter Germany for every film produced by German companies. As ninety percent of the films shown in Germany were American, such a law would amount to a de facto boycott of American films, Hays claimed.[8] On the basis of Hays's request the embassy in Berlin was promptly instructed to counter the proposed legislation.[9]

Despite American protests, the German contingent system came into force in 1925, stipulating that two foreign films could be released for every German film—a substantial modification of the originally proposed one-to-one quota. No decision was taken at this time regarding subsequent years. This modification, which was clearly favorable to American films, may have been a direct result of diplomatic pressure. If too few films were available to fill the demand of the movie houses, the contingency could be further modified with the introduction of so-called "compensation films." Only German distributors who could demonstrate that they were handling a German "compensation" film produced between 1923–1925 could present foreign films for censorship. In 1924, 241 motion pictures were made, which meant that about 500 foreign films could enter Germany, most of them ultimately American.[10] The diplomatic success, however, was, limited since only German distributors were allowed to handle foreign films.

In order to study why the European anti-American film "agitation" had increased, the MPPDA, in the summer of 1925, sent Oscar Solbert on a mission to Europe.[11] Solbert provided the MPPDA with the important information that the German government favored a continuation of the contingent system for 1926, as it seemed satisfied with the effects of the quota law. This information came up in a May 20, 1925, meeting between Solbert and Dr. Mulert, the film specialist of the German Department of Commerce, arranged by the American commercial attaché in Berlin. Solbert reported that although there had been no decision, the contingent system would most likely continue in 1926 because it could not be replaced by higher tariffs. Mulert confided that "no wall of tariff could be put up that was high enough to keep the American pictures from flooding the German market. Also that a high tariff would call for retaliatory tariffs on the part of other countries against German pictures."[12]

Lacking trust in the Germans, Solbert tried to dissuade American film companies from aiding German film export around the world by allowing them to use the American distribution system. When the American film companies Paramount and Metro-Goldwyn entered an alliance with the German company UFA in 1925 (Parufamet), with the purpose of handling each other's films, Solbert warned that the collaboration was a threat to Hollywood's dominant position, because UFA would gain access to the American market and to the world market as well using American agencies around the world. UFA, Solbert claimed, wished to continue the contingent system only until it could supply the home market, at which time the Germans would drop their liaison with the American companies. He recommended that the Americans should hint that the American market would be closed to the German companies, and that it would be possible for the American companies to undersell them in neutral markets so as to effectively lock them out. Solbert referred to the ruthlessness of German trusts that did not recognize any rule of fairness if they could obtain a monopoly. He argued that it would be useless to argue for fairness, the "big stick" being the only sure means of persuasion.

At a meeting with Oscar Solbert, the director of UFA, Erich Pommer defended the contingency measure by arguing that American film producers had not played fair in the German market and had consistently kept German films from being shown in America. Solbert seems to have agreed when he "hinted" that the strong American position was a result of the combined strength of the American producers in MPPDA, their influence with the American press, and their control of a large portion of the key theaters in the United States. Solbert also "hinted" that the United States might retaliate by keeping UFA films off the American market if a tariff system did not replace the contingency, and American loans to the German industry might cease.[13]

It was essential for the MPPDA, in order to carry out a successful foreign policy, to obtain extensive support from the State Department. Therefore, the MPPDA carefully selected the explanations presented to the civil servants as to why German films were not distributed in the United States. The MPPDA argued that German films were unsuitable for distribution in the United States, except in rare instances, and that American film companies only suffered serious losses by acquiring foreign films. The MPPDA never even hinted that the Hollywood companies had an almost total control of the monopolized American market.[14]

After Solbert's mission to Europe ended in the fall of 1925, the MPPDA discussed the results with Herbert Hoover in the Department of Commerce along with members of the Tariff Commission and the U.S. Chamber of Commerce in Washington. In the MPPDA's petition to the State Department of October 8, 1925, Oscar Solbert made a case for why Hollywood should receive support, which activated the civil servants in support of the MPPDA's film export policy:

> Let me analyze the situation as it was found upon intimate study in Europe and how it affects American trade abroad. There is one important and economic reason for antagonism to American pictures. This is the complete realization that trade now follows the film more than the flag. The American film is the greatest vehicle for free advertising ever known for American goods in every market of the world. It is for this reason that the industries in foreign countries are combining to demand of their governments legislation that will restrict the showing of American films in their markets and thus incidentally advertising American goods, and artificial protection for the growth of their own national film industries in order to thus establish advertising agencies of their own.— There is a second though lesser reason for objection to American films. This is the realization in high quarters of the influence of the United States as an example of a prosperous democracy, to a great extent illustrated through the medium of our moving pictures, upon the peoples of Europe in their struggle for a larger hand in their own government....The idea of Americanization is therefore played up by the press as a terrible bogey. Those still in power, both nationally and economically, in certain

foreign countries are becoming more and more aware of the influence that the United States exerts in the bloodless revolution going on in Europe of the gradual shifting of power from the few of the old regime to the whole people of the present and future. The youthful example of a powerful and prosperous republic ruled by the voice of the majority of all its people is helping materially to pry loose traditional and inherited control....

Coming back to the real business reason for anti-American motion picture propaganda we find that the remarkable degree to which American motion pictures are spreading the demand for American goods in the remotest corners of the world is nothing short of phenomenal.... [15]

Solbert's explanation that American films were "tacit salesmen" of American products and ideology was exactly the argument that would make the diplomats in the State Department actively support MPPDA's export policy. On October 26, 1925, Arthur N. Young, the State Department's Economic Advisor, reported that his bureau had forwarded Solbert's report to the embassy in Germany, which was requested to take up the matter with German authorities.[16]

But already in December 1925 the American film policy toward Germany was in ruins. The Embassy had learned that the German film industry had recommended a continuation of the contingent system for one more year, this time with even more drastic restrictions of foreign film imports, including a one-to-one quota. In the meantime UFA had received a loan of fifteen million marks from Universal, and the companies agreed to handle one-third of each other's films. The American ambassador said of the agreement that "UFA has made a breach among the ranks of American producers and has now secured one company which will be inclined to fall in with what they propose regarding the contingent system."[17] Representatives of Famous Players-Lasky had also negotiated with UFA about a loan, on the condition that the contingent system be abandoned. But UFA knew that it would not get a loan if the contingent system were abolished because the Americans would establish their own agencies instead. American companies were competing in trying to get UFA's support, which had thereby weakened the American position, Ambassador Jacob Gould Schurman claimed.

It was the MPPDA's policy to establish a united front of all American film companies to confront foreign competitors, and only the German film industry was successful in breaching U.S. ranks. The reason was that, unlike the situation in France, German producers, distributors, and exhibitors were united in the "Spitzenorganization der deutschen Filmindustrie" so that all parts of the film industry jointly promoted the quota policy. The MPPDA in 1924 and 1925, being relatively inexperienced in collaborating with the State Department and in operating its own foreign department, was therefore unable to neutralize German opposition by establishing a united front against the German film industry and its government.

The German contingency created hardships also for French producers, who entered into a collaboration arrangement with the Germans. A French article complained that the agreement was far more advantageous to German film producers than to the French due to the contingent restrictions.[18] The contract on common production signed by the two countries contained two important conditions. First, the exterior shots should be made in the country where the action took place, while the studio photos should be made in German studios. Second, the principal parts should be distributed between German and French actors. German films could enter France without hindrance, but as a result of the contingency the German borders were virtually closed to French movies. The result was that German studios produced most of the films, and all secondary roles were given to German actors.

As a consequence, the French film industry demanded that France should also introduce a contingency measure similar to the German one in order to save the French industry. The producers were complaining that contingency measures applied by other countries had led to a considerable development of the foreign film industries to the detriment of the unprotected French film industry, which could barely subsist. Without a quota policy, French producers were unable to negotiate more advantageous reciprocity agreements with foreign countries, which protected their film industries, whereas their films could enter an unrestricted French market.

France: Jean Sapène's quota initiatives, 1924–26

When the German film industry began to agitate for the introduction of film-quota legislation, the leaders of other European film industries also began to move toward introducing similar legislation. In France, Jean Sapène was the major advocate for quota protection for the French industry against the import of American films. He began these lobbying efforts in 1924, but his initial proposals elicited no response. Sapène made an unsuccessful motion in the "Chambre Syndicale de la Cinématographie Française" urging the government to require an export license for a French film for every import license for a foreign film. The background for his initiative was that the Pathé Company was being forced out of the American market, and his proposal aimed at forcing the American film industry to keep the market open for French films.

The Americans immediately discovered that Jean Sapène was the mastermind behind the quota agitation. In order to quell this uprising, ambassador Myron Herrick arranged a "get together" meeting in the embassy in December 1924 between officials from Famous Players-Lasky and representatives of Sapène and other French interests. During the meeting, the French requested a better treatment of their industry by the Americans.[19] The Americans did nothing further, and Herrick merely reported that his informal action had quieted down Sapène's anti-American agitation; apparently Sapène thought that he could in fact reach an arrangement with the Americans.

In actuality, when offering apparent explanations for not buying French films, the Americans were merely following a tactic of deception and delay. For example, when speaking to the French press the foreign director of Paramount's New York headquarters, Sydney R. Kent,[20] avowed that it was impossible for American film companies to buy French films because they were of such poor aesthetic quality they could not show them to the fastidious American spectators. It was not a question of the films' technical quality, Kent insisted, but the fact that the scenarios were simply not adapted to American "taste." Kent urged the journalists to fight the mistaken belief that American films were trying to replace the French, claiming that he personally would be delighted to buy a French production if it might interest American audiences. Kent urged the French to produce films with an idea of pleasing everybody; then they would be able to do business on a bigger scale. He even invited French film producers to study film production in Hollywood. The journalists swallowed the story, and even Jean Sapène seems to have swallowed the American propaganda, at least temporarily.[21]

One of the reasons Sapène appeared pacified in 1925 was that he had plans to overcome the American dominance by monopolizing French film distribution. Sapène controlled the patents for a new nonflammable safety film, and through his political contacts he influenced the government to issue a decree that prohibited the use of explosive nitrate film.[22]

The safety film was, however, not readily accepted because it had serious technical problems. To begin with the Pathé Company was unable to deliver sufficient quantities of safety film at a reasonable price by the date the decree became effective.[23] Moreover, the safety film did not last as long as the acetate film, and the quality was so poor it could barely be used. The consul stated that "the Pathé people" dreamed of securing an absolute monopoly over the exhibition of motion pictures in France, if not in all of continental Europe, by having the French government pass legislation forbidding the exhibition of nonflammable film. They believed that they had the only patents for nonflammable safety film extant and that consequently they could prevent other companies from manufacturing a competing product. This belief was translated into action by the decree of 1922 banning nitrate film.[24]

The decree was regularly postponed throughout the 1920s because of the poor quality of the safety film. When Kodak came out with a cheap acetate film in 1928–29, Sapène's dreams of empire crumbled. Sapène's drive for monopoly created distrust among film producers and a lack of solidarity with French exhibitors, which ultimately proved disastrous for the policies aimed at protecting French film production.

In September 1925, the MPPDA received information that Sapène and other film producers had resumed their pressure on the French government to have it introduce a reciprocity film quota policy. In the spring of 1925, a quota proposal had been defeated in the "Chambre Syndicale," but in September there was a new proposal of a quota arrangement. The MPPDA complained to the State Department that it would be a serious blow to American exports if enacted because it stipulated that import licenses would depend on how many export licenses were issued. The proposal was detrimental, the MPPDA claimed, because French films were only occasionally suitable for showing in the United States.[25]

The State Department reacted by immediately demanding that the embassy investigate the matter and give American interests all proper support.[26] The embassy replied that behind the proposal were only two men, Charles Pathé and Jean Sapène, both of whom were interested in promoting the exhibition of French films in the United States. It was almost certain that the government would not introduce import restrictions on its own initiative, since such restrictions would be injurious to French film exhibitors and theater owners. The best move American interests could make would be to try to placate Sapène by exhibiting some of his films in the United States. In other words, "a little tact on the part of American film interests, involving, perhaps, some small sacrifice in the putting on of French pictures, would close the whole question."[27]

As the "Chambre Syndicale" rejected his policy to protect French production, Sapène created his own organization, which he launched in November 1925 at a banquet of the cinematographic press in the presence of the minister of fine arts.[28] The organization's program included a proposal to prohibit imports, except for "contingents," to films from countries that imported French films. Import licenses should only be given to members of the syndicate that produced French films. The minister was baffled and did not comment on Sapène's proposal.[29] The contingent measure was published in Sapène's newspaper, Le Matin, under the name Pierre Gilles. He suggested that film imports should be limited to two meters for every meter of French film produced.[30]

Nothing came of the contingency plans because the other film producers were suspicious of Jean Sapène's motives. At first, the "Chambre Syndicale Française de la Cinématographie" found Gilles' proposal attractive, but it was soon realized that it favored only producers who were also importers, in other words Sapène, whereas it would be detrimental to others.[31] Herron explained to Vice Consul Alfred D. Cameron that the Pathé consortium was responsible for these attacks, and since Sapène was involved in both *Le Matin* and the Pathé consortium, it was reasonable to think that he was the instigator of the articles.[32]

The State Department Begins Fighting the Contingent

The State Department began officially to assist the MPPDA in fighting European film contingents following an instruction on January 30, 1926,[33] addressed to a number of embassies. They were requested to report any occurrence of agitation and governmental activities directed against American films. The embassy was also to determine whether discrimination occurred against American films as compared with other imported films. The instruction itself was a reaction to a letter from Will Hays, which stated that the agitation against American films threatened to spread throughout the world.

Chester Lloyd Jones, the commercial attaché in Paris, replied that agitation was carried out in France chiefly by "private interests" and was directed almost entirely at American films. He thought it would probably be impossible to protest potential legislation on the grounds of discrimination since it would be of a general nature. But since American films dominated the French markets, they would be most affected. The attaché doubted that drastic legislation would be introduced against American films since the prosperity of French distributors and exhibitors depended on a continuous, adequate supply of good films, which French producers were unable to provide. However, a minority of French producers (meaning Jean Sapène) might profit from restrictive measures, and their strength in political maneuvering might enable them to have harmful legislation passed. The embassy had also warned French authorities that drastic measures against American films might lead to retaliation.[34]

In February 1926 Jean Sapène suddenly dropped his quota agitation. American film companies had begun to follow up on the embassy's suggestion to buy his films. Universal purchased the films *Michel Strogoff* and *Les Misérables*, which were shown with great success in New York.[35] But such purchases were rare exceptions. American film companies also bought the films *Surcouf, Titi—King of the Kids, Captain Rascasse, Colette's Tears, Antoinette Sagbrier, Mademoiselle Josette My Wife,* and *Belphegor* for political reasons, but they were never released in the United States.[36] Sapène probably entered a contract with the Americans because he lacked funds. The American film industry did not purchase Sapène's films in order to make a profit, but for strategic reasons or as a kind of bribery in order to postpone the introduction of quota legislation. As Colonel Lowry from the MPPDA explained, Sapène "is a person to be reckoned with in the future development of business in France."[37]

Sapène realized that his association no longer served any purpose now that the Americans were buying his films, and he reentered the "Chambre Syndicale" as an honorary president.[38] Sapène stipulated that some action be taken to protect the French industry, but there is no evidence of any movement in this direction.[39]

In 1926, the federal government intensified its diplomatic support of Hollywood exports. In September George R. Canty became trade commissioner for motion pictures in Paris. Canty was responsible for gathering information about developments in the European film markets for the Motion Picture Division in the Department of Commerce, whereas the diplomats carried out film diplomacy and reported to the State Department.[40]

With Canty's arrival in Paris in 1926 the film diplomatic system reached its complete development, both with regard to gathering information and providing the MPPDA with diplomatic support if foreign governments encroached on the interests of the American film industry. Whereas the American film diplomacy was fully prepared to counter European interference in the American film exports, European governments were in general only marginally interested in the conditions of the national film industry. French film policy was almost exclusively confined to extracting amusement taxes from movie houses.

Film Europe: French-German collaboration, 1924–26

"In the face of the overwhelming prosperity of the American film industry any attempt at fighting back would seem to be like a pygmy up against a giant," was the New York Times' assessment of the situation.[41] European producers realized that cooperation among European industries was necessary in order to become competitive with Hollywood. Only Germany had been able to rival the position of the American films because it protected its market by the contingent system. But the contingent also stopped the import of films from other European countries. Therefore it was necessary to collaborate in exchanging films in Europe. Louis Aubert anticipated that economic collaboration would influence the political sphere and bring about "the United States of Europe." The movement towards international collaboration to prevent war was strong in the mid-1920s, and Edouard Herriot was also a major advocate of European integration.[42]

Throughout the 1920s European film production gradually increased, whereas American exports constantly decreased. The production of films in individual European countries was comparatively small, but taken together the size of European production was comparable to the American. If they collaborated and exchanged films, European film production would cover the demand of the European movie houses, and American films might be excluded.[43] The MPPDA was aware that European collaboration might reduce American exports, and therefore the association followed a tactic that aimed at destroying any attempt at European cooperation. The State Department labeled any such collaborative efforts as discrimination against American products.

According to William Victor Strauss, the European film producers could not obtain a profitable production based on the receipts in the home market alone, and therefore they had to export films to other countries. As the American market was in general closed to foreign films, the European producers could only increase the receipts by exchanging films with other European countries. Quota arrangements such as the German one, however, limited not only the import of American films, but also those from other European countries, and it was therefore necessary to arrange agreements of co-production.

To counter Hollywood's dominance, an international collaboration network was established in the 1920s, the so-called "Film Europe." It consisted of different European initiatives to promote co-production and reciprocal distribution agreements, especially between Germany and France in the years 1924 to 1928. The purpose was to create a "common market" for films by breaking down trade barriers, thereby obtaining a broader economic basis for film production than any single country could sustain. The movement was to give the European producers a dominant position within their own region as a precursor to a new expansion on the global market. In 1925 the collaboration was shaken when the UFA Company ran into economic difficulties and had to be rescued by the Americans. Ultimately, the collaboration proved much less advantageous to the French film producers than to the Germans.[44]

The American film diplomats learned about the first attempts at German-French collaboration in 1924 with the establishment of the German film trust, Westi-Film G.m.b.H. of Berlin.[45] Westi was founded in order to fight the competition from American films. The concept was to reproduce the conditions in America by distributing films in a wider European market, which would allow the films of the syndicate to amortize their over-head in Europe and compete at low prices overseas.[46] The company had gained control of several film production companies and cinemas every-where in Europe.[47] A merger of the Wengerow Company with the Stinnes concern established Westi-Film. The directors were Wladimir Wengerow, and Richard Becker and Leo Bagerow, the latter two from the Stinnes central agency. The aim of the Wengerow Company was to produce and sell films, especially to Russia, but before the establishment of the Westi-Film Company it lacked the strong capital of the Stinnes concern.

In February 1925 the Pathé Company entered an agreement to exchange films with the Westi group. The Westi companies would exhibit the Pathé films in their German theaters, and Pathé would show Westi productions in France. Both firms owned or controlled several hundred movie houses in their respective countries. Another agreement was supposedly entered be-tween Gaumont and UFA. A Paris representative of one of the leading American film producers thought that the arrangements would have little effect, because the only way they could oust the American film from its present predominant position in the European markets would be either to pool their efforts towards producing sufficient film of good quality, or to bring pressure to bear on their governments to tax foreign film out of existence.[48]

In January-February 1925, the German and French film industries entered two agreements of cooperation. The first was between Pathé and Westi, who both controlled the distribution of films to several hundred cinemas. The arrangement was that Westi would distribute Pathé films in Germany while Pathé would show Westi films in France. The other agreement was probably between UFA and Gaumont. However, in the autumn of 1926, before the Westi agreement could prove the value of international collaboration, Stinnes died and Westi went bankrupt.

The International Film Conference in Paris, 1926

The lack of unity among the various branches of the French cinema industry gave Sapène a unique opportunity to become the leader of the French industry, but with his arrangements with the American film industry he lost his opportunity.[49] As the leader of the French film industry, he would also have been one of the most outstanding leaders of a European film community that might have been established during the Film Conference in Paris in September 1926.

The Paris conference was arranged by the "Institut International de la Coopération Intellectuelle" (IICI) under the League of Nations. The aim of the conference was to study the cultural, aesthetic, and educational aspect of the cinema, but not its economic and industrial development. The American film industry refused to take part in the conference because, as Herron explained in a press release, "the conference might easily develop into an anti-American affair if we took part in it, and as the foreign situation is none too happy at present we did not want to complicate it."[50]

Sapène would have become the natural leader of a European campaign against American films if he had participated in the conference. Sapène's newspaper, Le Matin, did not even mention the congress until after it had taken place, and the Pathé Company, which was the most important group of French film producers, was not directly represented there. Le Matin finally took notice, declaring itself astonished that the principal magnates of the industry in France, England, the United States, and Italy were not among the delegates, because without their cooperation the resolutions of the congress could not be realized. For the congress to be successful, it should have been organized by those who had built up the French motion picture industry, who would have been the best equipped to outline a practical program and make decisions about the international film industry. The article concluded that without the support of the film industry, the resolutions of the congress were bound to be useless and without force.[51]

In reality, Sapène did not take part in the congress because he had entered into a deal with the Americans, apparently unaware that Universal had purchased a few of his films only to win his support and thereby prevent both European film cooperation and the passage of French quota legislation.[52] Aware of the threat of European collaboration to American film exports, the MPPDA opposed all attempts at European film agreements. Fredrick L. Herron later explained to the State Department that

> [t]he main purpose of the conference had been to get publicity for the movement in support of measures directed against American films. This movement had collapsed because arrangements had been made privately for restraining the French press from publishing the material in question. This matter had been attended to through Sapène. He was now hostile, apparently because American interests had rejected a scenario prepared by his wife, for which $150,000 was wanted.[53]

Sapène's main aim, however, was to open the American market for his own films, and European film collaboration and French quota legislation was of lower priority to him.[54] In fact, the MPPDA companies were determined to uphold their control and monopoly in the American film market, and their dealings with him were based on purely political considerations. In 1927, the Federal Trade Commission found the Famous Players-Lasky

Corporation guilty of a criminal conspiracy to violate the antitrust laws of the United States. In a complaint to the President of the United States, William Sheafe Chase, superintendent of the International Reform Federation, accused the MPPDA of being an unlawful combination in restraint of trade by monopolizing film exhibition.[55] But no action was taken against the MPPDA because Will Hays was a personal friend of the American presidents of the 1920s, Calvin Coolidge and Herbert Hoover.

The MPPDA actually had no hard evidence to support its opinion that the Paris congress was a mask for anti-American activities until November 1926, when the vice-consul, Harold L. Smith, found out that independent German film producers had had several meetings with French film producers in order to carry out a French-German collaboration in film production. UFA had not taken part in the negotiations, in which several kinds of collaboration were discussed. The most important form of collaboration was to produce films using mainly German funds but French directors and artists, and based on French scenarios. The Germans would distribute the films in Central Europe and in Scandinavia, and the French would distribute them in France, Belgium, Switzerland, the Latin countries, South America, and the Middle East. The advantage would be that the films would not be subject to the German contingent system that regulated the import of foreign film. Another advantage might be that the films would have an international character, which would enable them to compete with the American films. The Germans thought they could not make sufficient profits under the existing conditions; it would be futile to attempt to break into the American market, and therefore they could expand their market share only by producing and distributing films in collaboration with French film producers.

The congress had also set up a permanent commission to organize the next meeting, which was scheduled to take place in Berlin. The executive committee consisted of Aubert, Julien Luchaire (French director of the IICI), and Bausback, managing director of UFA.[56] The Americans watched with interest as they withdrew one after the other. Luchaire went first, because Sapène and Aubert had refused to supply funding for the institute. Bausback withdrew after having been approached by the Americans, but stated that he had never been keen on collaborating with the majority of the congress participants, which consisted of professors, school teachers, reformers, and other intellectuals.[57] In 1927 Louis Aubert was the only remaining member of the organizing committee, and the IICI had lost interest in organizing the next congress.

Jean Sapène seems also to have been one of the coordinators for the next film congress, but withdrew in February 1927, explaining that:

I believe that it is foolish for representatives of the motion picture industry to participate in the International Motion Picture Congress, as now constituted. I refused to accept membership in the organization Commission for the next Congress, to which I was recently elected. The results of the next Congress will be no more important than those of the last one, which accomplished nothing. I do not think the American industry should take part in the next Congress, and I do not intend to participate in it. Why should we, cinema industrial leaders, take part in a Congress where we would be outvoted by the numbers of delegates who have no connection with the industry? What can the Congress accomplish? Nothing! Copyright? There is only one thing to do and that is to induce the United States to accept the Berne Convention. There is no possibility of authors receiving royalties from the receipts of cinemas, which is now done in the case of the legitimate theater.

I want to be independent to make such agreements as I see fit between my company and American companies or those of any other country. A world organization could do nothing to divide up production, for the member companies would refuse to sacrifice themselves. We are in business to make money and not for philanthropic reasons. The Congress was organized by "fonctionnaires" to give them something to do, and with the hope of obtaining financial support from the motion picture industry.

A reunion of the leaders in the motion picture industry in France, Germany and the United States would be useful to solve artistic, technical and commercial problems common to all, but it should not be held until a definite program is drawn up....The United States is making a big mistake in not taking more European films.[58]

Still, the French politicians thought that France controlled the world cinema, for they lacked any real understanding of even their own film industry, which was being bested by the competition with Hollywood. It was symptomatic of this attitude that the minister of fine arts, Edouard Herriot (as reported by American Vice Consul Harold Smith), spoke naively about French cinema in the Chamber of Deputies without regard for the future of the film industry, stating that

[t]he cinema is an endless lesson with unbounded possibilities, and the best means to show the world to children. But I fear that up until the present time, it has been badly employed. When we follow closely with

interest, with affection, the state of mind of the youth of today, it is not without anxiety that we see that the modern cinema with its romantic films, of poor romance, causes the birth of dangerous germs. There are too many films which can sow bad ideas in the minds of the youth, and I, the guardian of the children of the nation, intend to protect them. I will insist that the educational authorities supervise closely the motion picture shows to which the youth of the school are invited. That is my criticism. I have told you what the cinema should not be. I must tell you what I think it should be. What shall replace the romantic conception which only results in the transcribing of poor novels to the screen? I have studied this question very thoroughly, and I think that I should first change the pedagogic museum, give to France something that she does not have, an institute of pedagogy, where we can investigate the possibilities of instruction by motion pictures. We could there show how to give a lesson by means of the movies. In other words, develop the pedagogy of motion pictures. Whatever happens, my ideas on the subject are very clear. I do not want to permit the use of an art against the welfare of youth when this art can render such marvelous services.[59]

Herriot's speech was loudly applauded. He had taken a great interest in the development of educational motion pictures. While he was mayor of Lyon, he had promoted the installation of projectors in many schools in his district, and he had even spent his own funds to promote educational films.

Herriot's attitude towards the French film industry was further revealed in his reply to the communist deputy Vaillant-Couturier, who suddenly demanded in the Chamber of Deputies on November 30, 1926, that the government should nationalize film production. The international film congress, Vaillant-Couturier declared, only caused private industry to strengthen its hold on motion pictures. He would not accept Aubert's definition of cinema, during the congress, as a box for expenses and a box for receipts. An advertisement in *La Cinématographie Française* had stated that the international motion picture congress had been propitious in aiding business among different countries, which Vaillant-Couturier certainly hoped was not the League of Nations' intention for the congress. In conclusion he stated that besides the Aubert enterprises—since the Gaumont Company had been absorbed by the American Metro-Goldwyn trust—the only production company worth mentioning was the Cinéromans-Pathé-Consortium. And even Herriot himself had criticized the quality of that company's films. The cinema could develop only once it was liberated from the film magnates. The theaters were subsidized, so why not the movie houses?

In his reply, Herriot did not defend the interests of the French film industry, which Harold L. Smith took as ample evidence that the government had no intention of interfering in the conditions of the private film industry. Herriot mainly dwelled upon his agenda, the promotion of pedagogical films. He stated that he would support and guarantee the artistic freedom of the artists who wanted to devote themselves to careers within the motion picture industry. Moreover, he would introduce a film professorate, and he would open discussions with the industry to make it possible for artists to study film art under the auspices of the state. But he would not nationalize the film industry, which he thought would only prosper in freedom.

The Emergence of the French Quota Legislation,

1927–28

HOLLYWOOD HAS A FOREIGN WAR
Export of American Films Is Curtailed by
Many Nations as Undesirable Influence—
Our Cinema "Art" Is Criticized
—Headline, *New York Times*,
March 4, 1928

The absence of the Americans at the international congress in Paris in 1926 seems to have opened the eyes of the Europeans to the true American strategy. The *New York Times'* Paris correspondent[60] noticed a growing bitterness among European film producers and distributors over American control of the world market for motion pictures, and even though the aim of the congress was not to deal with business problems, they lay in the background. Steps were taken to establish a permanent international organization of especially European interests in order to counter the American influence, which they felt threatened their very existence. Unfortunately, such cooperation was impeded by the introduction of quota policies.

In 1926 there were no signs that France might introduce a contingency system similar to the German one. But in the beginning of 1927 the French began to awaken and become suspicious of the American strategy. For example, the director of Films-Albatros, A. Kamenka,[61] wrote that the American film industry had decided to annex the European film industry. The plan was to destroy the European film industry by taking away its personnel and organizing the exhibition of American films in Europe. The American strategy was to squash the competitor who had started to become dangerous by conquering its markets.

At the end of February 1927, the minister of fine arts, Edouard Herriot, decided immediately to set up a film commission in order to study all aspects of the motion picture industry. The commission had around fifty members, who represented other ministries, film organizations, manuscript authors, the film press, exhibitors, and projectionists. An advisory board would examine how the proposals could be carried out. Harold L. Smith commented that Herriot had always shown a great interest in educational films, but now his plans were to take an active interest in all parts of the film industry.[62] Several French film producers had started to demand that the American film industry collaborate with them, either by purchasing a larger number of French films or by producing films in France. Such assistance would be a philanthropic aid to the French industry, because in both cases the Americans would probably lose money.[63]

The campaign in favor of a quota system to protect French films reopened in March 1927 with the publication of three editorials in the film journal *l'Intransigeant*.[64] The idea of protection had become almost a dead issue because the government had not shown any active interest in it, but the passage of the British "Quota Act" in April 1927 raised the question again. The American consul Alphonse Gaulin thought that the interest several ministers took in the film industry indicated that something definite might result, most likely in the form of higher import duties or a contingent system similar to that of the Germans.[65] Harold L. Smith explained that Léon Bailby had written the editorials in *l'Intransigeant* on behalf of Sapène.

The arguments Bailby used to activate the French government were in principle the same as those used by the MPPDA to induce the State Department to give the American film industry diplomatic support. That is, the Americans understood that films could be used to make propaganda for themselves, their country, and their government, and that even their language served to convince the world that the United States was the foremost country and culture. Aubert had stated that motion pictures were a means of economic colonization: "When we take up the defense of French motion pictures, we do it not only on account of patriotism, but because we see a real danger; four million French people spend an entire evening at a course on American 'culture' and take a lesson in American propaganda once a week. Within a short while, if the French Government does not intervene, there will be no obstacle to this propaganda of colonization; French production of motion pictures, ruined by an overbearing competition, will cease." France had done nothing to protect its film industry and culture.

Bailby also explained that the French film industry was not competitive due to unfair market conditions, rather than as a result of deficiencies in film quality. With the exception of the extraordinary films by Chaplin

Fairbanks, and De Mille, most American films were childish, with silly scenarios that were inferior to French or German films of the same category. Often the artists were mediocre, but they were well publicized by the French press. American films had the advantage that their production costs could be fully recuperated in the home market. Something had to be done to limit the dominance of American films for the protection of the production of French films. But to the government the film industry was only a milk cow which could be milked without ever being fed.[66]

The propaganda continued on April 6, 1927, when *Ciné-Comædia* published interviews with Jean Sapène,[67] Léon Brezillon, and Marcel l'Herbier about how they thought French film might be protected. Sapène thought protection was necessary, and that it could be implemented in two ways, either by introducing a quota arrangement, or by increasing tariffs on foreign films. To function efficiently, the quota arrangement had to be planned carefully. An increase in tariffs might be efficient if it was high enough to stop the import of films that already had recovered their costs. A tariff increase might prevent the worst films from entering France, the ones that were offered to the movie houses at low rental prices, creating a disastrous competition for French film production. It would be possible to promote the production of French films by making the import of films free to an extent comparable to the value of the French films that foreigners bought. Sapène also recommended that the film industry also demand a reduction of the exorbitant amusement taxes, which would enable the movie houses to pay a higher film rental. He thought it necessary to expand the number of movie houses, since more than fourteen million French people, one-third of the population, had no access to cinemas because they lived in the countryside.

The director of the French cinema owner's organization, Léon Brezillon, thought that a contingent measure might result in an increase in French film production, but that it would also be necessary to reform film distribution. He advocated a prohibition of the block-booking practiced by certain American film companies because it limited the film selection.

Vice Consul Smith interviewed Louis Nalpas, Sapène's right hand man, in the beginning of April 1927. [68] Nalpas stated that it was an important time because Sapène was working on a plan to be submitted to the French government. He thought that he had given the American industry plenty of time to enter an agreement about the distribution of more French films in the U.S., and he had been unable to achieve any permanent results. He thought that a solution depended on the half-dozen big companies that controlled the market in the United States, and that if they wanted they could release French movies and induce the public to see them.

Smith also noticed that the French minister of commerce, Bokanowski, refused to introduce a film quota policy. At a banquet for Louis Aubert, Bokanowski stated that he constantly received propositions to protect the film industry; a quota arrangement or tariff increase could be useful, but would be only a palliative measure. Instead he suggested that the French industry should attempt to find a solution through better organization and combination. He chided the producers for being badly organized and competing with foreign film in many separate units, and he advised them to form a central organization that might become the nucleus of a European organization. With such an organization the French industry would be invincible.

On April 19, Harold L. Smith informed the State Department that the movement for the protection of the French film industry had become serious.[69] Leaders of French film production were working on proposed legislation that would be presented to the French government for adoption. They felt that the American industry had failed to buy or distribute a sufficient number of French films, considering the great number of American films shown in France. Jean Sapène was behind the movement. The background for the alarming news was that Léon Bailby had published yet another feature article in l'Intransigeant, in which he stated "if we don't do something to protect the French motion picture industry, it is condemned to death." The leaders of the film industry had reached an agreement to recommend Sapène's contingent system.

But in May 1927, following a visit by C.C. Pettijohn, the general counsel of the MPPDA, Sapène decided to withhold his quota legislation campaign for several months. Pettijohn had promised to put Sapène's demands to the American industry to seek an accommodation. If three or four of his films were distributed in the United States per year Sapène would be satisfied, Vice Consul Smith reported confidentially, and if Sapène was quieted the agitation would no longer be serious, because he was the only politically influential public figure in the French industry, as none of the others in the industry had his influence or standing.[70] Shortly after, the consulate reported that Sapène's latest feature film, Casanova, was sold to Universal for distribution in America, and the purchase of Princesse Marsha, in which Mrs. Sapène starred under the name Claudia Victrix, was also being contemplated.[71]

Herriot's cinema commission met in the beginning of May 1927 to discuss the general situation in the French industry, as well as the proposed means for the protection of the French production industry. The embassy had no knowledge of what took place at the meeting. It seems most likely that the exhibitors' representatives disagreed among themselves on which policy to adopt. After the meeting, the exhibitors organized into three different groups according to size, which would then report their opinions to the French syndicate of Motion Picture Exhibitors. For the large theaters, the president was Léon Brézillon, the medium-sized cinemas were led by Jean Chatagnier, and Morel represented the small cinemas.

It also seems likely that the exhibitors' opposition to the producers' demands for protection began at the meeting of the cinema commission. The critic Boisyvon[72] explained in l'Intransigeant that there was a movement among the French exhibitors to oppose any measures for the protection of the French production industry. They were specifically opposed to any palliative measures, which they believed would result in protected French movies becoming prohibitively expensive if a film shortage emerged. The minor French exhibitors, in particular, were not anxious to sacrifice themselves to aid the French producers, who had never shown any inclination to favor them. Many exhibitors disliked Sapène and, recalling his heavy-handed methods in the handling of the safety film question, criticized him for endeavoring to become further entrenched in all branches of the film industry at the expense of the exhibitors.[73] Harold Smith also informed the MPPDA about an interview he had had with Charles Burguet, who had been appointed to represent the screenwriters in the cinema commission. Burguet stated that he was strongly in favor of a contingent system.

The exhibitors united for common action in favor of a reduction of both movie rental prices and the special taxes on those movie houses which had gross receipts of less than seven-thousand francs a month. They also wanted to limit advance booking to three months and do away with block-booking. All important distributors rented films a year in advance, which to a certain extent involved block-booking. The exhibitors hoped to break up this practice and thereby obtain lower film rentals. It was surprising to Harold L. Smith that more of them had not realized that the contingent system would result in a considerable increase in film rentals.[74] Foreign films would cost more on account of the limited numbers imported or as a result of the increased import duties, depending on the plan that was adopted. The French producers would also increase prices in order to obtain a greater return for their productions.

Alphonse Gaulin, the American general consul, observed that in June 1927, Sapène had become the leader of a movement to have the special taxes on the exhibitors reduced, and to compensate the loss to the French treasury he proposed that the import duties on films could be raised.[75] Sapène stated that the import duties were ridiculously low for the benefit of the French film printing industry. He also suggested that French cinemas be required to show French films twenty-five weeks in a year, which the consul thought would be a tremendous blow to the American industry.

When Parliament discussed the finance bill in June 1927, the deputy André François-Poncet proposed to increase tariffs as well as to limit the import of foreign films to three-fourths of the average number of films shown in France during the years 1924, 1925, and 1926. The consul calculated that the proposal would limit the number of foreign films to 450, thereby limiting the American share to 405 films per year. [76] The proposition caused a great deal of discussion, but it came too late to be considered by the cinema commission, and the proposal seems not to have been adopted before the session ended prior to the summer holidays.

After the summer, on October 2, 1927, the minister of fine arts appointed a cinema commission. The commission had forty-four members representing different departments of the government, producers, exhibitors, artists, authors, and practically every branch of the industry.[77] At a meeting on November 10th, Edouard Herriot decided to form three subcommissions, the first to report on film production, the second on the exhibition and distribution of films, and the third on use of films in education. Herriot explained in the Senate that he was shocked to discover in the customs statistics the number of films imported from the United States, when France might produce enough for its own needs. "France would soon be colonized by foreign motion picture interests if we do not do something about it."[78] Charles Burguet, the French author, movie director, and president of the Film Authors' Society confided to the American consul, Harold L. Smith, that "Herriot knows very little about motion pictures, and must rely upon the Cinema Commission for guidance."[79]

At first Jean Sapène was unwilling to collaborate with the Cinema Commission while he was still attempting to reach an agreement with the Americans, but in October he began to be in favor of the contingency project. He may have changed his mind because Nalpas and Knecht, during their stay in the United States, had been unable to sell the film Casanova to any American film company. Fredrick L. Herron from the MPPDA had talked to them several times, and he explained to Gaulin that one could not expect that film companies would buy a film that could not be sold to the public, and the passage of the quota law would mean the end to French films in America.[80] Herron assured the consul that Sapène's new policy was entirely uncalled for: "We have in the last year taken six French pictures in this market for distribution—two by Universal, two by Metro and two by Paramount. Of these six, four are M. Sapène's own pictures. This goes very plainly to show that no matter what you do for these French motion picture people, they demand something new in addition."[81] Herron neglected to mention that France at the same time had bought 565 films from the United States in 1926.

Herron thought that it was out of the question to buy a certain number of French pictures each year in order to fend off the French quota legislation, because then other countries would demand similar concessions. As Herron argued, "we can no more do this for France than we can for England, Czechoslovakia, Poland, Russia, Italy, Spain or any other country of the world."[82] The MPPDA companies clearly had total control of the American film market.

On November 24, 1927, Sapène became the chairman of the first subcommittee dealing with film production, and he drew up the contingency plan together with Charles Burguet. The central point was that distributors of foreign films would have to export a French film in order to obtain permission to release a certain number of their films in France. The ratio mentioned was seven-to-one, or maybe ten-to-one. The report of the subcommission of distributors and exhibitors, however, was completely opposed to any contingent measure, and most of the commission, including Herriot, opposed it. On December 29, 1927, a compromise proposal, put forward by Léon Gaumont, was agreed to, which limited the releases of foreign films to nine meters for every one meter of French film produced.[83]

The Herriot Decree, 1928

On January 11, 1928, the Cinema Commission considered the report of the second subcommission on the problems of the distributors and exhibitors, and attempted to determine which parts of the contingent project could be enacted by decree rather than requiring the passage of legislation. There was also some discussion of how many permits a producer would obtain for the release of a French film in foreign countries.[84] During the meeting, Serruys, the expert from the Ministry of Commerce, pointed out that there were certain discrepancies between the contingent project and the decisions at the Economic Conference on Import Restrictions held in Geneva in October and November 1927. The quota project would violate the Geneva Convention of the *International Conference for the Abolition of Import and Export Prohibitions and Restrictions.*

The aim of the Geneva conference was to maintain international free trade. France had signed the convention, but the United States had not. France had not, however, included films in the list of products which should continue to be restricted. The Cinema Commission had given little thought to the decisions of this conference, believing that the contingent project was entirely an internal French matter, since no restriction on the import of films was imposed; the proposition was to limit the release of foreign films in France. England, Germany, and Italy had also signed the conference convention and upheld contingent laws at the same time, and it was unthinkable that France would not be able to introduce similar measures. In addition, since the United States had prohibited the import of French wines on the basis of protecting the health of its citizens, the commission thought that France would have the right to limit the number of American films released in order to protect the minds of the youth of the nation. Although the proposed decree caused a storm of protest in cinematographic circles, on January 15 the Chambre Syndicale resolved to authorize its members in the first sub-commission to vote for the contingent decree if the nine-meters-to-one measure adopted by the first subcommission was carried out. With this decision and a promise to the exhibitors that they would have sufficient film for their programs, the Cinema Commission decided to accept the decree proposed by Herriot, with one dissenting vote. According to Harold L. Smith, "The meeting was not without incident, for Mr. Sapène and one of the representatives of the exhibitors came to blows and the latter was floored."[85]

The decree was issued on February 18, 1928 and went into effect on March 1. It consisted of three essential parts. First, it assimilated the cinema laws to those of the theater. The cinemas wanted treatment as favorable as the theaters received, especially in regard to taxation. The decree also reduced the arbitrary local control over the licensing of French movie houses, which increased in number and quality in the following years. The Ministère de l'Instruction Publique censored the films, but the local police could still prohibit shows according to the laws of 1884 and 1790, a power they retained up to the 1960s.[86] Second, the decree gave autocratic powers to the new Cinema Control Commission regarding the release and censoring of all films. All films from a company which had produced an "anti-French" film might be barred from French screens. Finally, the decree gave the commission the power to compel foreign film producers to buy French films in order to release their films in France. Herriot had by then abandoned his plan for parliament to pass a contingent measure, but instead he gave the Cinema Control Commission arbitrary powers to regulate the release of foreign films in France.

Consul General A. Gaulin told Herron that the decree would be extremely annoying for the distribution of American films in France, besides being a clear violation at least of the spirit of the Geneva convention. His interpretation seemed to be confirmed by Herriot's declaration that the primary objective of the decree was to limit the release of foreign films in France to control the release of foreign films treating French subjects, and to compel foreign producers to buy French films.[87]

The envoy Edward G. Lowry represented the MPPDA,[88] but had problems collaborating with the diplomats, and his health was failing. Therefore, he did not meet with Herriot until February 18, 1928, the date the decree was issued. The diplomats and the civil servants of the Department of Commerce and the State Department constantly complained that Lowry refused to cooperate with them to resolve the French situation.[89] In fact, it seems the federal administration was more willing to serve the interests of Hollywood than the MPPDA wanted.

Herriot, in a meeting with Lowry and the commercial attaché Henry MacLean, claimed not to understand why the foreign film industries, American, German, Italian, and others, were so anxious about the decree.[90] He claimed that the decree was not a contingent in any respect. The problem was that the French producers had encountered difficulties selling their products abroad, and he thought they should be protected in some way. The aim of the decree was to help French production. Foreign companies that bought French films would get preference in obtaining visas. The new film commission was only a stronger censorship board, and the only difference was that representatives of the French film industry had been called upon to cooperate on it. Herriot emphasized that the government did not show any unfriendly feeling toward the U.S.; it simply desired to help French production. Herriot also wanted the American industry to take more interest in French production.

The decree was an administrative measure that did not require the approval of the Chamber of Deputies. Under its terms a special commission of thirty-two members was created. All foreign films had to receive a visa from this board before they could be shown in France. No visas would be granted to films that were offensive to French traditions and customs. The commission would also take into consideration whether the company was prepared to distribute French films for exhibition in the United States or other countries. The commission would not grant more than seven visas on foreign films for each French film exported. The French restriction was the strictest ever instituted in Europe; arbitrary power was given to the commission to reject any films with the result that no American company would know how many films it could release in France in a given year.[91]

The commission started to issue visas immediately. On March 12, 1928 Lowry succeeded in obtaining a copy of the film control commission's internal guidelines, which he immediately sent to Will Hays. On March 13, Lowry had lunch with the representatives of the American film companies, who all agreed that the situation was serious, and that it could expand to the rest of Europe. He succeeded in persuading them not to buy any contingents or visas before they obtained instructions from New York.

Lowry and Miles from the International Chamber of Commerce had an interview with Paul Léon, president of the Film Commission, on March 13, 1928. According to Lowry's memorandum,[92] Léon stated that the motive of the decree was not hostility towards foreign films or foreign countries, but simply a desire to preserve French film industry from ruin. Léon supposed that Lowry had heard of the regulations in an outline that had not yet been accepted by Herriot. Lowry asked if it was true that the regulations limited the number of films admitted into France. Léon replied that this was true to a certain extent, and that the regulations had a resemblance to a contingent, but it was not really a contingent and would not be rigid. The quantity of foreign films entering France would vary in accordance with the development of French production, which could decrease and increase. The French exhibitors' need to obtain a sufficient number of American films would also be taken into account. The companies that facilitated the purchase of French films abroad would obtain visas more easily than others, as the decree intended to increase French production. Léon preferred to call the regulations a "direction d'idées" rather than a contingent. He thought that a close collaboration of American and French individual companies on the basis of film exchange would be the most desirable solution. The French would thus learn what kinds of films they should produce to get into the American market, and the American company would have the advantage of being able to export more films to France.

Léon then stated that the plan was to fix a seven-to-one quota, which meant that the Americans were obliged to buy one film in order to obtain seven export licenses. He estimated that France needed about six-hundred films a year and produced about one hundred, a number he thought would increase. Five hundred and twenty visas had been issued, which the commission thought would last to September 1928, and the commission could issue visas in case French films were purchased. Herriot would sign the regulations within three or four days and they would then be ratified by the Senate. Colonel Lowry stated that the American industry would be glad to obey the laws of any country in which it operated if this could be done without loss or injury.

The French regulations were approved on March 16 and appeared in *Le Matin* on March 18. The American commercial attaché to Switzerland, Charles E. Lyon, thought they violated the Geneva Convention but only considered articles 2, 6, and 7 as evidence of discrimination.[93] Article 2 stated: "All French films (except such as offend morals and public security) will receive from the Control Commission the visa necessary for their exploitation in France, the Colonies and Protectorates." Lyon thought that this condition violated the Geneva statement that exceptions to the treaty are permissible so long as they extend to foreign products the same regimen applied to native products. The visa regulations were quite different for foreign films.

Article 6 stated: "In view of the large number of films that recently received visas from the Control Commission (520 films) this Commission establishes the number of 500 foreign films which will be introduced in France during the period from March 1, 1928 to September 30, 1929. This total may be changed at any time, if necessary, to assure the number of films necessary for French exploitation."

Article 7 stated: "Producers who give evidence of having sold one major French film in foreign countries that are themselves producers of films and where French films find it hard to gain a footing, will receive from the Commission authority to show in France, the Colonies and Protectorates seven foreign films for each of the domestic French films thus sold." Lyon concluded that the regulation was carefully worded in order not to appear to be in conflict with the Geneva treaty.

Will Hays decided to go to Paris to negotiate personally probably because Lowry was unable to keep track of the developments and was unwilling to collaborate with the commercial attachés of the embassy.[94] The commercial attaché MacLean[95] complained that Lowry incorrectly reported from the meeting on March 12, 1928, with Edouard Herriot that the regulations had been submitted to parliament for its approval and that action was imminent. The result was that Hays asked the State Department to take action; the embassy was asked for a report and to advise whether there existed any basis for formal or informal action. Even a week after the meeting had taken place, Lowry was still unable to say what the status of the regulations were or what procedure should be followed if they were to be put into effect. Colonel Lowry's assertion that no decree would be passed until he had had a further chance to confer with Herriot was also wrong. Lowry had given the State Department the impression that the decree would not do much harm, and that the American companies did not care about the French market. This error was exposed when Herron came down to Washington to confer with the State Department and the Department of Commerce. Nor had Lowry understood that the seven-to-one ratio was not an integral part of the decree, but an internal decision of the commission.[96] The problems of representation in France seem to have induced Will Hays to appoint Vice Consul Harold L. Smith as the MPPDA's European representative in April 1928.[97]

[1] Confidential report from Oscar Solbert to Will Hays, Berlin, May 20, 1925, *Will Hays Papers.*

[2] Thomas J. Saunders, *Hollywood in Berlin* (Berkeley, CA, 1994), p. 54.

[3] Translation of an article in *Tägliche Rundschau*, August 3, 1926, in letter from L. Domeratzky, Chief, Division of Foreign Tariffs, to J. S. Connolly, MPPDA, Washington, Jan. 17, 1921, USDC.

[4] Ambassador Jacob Gould Schurman, U.S. Embassy Germany, August 6, 1926, USDS.

[5] Report to the USDC from Douglas Miller, U.S. Trade Commissioner Germany, Sept. 12, 1924 , in letter from Will Hays to Under Secretary of State Joseph C. Grew, Nov. 11, 1924,, USDS.

[6] In 1922 there had been 351 German film producers, but in 1923 there were only 214, and in 1924 the number had decreased even further. German companies had produced 1,221,289 meters of film in 1922—which was a drop of 65% from the 1921 level—and from 1922 to 1923 production dropped another 33.3%. In the first six months of 1924 the German film production was 223,000 meters, but twice as much film was imported. In 1920 the film import had only been 736,838 meters, but in 1922 the number increased to 2,480,811 meters.

[7] Letter from Will Hays, MPPDA, to Arthur N. Young, Economic Advisor, New York, October 8, 1926, USDS.

[8] "Proposed legislation by Germany adverse to American motion picture interests." Conversation (Memo) with Will H. Hays. Nov. 10, 1924, USDS.

[9] Telegram from Charles E. Hughes, USDS, to U.S. Embassy Germany. Washington, DC, Nov. 14, 1924, USDS.

[10] Letter no. 934 from Matthew E. Hanna, First Secretary of Embassy, U.S. Embassy Germany, Feb. 3, 1925, USDS.

[11] Solbert was born in Sweden in 1885. He was tall and impressive looking with his many decorations from his service as military attaché. As a colonel in the U.S. Army he was assigned to duty in Copenhagen on Jan. 25, 1918. He was promoted to major and assigned to duty as military attaché at London from 1919 to 1924. In 1923 he met Will Hays, who together with Chief Justice William Howard Taft helped him become military aide to President Coolidge in 1924/25. After his 1925 mission for the MPPDA, Solbert became the first director of the George Eastman House, the International Museum of Photography and Film in Rochester, NY, remaining in that function until his death from a heart attack in the museum's elevator in 1958. *Register of the Department of State* (Washington, DC, GPO, 1918, 1919, 1924, 1925); "Oscar Solbert," in *Who Was Who in America*, vol. 3. (1960), p. 803; *New York Times* obituary (April 17, 1958); Edward P. Curtis, "Oscar N. Solbert," in *Image*, 7, no. 7 (Rochester, NY, Sept. 1958):148–51.

[12] Report from Oscar Solbert, Berlin, May 20, 1925, *Will Hays Papers.*

[13] Ibid., June 4, 1925.

[14] Letter from Jack S. Connolly, MPPDA, Washington, DC, to Frank B. Kellogg, Secretary of State, Dec. 9, 1925, USDS.

[15] Report from Oscar Solbert, part II, "Confidential and unofficial," to State Department's economic advisor Arthur N. Young, New York, Oct. 8, 1925, USDS, Germany.

[16] Letter from Arthur N. Young to Solbert, Washington, DC, Oct. 26, 1925, USDS. Instruction No. 146 to Ambassador Jacob Gould Schurman, Oct. 27, 1925), USDS.

[17] Letter no. 586 from Schurman, U.S. Embassy Germany, Dec. 21, 1925, USDS.

[18] Clipping from *Paris-Midi*, Nov. 14, 1925, USEF.

[19] Sheldon Whitehouse, Charge d'Affaires interim, USEF, Oct. 7, 1925, USDS.

[20] Stenographic report of an interview Mr. Kent gave to the newspapermen, Paris, Nov. 11, 1924, USEF.

[21] Jean Sapène wrote in a pamphlet: "We shall make French films, purely French, with our qualities and our defects, and we shall only produce the works conceived by ourselves and we shall eventually find a place for our productions.... Don't you understand that

when you ask us to make films to the taste of your [American] audiences it means the negation of all effort of originality and that it is stupid?" Translated by Edward G. Lowry (July 5, 1926), *Will Hays Papers.*

[22] Exhibition of inflammable moving picture films was prohibited after Jan. 1, 1925, according to an Ordinance of April 10, 1922 from the Prefect of Police of Paris. The letter has a confidential section: "It is generally understood in Paris moving picture circles that this prohibition is the result of the efforts of the 'Société Pathé-Cinema' to control the film trade, since it claims to be the only manufacturer of non-inflammable films. This opinion is supported by the reference in the first paragraph of the Ministerial Circular to a circular request made to the Departmental Prefects by the 'Société Pathé-Cinema' that Orders be issued making the use of non-inflammatory films obligatory within a maximum period of two years." USCP, May 11, 1922.

[23] Motion Picture Situation, report from Vice Consul Alfred D. Cameron, Paris, Jan. 19, 1926, USDS.

[24] Ibid.

[25] Letter from Jack S. Connoly, MPPDA, to the secretary of state, Washington, DC, Sept. 30, 1925; telegram from Secretary of State Kellogg to USEF, Oct. 1, 1925, USDS.

[26] Telegram from Kellogg to the American embassy in France, Oct. 1, 1925, USDS.

[27] Sheldon Whitehouse, Charge d'Affaires interim, USEF, Oct. 7, 1925, USDS.

[28] Vice Consul Alfred D. Cameron, "Postponement of Decree Prohibiting Inflammable Motion Picture Films," Paris, Nov. 10, 1925, USEF.

[29] Cameron, Report: "Motion Picture Situation," Paris, Jan. 19, 1926, USDS.

[30] Pierre Gilles, "Pour la Cinematographie française. Du Contingentement" *Le Matin.* Paris, Nov. 27, 1925, USDS.

[31] "Protection du Film Français," *Bulletin Officiel de la Chambre Syndicale de la cinématographie et des Industries que s'y Rattachent.* Enclosure to despatch, Paris, Jan. 15, 1926, USEF.

[32] Letter from Fredrick L. Herron, MPPDA, to Vice Consul Alfred D. Cameron, New York, Dec. 5, 1925, USEF.

[33] Leland Harrison, the Department of State, unnumbered Instruction to several American embassies in Europe, Jan. 30, 1926, USDS.

[34] Chester Lloyd Jones, Commercial Attaché, Memorandum: "Agitation against American Films in France" Paris, March 1, 1926, USDS.

[35] "Universal's friendly dealings with Sapène...were one of the interesting developments of the year insofar as the American industry and France were concerned. 'Les Misérables' and 'Michael Strogoff' were released by Universal in America, the latter opening for an engagement at the Cohan theater, New York city on Dec. 5." *Film Yearbook* (New York, 1927), p. 937.

[36] Harold L. Smith: "Motion picture Notes." Paris, Feb. 18, 1927, USDS.

[37] Letter from Edward G. Lowry to Will Hays (London, July 5, 1926). *Will Hays Papers.*

[38] Comite de Direction de la Chambre Syndicale Francaise de la Cinématographie. Reunion du vendredi 19 fevr. 1926, USEF.

[39] Chester Lloyd Jones, Commercial Attaché, memorandum: "Agitation against American Films in France," Paris, March 1, 1926, USDS.

[40] Letter from General Consul Robert P. Skinner, Paris, Sept. 22, 1926, USDS.

[41] Martha Gruening, "European Revolt against Our Films," *New York Times* (Oct. 30, 1926).

[42] Edouard Herriot, *Europe* (New York, 1930).

[43] William Victor Strauss, "Foreign Distribution of American Motion Pictures," *Harvard Business Review,* 8 (1929): 307–15.

[44] Ruth Vasey, "The World-Wide Spread of Cinema," in Geoffrey Nowell-Smith, *The Oxford History of World Cinema* (Oxford, 1996), p. 59. For an extensive description of "Film Europe" see Andrew Higson and Richard Maltby, *Film Europe and Film America* (Exeter, 1999).

[45] John Dyvelen Prince, U.S. Legation, Denmark, "Formation of a European Film Trust," Copenhagen, August 21, 1924, USDS (Germany).

[46] Letter from Will Hays to Under secretary of State Joseph C. Grew, New York, Nov. 11, 1924, citing a report from trade commissioner Douglas Miller (Berlin, Sept. 12, 1924), USDS (Germany).

[47] Prince, "Formation of a European Film trust."

[48] Robert P. Skinner, "Franco-German Cinematograph Agreements," *American Foreign Service Report* 83, Paris, Feb. 4, 1925, USEF.

[49] Fredrick L. Herron, Memorandum for Mr. Hays, New York, July 11, 1927, *Will Hays Papers.*

[50] Press release from Fredrick L. Herron, MPPDA, Telegram, New York, July 2, 1926, *Will Hays Papers.*

[51] Translation of the article in "Comment of *Le Matin*, unfavorable to the Congress," Paris, March 3, 1926, USEF.

[52] "Universal's friendly dealings with Sapène...were one of the interesting developments of the year insofar as the American industry and France were concerned. 'Les Misérables' and 'Michael Strogoff' were released by Universal in America, the latter opening for an engagement at the Cohan theater, New York city on Dec. 5." *Film Yearbook* (New York, 1927), p. 937.

[53] Conversation: Major Herron. Subject: Motion Picture Situation, USDS, Office of the Economic Adviser, Feb. 13, 1928, USDS.

[54] Fredrick L. Herron, MPPDA, "Memorandum for Mr. Hays," New York, July 11, 1927, *Will Hays Papers.*

[55] Letter from William Sheafe Chase, Superintendent of the International Reform Federation to the President, Washington, DC, July 14, 1927, USDS.
"The Movie Trust," Kokomo Ind. Dispatch (July 12, 1927), *Will Hays Papers.*

[56] Letter to Fredrick L. Herron, MPPDA, from Vice Consul Harold L. Smith, Paris, May 2, 1927, USEF.

[57] Harold L. Smith, "Recent Developments in French Motion Picture World," Paris, March 2, 1926, USDS.

[58] Harold L. Smith, "Interview with Mr. Jean Sapène on Feb. 4, 1927," in "Recent Development in French Motion Picture World" Paris, March 2, 1927, p. 16, USDS.

[59] Harold L. Smith, "Motion Pictures Discussed in the Chamber of Deputies," Paris, Dec. 7, 1926, USDS.

[60] Martha Gruening, "European Revolt against Our Films."

[61] A. Kamenka, "Un nouveau cri d'alarme," *La Cinématographie française* (Jan. 22, 1927): 3–4.

[62] Harold L. Smith, "French Minister to Appoint Motion Picture Commission," Feb. 25, 1927, USDS.

[63] Harold L. Smith, "Recent Developments in French Motion Picture World," March 2, 1927, USDS.

[64] Translation of the three articles in *L'Intransigeant* (March 14, 24, 25, 1927) in letter from the American general consul Alphonse Gaulin to Fredrick L. Herron, MPPDA, April 6, 1927 USCP.

[65] A. Gaulin, American Consulate, to F.L. Herron, April 6, 1927, USCP.

[66] Leon Bailby, "What About Us?" Translation of article in French in *L'Intransigeant*, March 24 1927, USEF.

[67] Interviews with Sapène and Bressillon were published in *Ciné-Comædia* (April, 6, 1927).

[68] General Consul A. Gaulin reported Smith's interview of Nalpas. Paris, April 14, 1927, USCP.

[69] Léon Bailby, "Notre cinema," *L'Intransigeant* (April 18, 1927), translated by Harold L. Smith in "Campaign for the Protection of the French Motion Picture Industry," April 19, 1927, USDS.

[70] Letter from Harold L. Smith to Fredrick L. Herron , Paris, May 2, 1927, USEF.

[71] Harold L. Smith, "Exhibitor's Opinion on the Proposed Measures for the Protection of the French Motion Picture Producing Industry," May 6, 1927, p. 5, USDS. *Princesse Marscha* was sent to America, but no letter shows that the Americans bought it.

[72] Boisyvon, "For French Films" and "Who Should Begin," in *L'Intransigeant* (April 30, 1927), cited in report by Harold L. Smith, May 2, 1927, USDS.

[73] Smith, "Situation of French Motion Picture Industry in France"; letter from Consul General A. Gaulin to Herron, Paris June 3, 1927, USEF.

[74] Harold L. Smith, "Resolutions of the Exhibitors' Syndicate," Paris, May 6, 1927, USDS.

[75] A. Gaulin to Herron, Paris, June 3 and 14, USCP.

[76] Gaulin to Herron, Paris, July 2, 1927, USCP.

[77] Despatch from Harold L. Smith, Jan. 9, 1928, USDS.

[78] Letter from the Embassy to Herron, Paris, Nov. 28, 1927, USEF.

[79] Letters from Smith to Herron, Paris, Dec. 15, 1927; Jan. 9, 1928, USCP.

[80] Letter from Herron to Gaulin, New York, Dec. 12, 1927, USCP.

[81] Ibid., Dec. 23, 1927, USCP.

[82] Ibid.

[83] Letters from Gaulin to Herron, Paris Dec. 12, 23, 1927, USCP. Smith, "Motion Picture Contingent Project Approved by Cinema Commission," Paris, Jan. 9, 1928, USDS.

[84] Harold L. Smith, "Developments in Motion Picture Contingent Agitation in France: Meeting of the Cinema Commission on Jan. 11, 1928," Paris, Jan. 16, 1928, USDS.

[85] Smith, "Formation of a French Motion Picture Control Commission," Paris, Feb. 20, 1928, USDS.

[86] Marcel Nussy, *Le Cinématographe et la censure* (Montpellier, 1929), p. 67.

[87] Article in *Le Matin*, cited in an editorial by Léon Bailby, *L'Intransigeant* (Feb. 19, 1928). Letter from General Gaulin to Herron, Paris, Feb. 14, 1928, USCP.

[88] Letter to Will Hays from Edward G. Lowry, Paris, March 14, 1928; letter from Herron to Hays, New York, April 4, 1928, *Will Hays Papers*.

[89] C.J. North, Chief, Motion Picture Section, Specialties Division, USDC to George R. Canty, Trade Commissioner, Paris (Washington, DC, April 7, 1928), USDC.

    North had a conversation with Herron and Pettijohn, MPPDA, in New York in which he presented the complaints about "Colonel Lowry's utter lack of co-operation with us in the French situation. I went after this strong and as a matter of fact I found the Major [Herron] considerably more sympathetic to this kick on our part than I had hoped. Whether anything tangible will come out of it or not I don't know but he has written some sort of a letter to Mr. Hays and also to the Colonel himself."

[90] Edward G. Lowry, "Memorandum of what M. Herriot said at interview of March 10, 1928," *Will Hays Papers*.

[91] Letter from C.J. North to Assistant Secretary of Commerce, Julius Klein, Washington, March 14, 1928, USDC France.

[92] Edward G. Lowry, "Memorandum of Interview with M. Paul Leon, Chairman of the Cinema Control Commission," Paris, March 13, 1928, *Will Hays Papers*.

[93] Charles E. Lyon, Commercial Attaché, Switzerland, "French Films and the Geneva Treaty," Berne, March 20, 1928, *Will Hays Papers*.

[94] Letter from C.J. North to the commercial attaché H.C. MacLean, USEF, Washington, March 29, 1928, USDC, France.

[95] H.C. MacLean, "Regulations adopted by the Film Control Commission," memorandum to Dr. Klein, dated by Will Hays March 28, 1928, *Will Hays Archives*.

[96] Letter from C. J. North to H.C. MacLean, USEF, Washington, April 10?, 1928, USDC, France.

[97] Harold L. Smith's last letter as vice consul was dated March 5, 1928; his first correspondence as MPPDA representative was dated May 1, 1928.

6

The Herriot-Hays Agreement, 1928-1930

Since the Americans did not buy the required number of French films, their imports were held up. The French producers were determined to force the Americans to buy French films, whereas the Americans were equally determined not to enter such an agreement.[1]

Will Hays sailed to France on March 28, 1928,[2] and sent out a press release when he arrived in Paris on April 4. The release did not reflect his concerns, but was written in language that journalists would like to hear:

> My chief concern is to make it possible for the motion picture to play worthily the great part which is reserved for it in the world of to-day, and to prepare it for those noble roles which lie before it in the future. For it is today the greatest single expression of the world, and it has it within its power to foster and strengthen those common ties which must ultimately triumph in the peace and brotherhood of the world....Far beyond the physical or commercial importance of motion pictures is their importance as an influence upon the ideas and ideals, upon the conduct and customs of those who see them....[3]

Hays ingeniously turned the focus away from the commercial conflict, and concentrated attention instead on the problem of the intellectual effects of Hollywood films on the spectators. But ambassador Myron Herrick was not carried away by Will Hays's propaganda, since he regarded the situation as a business dispute between the American film industry and the French producers.[4]

Hays's critics argued that the public at large should be less inclined to listen to his speeches on the purely altruistic purposes of the industry. Hays had become the supervisor of screen morals, but he was himself uninterested in the motion picture itself, in books, in plays, or in any other form of art. He was quite untouched by such matters, for they were not a part of his job. "His zeal in barring extreme salaciousness is based on the universal motion picture terror of further censorship, federal or state. He was hired to block additional government supervision, to tame radical spirits among the producers, to prevent trade practices which cause expensive litigation, to use his influence as an important politician of the party in power, and it is said, to prevent the Actors' Equity Association from organizing motion picture actors and extras."[5]

Having success with the French was of vital importance for Hays's ability to stay on as head of the film industry, since his position was threatened by his involvement in the Teapot Dome scandal. In 1921, during the administration of President Harding, Secretary of the Interior Albert B. Fall secretly leased the naval oil reserves at Teapot Dome, Wyoming, and Elk Hills, California without competitive bidding. A Senate investigation in 1922–23 revealed that Edward L. Doheny, who had leased the Elk Hills oil field, had also "loaned" Fall large sums of money without interest, as had Harry F. Sinclair, the recipient of the Teapot Dome lease. Will Hays was charged with involvement in the scandal. He had obtained an advance of $260,000 in Liberty bonds from Sinclair to cover the Republican National Committee's campaign deficit.[6] Hays was called to testify in the Senate on February 10, 1928,[7] but after his successful mission to France he was not called upon again.

It is not clear what regulations the French cinema commission had actually instituted. On April 4, 1928 the commission defined the ratio in the import regulations of seven imported films to one French as meaning that of the seven, four films would be American, two would be from Germany, and Great Britain would receive one permit.[8]

But already on April 5, 1928, the day after Will Hays's arrival, the *Evening World* reported that the quota plan had been dropped temporarily.[9] The film committee decided not to recommend the quota system, and would allow foreign films to enter on the same basis as the previous year's sales, which would not restrict imports. It was the French theater owners who brought about the decision, claiming that French producers were not in a position to supply enough films, having produced only seventy features in 1927. Will Hays had not even seen Herriot before the decision was made.

When Edouard Herriot met Will Hays during Easter (most likely on April 9), he claimed that he had no desire to drive American films out of France, but that he did not want to let the French industry die unprotected. He asked Hays to prepare a proposal for a solution and to send it to him in Lyon, where he was campaigning for election on April 22 and 29.[10] Jean Sapène did not take part in the negotiations because he went to Morocco one week after Will Hays arrived in Paris.

The American embassy provided Hays with full support to work out the proposal.[11] In response, Will Hays submitted his "ultimatum" on April 20, 1928, in which he stated that the American companies were unable to operate in France under the regulations created by the cinema control commission. Hays had three proposals. First, he assured his hosts that American films would be devoid of scenes offensive to French national feelings. To fulfill such a promise, the American film industry adopted a self-censorship regulation, the so-called "Hays Code." Second, Hays proposed to institute a study concerning the ways and means by which the industries in France and America could cooperate more closely, to their mutual advantage. He would give free access to representatives of the French film industry to the American production plants so that they might study the production of American films. Finally, Hays promised that the organized American industry would look with favor upon the circulation in the United States of French films that would be suitable for world distribution.

As a precondition for putting the proposals into effect Hays requested that Herriot repealed the decree of March 12, 1928 (along with the extensions of April 4 by the cinema control commission) or at least held in abeyance during the period of study. He also requested that paragraph 4 of article 4 of the decree of February 18, 1928, concerning censorship of foreign films, would not be applied in a manner adverse to importers of American pictures.

On April 19, 1928, Will Hays addressed the American Club of Paris. He was introduced by the president of the club as "a man known for his exalted ideals."[12] Hays's talk met the idealistic expectations when he stated that he brought "a word of that greatest of all ambassadors of understanding, the motion picture. I refer not for one second to American motion pictures, but to all motion pictures wheresoever made. The only competition I recognize is not competition between France and America, or Germany and America, or England and America, no:—but between good pictures and better pictures wherever they are made....To you of France, I bring this offer of cooperation from a group whose only wish is that we help each other to develop the maximum usefulness of motion pictures."[13]

In contrast to Will Hays's statements, *The New York Times* explained more candidly that the Americans thought it was necessary to take a strong stand in the conflict with France because the French situation had the attention of all other film-importing countries in Europe and its eventual solution would influence film regulations in these countries as well.[14] The American position was not a bluff, since no films had been sold since March 1, and the possibility that eight- to ten-thousand French would be unemployed if the movie houses were forced to close for lack of films was said to have influenced government officials considerably.

The other members of the government let Herriot grapple with the difficult situation. Herriot did not return to Paris before April 30, 1928. In the meantime, Ambassador Herrick wrote to Herriot explaining that the regulations would force the American motion picture industry to suspend its operations in France.[15] The American film companies there supported Hays's course of action, and if he did not obtain an agreement for the suspension of the regulations, they would cease doing business in France.[16] Sapène, knowing the content of the "ultimatum," cabled the minister and the other leaders of the film industry from Morocco, urging them to seek a compromise.[17]

The decisive discussions leading to the Herriot-Hays agreement took place at a meeting of the Sous-Commission de Controle du Cinema with Will Hays on May 3, 1928. Louis Lumière was the chairman of the commission, which had the following members: Aubert, Bernede, Delac, Brezillon, Burguet, Gallo, Germain Dulac, Lussiez, Hurel, Crouzet, Nalpas, Jean Toulout, and René Gadave.

In this meeting Hays objected to article 7 of the regulations, which obliged American companies to buy French films as a precondition for distributing American films in France. The chairman then read a new redaction of article 7, which stipulated that all producers who had produced a French film of the "first category" would receive seven permits for importation of foreign films. If they could demonstrate the exportation of a French film to "major production countries" they would receive two permits. In a concession later that evening, the commission increased the number of films that could be imported without restrictions from forty to sixty percent of the number of films imported in the previous year. [18]

Hays met Herriot in the morning of May 4 to sign the agreement. In its final form it allowed the import of seven foreign films for every film produced in France. In addition, sixty percent of the American films shown in France during 1927 could be imported without being subject to contingent restrictions, and the obligatory purchase of French films for distribution in the United States was repealed. The agreement called for renegotiations after one year.[19]

Yet, after the agreement had been made and Hays had returned to New York, he ignored his promises to study the film situation and to promote the distribution of French films in the United States. To his great irritation, the French insisted that Hollywood hire the French literary critic Victor Mandelstamm as a reporter to ensure that French themes would be treated adequately. Hays reluctantly helped to establish Mandelstamm's authority within the Production Code Administration.[20]

The Herriot agreement crushed the French attempts to protect their film industry. The French quota was so generous that the American film imports to France never reached the ceiling; the Americans could have sent almost twice as many films as were actually exported. French politicians nevertheless considered the quota policy a decisive factor in reducing the dominant position of the American film industry, because the number of American films imported declined considerably towards the end of the 1920s. (See appendix B). As we have already seen, the statistics show a general decline in the American exports to several European countries in this period. But the decline was not a result of the French quota policy, whose effects cannot be established. At best, the French quota "restrictions" had only a limited effect and even that did not occur until later in the 1930s.

Conference for the Abolition of Import and Export Prohibitions and Restrictions, Geneva, 1928

Even though Will Hays had just entered the quota agreement with Herriot, the MPPDA continued to combat European quotas at the "Second Conference for the Abolition of Import and Export Prohibitions and Restrictions," held in Geneva in July 1928.[21] On that occasion, the confrontations between the United States and France over the "cultural exception" or "cultural diversity"(which again became prominent at the GATT negotiations in 1993–94) emerged for the first time. The Americans insisted that films were merely commercial products, whereas the French delegate, Daniel Serruys, claimed that film contingents and quotas were legitimate means of cultural protection. The arguments presented in the 1990s were strikingly similar to those used in 1928.

The background for the controversy was that France had not exempted motion pictures from free trade before signing the convention of the "First International Conference for the Abolition of Import and Export Prohibitions and Restrictions," held in Geneva between October 17 and November 8, 1927. The American consulate thought the French quota arrangements violated article 3 of the convention:

> Should the High Contracting Parties, in pursuance of their legislation, subject the importation or exportation of goods to certain regulations in respect of the name, form or place of importation or exportation, or the imposition of marks, or to other formalities or conditions, they undertake that such regulations shall not be made a means of disguised prohibition or arbitrary restriction. [The consul's underlining][22]

Already in March 1928, the MPPDA officers decided to protest the French quota policy at the Geneva conference that would take place in July. Fredrick Herron contacted Arthur N. Young, the State Department's economic advisor, in order to develop a campaign, stating that France was upholding the quota restrictions in violation of the convention.[23] Herron thought that France would probably argue that the Americans had restricted the distribution of foreign films, which, he said, was not the case. He claimed that

To Will Hays with admiration Oscar Solbert

Oscar Solbert. Military Attaché to Denmark, Sweden and Great Britain during World War I to 1924. Led the Mission to Europe for the MPPDA in 1925. He became the first director of the Eastman House in Rochester 1949 to 1958.
Courtesy of the Will Hays Collection, Indiana State Archive.

Clair Wilcox, director of the Office of International Trade Policy, 1945-1947.
Negotiator of the Blum-Byrnes Film Agreement of May 26, 1946.
Courtesy of National Archives, Washington, D.C.

M. Jean Sapène éloquent apôtre d'une Union Nationale Cinématographique Française.

Jean Sapène, ca. 1928. Born March 19, 1867 in Bagnéres-de-Luchon, Haute Garonne. Directeur Général des Services du Matin; of Pathé Consortium Cinéma, and of Pathé-Westi. Director of Societé des Cinéromans, and Companie Général de Publicité Parisienne. Courtesy of the Archive of the Ministére des Beaux-Arts, Archives Nationales, Paris.

Will H. Hays, director of the MPPDA 1922 to 1945, in his office, around 1945. Hays is famous for the Hays' Code that censored Hollywood films, but in fact he did not cut films or manuscripts personally. Courtesy of the Will Hays Collection, Indiana State Archive.

Will H. Hays onboard the Lusitania in March 1928 en route to France to discuss the film situation leading to the Hays-Herriot agreement.
Photo courtesy of the office of Will H. Hays Jr. in Crawfordsville, Indiana.

Claudia Victrix, wife of Jean Sapène, starring in *Princesse Marscha*, 1928. Her outdated acting style was detrimental to the reputation of the Pathé company. Courtesy of the Danish Film Archive.

Will Hays visiting George Eastman, probably on the occasion when Hays gave the opening talk at the Eastman Theater in 1922. Photographed in the West Garden of the Eastman House, Rochester. Courtesy of the Will Hays Collection, Indiana State Archive

ric Johnston, successor to Will Hays as chairman of the Motion Picture Association of America, 45-1962. He is being sworn in as directing supervisor of the European Recovery Administration CA), i.e. the Marshall Plan. His double position as head of the MPAA and official representative the U.S. confused foreign governments. Consequently, they were reluctant to challenge ollywood's position for fear that it would lead to a reduction of the Marshall relief. urtesy of the National Archives and Record Administration, NARA, Washington, D.C.

Fredrick L. Herron, director of the foreign office of the MPPDA, 1923-1943. Photographer Irving Chidnoff. Courtesy of the Quigley Photographic Archive, Special Collections, Georgetown University Library, Washington, D.C.

foreign films had just as many opportunities for distribution in the United States as domestic pictures. If a film just had the "proper drawing value" it would be put on the American market immediately, but foreigners often failed to make such a successful film. Herron thought that a good example of this was the case of a French producer who had brought Carl Th. Dreyer's *La Passion de Jeanne d'Arc* (1927) to America and tried to sell it to the distributors. "The title alone would cause every censor board in the country to prohibit the showing of the picture. The picture itself does not measure up at all to our standards of what the public demands." The French producer thought the American distributors conspired to prevent him from having the film distributed. To Herron, it was just "the old war cry."

On March 20 the American commercial attaché in Bern, Charles E. Lyon, requested instructions from the secretary of commerce as to which stand the American delegation should take when film regulations were discussed, in order to optimally promote American film interests. [24] He thought that articles 2, 6, and 7 of the French quota regulations conflicted with the spirit of the Geneva treaty, to which France was a signatory. The articles were ingeniously worded and had a bearing that did not appear on casual reading. Harold L. Smith knew that they were drawn up by an eminent jurist, Grunebaum-Ballin, who had worded them very carefully to avoid conflict with the Geneva agreement.[25] The French had not established a direct import quota, Lyon stated, but in reality the regulations might constitute a complete blockade of American films—if the French desired to interpret the article in that light. He believed that the ratio planned between American, British, and German films was most discriminatory against the Americans. Lyon also reported that the French had written to the Secretariat of the League of Nations to ask whether the treaty would permit the film restrictions they had in mind, but the League was not in a position to interpret the bearing of treaties.

The New York Times reported that on April 11, 1928, Will Hays had a long discussion with the American ambassador to Switzerland, Hugh Wilson, who came to Paris to discuss the upcoming session of the Geneva conference.[26] Many experts who had examined French and other European restrictions directed against American motion pictures were convinced that they constituted a direct violation of the Geneva protocol signed the previous year by France, Great Britain, the United States, and twenty other nations. In the same article the newspaper announced that Jean Sapène had signed through the Pathé-Cinéromans Company an agreement with British and German film interests for close cooperation involving an exchange of films and other mutual arrangements. The stated aim of the collaboration was "breaking the stranglehold of Hollywood." The potential possibilities of such an accord were taken very serious by American interests. However, with the limited production facilities of France, Britain, and Germany in relation to the needs of the three markets, such a European combine would be unable to force out American productions for many years, the *Times* concluded.

H. C. MacLean told Hugh Wilson that the French regulations conflicted with the Geneva Convention at least in spirit.[27] Hays had also made it clear that the American film industry wanted entire freedom of trade; hence, the MPPDA would not "agree" to the regulations even in the new form because they clearly represented a definite limitation of activity. It was difficult to protest the regulations because they did not represent an official act by the French Government as such, but merely administrative measures adopted by the commission created by the decree of February 18, 1928. As the decree was very carefully worded, MacLean did not feel prepared to decide whether the regulations constituted a technical violation of the Geneva Convention.

In preparation for the conference the MPPDA installed its own delegation in Switzerland. The organization hired an internationally renowned Austrian lawyer, Dr. Koretz,[28] who understood southern and central European distribution from a governmental standpoint. Just before the conference opened, Koretz joined Edward G. Lowry in Montreux, in order not to be conspicuously present at the conference and yet still be within reach.[29] They were able to furnish Wilson with a number of strong, valid legal arguments "in the nick of time" before the debate at the convention of July 7, 1928. (Koretz later claimed that his work had led to favorable results, as the conference refused to pass a resolution sanctioning the French demands).[30]

Hugh Wilson was well instructed when, at the "Second International Conference for the Abolition of Import and Export Prohibitions and Restrictions," he charged that the French film quota arrangements between Herriot and Hays were an obstruction of commerce in violation of the convention of the first conference, and he caught the French delegate Daniel Serruys completely by surprise. On July 2, 1928, Wilson complained that an American producer, in order to obtain the right to have film shown in France, had to either purchase and show a French film or, by arranging with a French producer, obtain a visa, which Wilson considered prohibition or restriction in violation with the Geneva agreement. The French decree regulating the cinema ruled that the cinema commission could change the stipulations from day to day or from hour to hour, and such fluid conditions made it almost impossible to do business with success. American companies had established at great cost a distribution service on a fixed basis for a year's distribution and the whole basis for their distribution system may be altered overnight.[31]

In his memoirs, Wilson wrote that the European diplomats at Geneva were not accustomed to such directness of statement. Daniel Serruys demanded the floor before the translation was completed, and answered in bitter sarcasm.[32] He claimed that the restrictions were manifestations of a spiritual defense to protect the manners, morals, and traditions of the French people. To accomplish this object censorship alone was insufficient and a certain national industry was essential. He agreed that there should be no administrative measures for economic purposes and insisted that his regulations had only cultural ends in view. He accused the United States of using sanitary and pure food regulations to disguise economic purposes. Serruys also denied that there was an analogy between films, which had cultural substance, and other commodities. He ended by stating that the regulations Wilson referred to no longer existed, although some similar regulations would be necessary.

The German delegate then made a speech pointing out that the conference could not make a decision in the matter. He agreed, however, with many points of Serruys's cultural arguments, and reserved Germany's right to impose measures in the future to protect Germany's traditions. Austria, Italy, and India made similar declarations. If a decision had been possible, Wilson thought it would have stated that nations have a right to maintain some form of protection for their culture and traditions.

At the second session, the Geneva conference achieved agreement on a treaty to deal with the international economic problems, and Hugh Wilson thought that had it become generally applicable it could have forestalled or retarded the rapid development of autarchic and controlled economy after 1930. But unfortunately, Poland failed to ratify the treaty, effectively torpedoing it, and it never came into general force.[33]

Despite its tenacity the MPPDA did not succeed diplomatically in convincing the Europeans to remove the film quota regulations. As before, France and the United States were the two major adversaries. The Americans claimed that films were merely commercial products, whereas the French claimed that film quotas were a legitimate means of cultural protection, a view that the other European countries supported. The situation ended in a stalemate, which has continued until today. The arguments used in 1928 thus have a striking similarity to those that were used at the negotiations of the GATT-Uruguay round in 1993–94.

The Quota Agreement, 1929

The confrontations between the United States and France resumed when the quota year ended on March 1, 1929. On February 27, 1929, the Chambre Syndicale agreed that it was necessary to restrict imports to three American films for every French produced because, as Charles Delac pointed out, the regulations had failed to protect the French industry.

Ambassador Herrick considered that the best American tactic would be to refrain from negotiations. He claimed that French film interests were trying to bluff and French cinemas would not be able to carry on without American films.[34] The MPPDA decided to follow a policy of confrontation, which meant that the American film companies would withdraw collectively from France. They claimed to be unable to operate profitably under the new conditions, but at the same time they knew that the French movie houses could not survive without substantial imports of American movies. On April 10, 1929, the American film companies announced collectively that they would suspend their activities in France.[35] The American representatives in Paris were confident that after a six-month cessation of sales, they would be able to defeat the quota system completely.[36] Will Hays wanted to test the new united front strategy toward the French film industry and its government. The American film companies only hesitantly agreed to the policy to boycott the French market. Furthermore, they wanted to bring in Western Electric and the Radio Corporation of America (RCA), which sold sound equipment, to take part in the boycott, believing that a shorter but more effective boycott would be in the best interests of all involved.[37]

The policy of the MPPDA had the full support of the State Department. On April 12, 1929, the department instructed the embassies of seven countries to hand in protests against the regulations and restrictions on American film export. The instructions, which were published in *The New York Times*, declared that the United States favored the freest possible film trade. The aim of the démarches was also to indicate to foreign governments that the MPPDA had the vigorous support of the State Department.

American critic of the film industry William Marston Seabury protested sharply against the policy of the State Department as it appeared in the *Times*.[38] In his opinion the United States was not in a position to protest the import restrictions imposed by other countries because the ineffective enforcement of the domestic antitrust laws allowed the American film industry to carry out monopolistic trade practices in the United States. The MPPDA companies controlled almost 100% of the American market, about 98% in Canada, more than 95% in Australia, about 90% in Great Britain, and 90% or more in many of the Latin American republics and in other countries. The members of the MPPDA controlled more than 75% of the first-run theaters in America. The monopolization of the film trade was being investigated by the Department of Justice, which had instituted five suits against the MPPDA and its member companies, charging them with carrying out various criminal and conspiratorial practices to monopolize and restrain interstate trade in the motion picture industry in violation of antitrust laws. Seabury also referred to the 17,000 pages of testimony taken by the Federal Trade Commission in its case No. 835 against the film industry, adding that the federal government ought not to support an organization that violated the antitrust legislation of the United States. The representations made by American diplomats abroad did not conform to the facts; even successful foreign movies that had entered the United States could not be marketed on a "free competitive basis."

Seabury's arguments made no official impression, and he received no reply. The State Department and the American embassies continued to stand behind the American film industry represented by the MPPDA.

For the MPPDA boycott policy to appear credible all the American film companies had to participate. As all representatives of American film companies joined the blockade, MacLean was confident that the quota system could be demolished. He thought that even if the present system could be continued it would be possible to operate at a profit.[39] But on April 26, 1929, Warner Brothers suddenly decided to resume sales, undermining the MPPDA's strategy and the position that the Americans could not operate in the French market at a profit. The action would give Warner an important advantage in the French market, and the other American companies would no doubt have followed Warner's example. But strong pressure from the MPPDA and the State Department brought Warner Brothers back into line.[40] Will Hays's idea was that by withdrawing totally, the French public would ask them back after a few months, and when they returned they would be able to dictate the conditions.[41]

The fight of the French film industry to obtain better protection was fundamentally undermined when two thousand French provincial exhibitors at a conference in Nice signed a petition urging the government to abandon the quota restrictions on the import of American films.[42] At the same time they protested the high amusement taxes and threatened to close the movie houses on June 15, 1929, in protest against the national budget proposal.

During the Nice conference, a huge poster was distributed to the cinema owners with the title, "La France colonisée par le film américain," which the chargé d'Affaires Norman Armour characterized as "a vicious and scurrilous attack upon the United States, its manners and customs, diverted more specifically into the channel of assertion that their representation upon the screen is harmful to French education, culture and traditions."[43] Immediately, American diplomats began to search for the posters in the streets of Paris, requesting the police to remove them. The poster was published by the obscure "Ligue de Défense de l'idée Française" as a supplement to *Semaine Cinématographique* on April 27, 1929. Herron knew that Max Dianville, who arrived at the conference together with Delac, the president of the Chambre Syndicale, had brought the poster to the conference.[44] Delac must have known of the poster in advance, Herron concluded.

On May 17, 1929 Herron informed the State Department that the French situation was going well.[45] It had come to a deadlock between the two industries, but the French government officials had been very favorably inclined to the American side, and Herron felt that if only Sapène could be eliminated in some way, the Americans would win the battle. He believed that the French government was still very much afraid of offending him, which might hold up the settlement of the negotiations for some time.

Towards the end of May 1929, Herron noticed that the film question had become a problem for the French government.[46] W.R. Castle at the State Department knew that at a meeting with French exhibitors, the new Undersecretary of the Ministry of Fine Arts, André François-Poncet, had declared that he was in favor of a custom tax, but Sapène stood in the way of any solution except a contingent.[47] François-Poncet had even expressed a very low opinion of Sapène to MPPDA's representative, Harold Smith, explaining that the Chambre Syndicale insisted that the quota system should be upheld in its strictest form, as requested by Jean Sapène. He had considerable power both with the press and politically, and it was extremely difficult for the government to reject the proposals of the Chambre Syndicale. François-Poncet had also asked if the American film companies would resume business in France if the status quo were prolonged. Consul MacLean replied that only the complete abolition of the objectionable contingent system would be acceptable. However, MacLean personally thought that American interests might be willing to resume their sales if the maintenance of the status quo was the only possible temporary solution for keeping the way open for the eventual adoption of another system.

The policy of the French film industry received another blow when the chairman of the provincial exhibitors' union, M.G. Madret-Lafage, sent a memorandum on behalf of all exhibitors assembled at their conference in Bordeaux on June 7, 1929, to François-Poncet, along with copies to all French senators and deputies.[48] The exhibitors complained that the contingent proposal, which the producers promoted, would deal a death blow to three thousand French cinemas. The exhibitors employed one hundred thousand French citizens, and they would be ruined if the minister followed the proposal of a few producers, whom they accused of seeking only personal profit. The producers' proposal would establish a regime that would put the exhibitors at the mercy of three or four French companies, which collectively did not produce more than a hundred films a year. Therefore they were forced to import a great number of foreign films which would be of little value to the public.

Behind the exhibitors' arguments, another consequence of the American boycott was that Sapène tried to arrange for closer collaboration with the German film industry. German films had increased access to France as a result of the Dawes plan, which arranged for the payment of war reparations in kind. The Germans delivered motion pictures at a value of 2,410,000 gold marks, or $575,500.[49] The French entered an agreement with the "Spitzenorganisation der deutschen Filmindustrie" in August 1930, which was prolonged until June 1932, allowing the French to export twenty-three films to Germany, while the Germans could export fifty films to France.[50]

In June 1929, the American film distributors in France stepped up the confrontation by declaring that they had started firing their staff because they had no use for them.[51] In reality, the announcement was only a political maneuver designed to put pressure on the French government. No one was sacked, it seems. They were busy booking old films to the movie houses,[52] delaying the booking of new films.

When Jean Sapène withdrew from film production in July 1929, selling the Pathé-Cinéromans company to the politically less adept Bernard Natan, François-Poncet saw a solution to the conflict in maintaining status quo. He expressed dissatisfaction with the quota system several times and wanted it supplanted by an increased customs duty. While Sapène was influential, he could not disregard the opinion of the Chambre Syndicale, which was under his influence.[53] François-Poncet, however, would not enter any agreement before the reparations talks, which took place during the summer of 1929, had been concluded.

The conflict was settled by an agreement of September 19, 1929, which prolonged the Herriot-Hays agreement until October 1, 1930, and if no arrangement were reached before May 1, 1930, it would be further prolonged to October 1, 1931. The American diplomats wanted the French to commit themselves to abolishing the quota system, but the final agreement only stated that a future arrangement should be based on "a method of protection different from the present principle."[54]

The continuation of the seven-to-one quota meant that in reality the quota system was abolished as a protection of the French film industry. The

American Consul Alfred D. Cameron stated that the number of films that could be imported under the quota was about twelve hundred annually, while the maximum requirement of the French market for foreign films was around eight hundred.[55] The immediate results of the accord were that friendly relations between the French and American film industries resumed; it also meant the de facto death of the quota principle not only in France, but in other European countries as well. Finally, the French recognized the futility of the quota system and recommended the introduction of a different system within two years, which assured the Americans that no new regulations would be adopted without their consent in that period.[56]

However, the advent of sound in 1929 persuaded the leaders of the French film industry that they would be protected by the French language, and therefore they chose to enter the new agreement. Unfortunately, the language barrier did not provide any protection against Hollywood competition. When hundreds of American films were dubbed into French, linguistic protection disappeared.

The State Department considered the 1929 film quota accord to be one of its most important achievements in the fight against European quotas and contingent regulations, not only for the American film industry but for all American exporters. The contingent principle was spreading like a disease, and had already been used to limit the import of American cars. If it were upheld, the quota principle would sooner or later have been applied to other products on a much more extensive scale.

---

[1] *New York Times*, April 5, 1928.

[2] Department of State, Office of the Economic Advisor, March 17, 1928, USDS.

[3] Will Hays's press release, Paris, April 4, 1928, *Will Hays Papers*.

[4] Ambassador Myron T. Herrick, Paris, April 27, 1928, USDS.

[5] Henry F. Pringle, "Will Hays's Reason for Becoming Czar of the Silver Screen: Will His Status Be Ruined Now?" *Brooklyn Daily Eagle*, April 7, 1928, *Will Hays Papers*.

[6] "Fall Blames Hays for Letter: GOP Chairman Forced Him to Use MacLean to Hide Doheny, He Says," *Daily Mirror*, April 5, 1928, *Will Hays Papers*.

[7] "Further Testimony of Will H. Hays," Senate hearings, Feb. 10, 1928, pp. 34–39, *Will Hays Papers*. Also: *American Review of Reviews* (April 1928): 350–51. Hays's archive has a large number of newspaper clippings concerning the Teapot Dome investigations, *Will Hays Papers*.

[8] Letter to Saul E. Rogers, Fox, New York from the MPPDA, New York, June 2, 1928, MPPDA's microfilm belonging to Richard Maltby. The four-to-one film quota is also mentioned in *The New York Times*, May 1 and 4, 1928.

[9] "French Abandon American Movie Embargo Scheme," *Evening World*, April 5, 1928, *Will Hays Papers*.

[10] Letter from Will Hays to F.L. Herron, Paris, April 20, 1928, *Will Hays Papers*.

[11] Hays sent a copy of his proposal to Fredrick L. Herron, with a letter dated April 27, 1928, *Will Hays Papers*.

[12] "Will Hays Speaks At American Club," *Paris Times*, April 19, 1928, *Will Hays Papers*.

[13] Address of Will H. Hays at the American Club, Paris, April 19, 1928, *Will Hays Papers*.

[14] "Truce is Expected on French Films," *New York Times*, May 1, 1928, p. 13.

[15] Letter from Ambassador Myron T. Herrick to Edouard Herriot and Will H. Hays, Paris, May 1, 1928, USEF.

[16] Myron T. Herrick to Herriot, Paris, April 27, 1928, USDS.

[17] Cablegram from Canty to North, Paris, April 25, 1925, USDC.

[18] Minutes of the meeting of the Sous-Commission de Controle du Cinématographie. Séance du 3 Mai 1928 à 17 heures, and Séance du 4 Mai, à 10 heures. Archive of the Ministère de Beaux-Arts, F21, Archives Nationales, Paris.

[19] Two cablegram from Canty to North, Paris, April 25 and May 4, 1925, USDC.

[20] For a description of Victor Mandelstamm's position within the code administration, see Ruth Vasey, *The World According to Hollywood* (Exeter, 1997).

[21] League of Nations, *Abolition of Import and Export Prohibitions and Restrictions: Convention and Protocol between the United States and Other Powers* (Washington, DC, 1930), Treaty Series No. 811, - See also: Richard Maltby, "Cinema and the League of Nations" in Higson & Maltby's Film Europe, pp. 82-116.

[22] Vice Consul Harold L. Smith, Paris, date of preparation, Feb. 20, 1928, date of mailing, Feb. 21, 1928, USDS. Letter from consul Gaulin to Herron, Paris, Feb. 14, 1928, USCP.

[23] Letter from Herron to Arthur N. Young, New York, March 7, 1928, USDS.

[24] Letter from Charles E. Lyon, Commercial Attaché, U.S. Embassy, Switzerland, "French Films and the Geneva Treaty," Bern, March 20, 1928, *Will Hays Papers*.

[25] Harold L. Smith," Reaction to the Motion Picture Decree of Feb. 19, 1928," Paris, Feb. 27, 1928, USDS.

[26] "Hays and Wilson Confer on Films," *New York Times* (April 12, 1928), *Will Hays Papers*, and USDS.

[27] Letter from H.C. MacLean, U.S. Embassy Paris, to Hugh Wilson, U.S. Embassy Switzerland; Paris, May 9, 1928, USDS.

[28] Letter from Herron to Will Hays, New York, June 2, 1928, MPPDA microfilms belonging to Richard Maltby.

[29] Telegram from Will Hays to Edward G. Lowry, New York, July 2, 1928, MPPDA microfilms belonging to Richard Maltby.

[30] Letter from Koretz to Will Hays, Wien, July 19, 1928. One might suspect that Koretz wanted to show that his efforts was worth his fee of $5,000, which is mentioned in a letter from Saul E. Rogers, Fox, to Will Hays, New York, Oct. 11, 1928, MPPDA microfilms belonging to Richard Maltby.

[31] "Wilson, Geneva, Green," telegram to the secretary of state, Geneva, July 2, 1928, USDS.

[32] Hugh R. Wilson, *Diplomat between Wars* (New York, 1941), p. 226.

[33] Wilson, *Diplomat between Wars*, p. 227.

[34] Telegram 76 from Ambassador Myron Herrick, Paris, March 1, 1929, USDS.

[35] Vice-Consul Alfred D. Cameron, "Motion Picture Quota Situation," Paris, April 13, 1929, USDS.

[36] Cablegram from MacLean, Paris, May 2, 1929, USDS.

[37] "The following cable has just been received from Harold Smith in our Paris office, which I think you will be interested in seeing:
Meeting our people. Seidelman, Warner present. Agreed stand pat and await action of the governments and refrain from further conversations with the French industry.

The opinion is unanimous that Western Electric and Radio Corporation should conform with policy by stopping sales of equipment and Heyl, of Radio Corporation, and Latham, of Western Electric, will cable their home offices for instructions. Heyl thoroughly approves. Latham thinks perhaps better sell equipment and thus gain supporters for our cause since purchasers will need our films. Herrick note not yet presented. Sapène ready for a compromise of forty per cent. Our people are opposed to any compromise and the situation looks better than ever for a finish fight. Spirit splendid. Seidelman has done fine work. Sapène is peeved about 'Times articles and insists you brought paper over there. [signed] Smith

Letter from Herron, MPPDA, to Undersecretary William Castle, New York, April 12, 1929, USDS.

[38] Letter from William Marston Seabury to the secretary of state (New York, May 1, 1929), USDS.

[39] Cablegram from Commercial Attaché H. MacLean, Paris, May 2, 1929, USEF.

[40] Office of the Economic Adviser,"Memorandum," Washington, DC, May 2, 1929, USDS.

[41] W.R. Castle, to Norman Armour, USEF, Washington, D.C., June 10, 1929, USDS.

[42] Alfred D. Cameron, "New Film Quota Agitation," Paris, March 2, 1929, USDS. *New York Herald* (March 9, 1929).

[43] Norman Armour, Chargé d'Affaires ad interim, to Alphonse Gaulin, American Consul, Paris, April 29, 1929. USEF. The poster is found in the archive of the Ministère des Beaux Arts, Archives Nationales, Paris.

[44] Letter and translation of the poster from Fredrick L. Herron to Frederick Livesy, Acting Economic Advisor, New York, May 16, 1929, USDS.

[45] Letter from Herron to Castle, New York, May 17, 1929, USDS.

[46] Ibid., May 29th, 1929.

[47] Letter from Castle to Hays, Washington, DC, June 4, 1929, USDS.

[48] Harold L. Smith, "Translation of a letter from Mr. M. G. MADRET-LAFAGE, President of the General Federation of Associations of Directors of Amusement Entertainment of the Provinces, The largest and most important organization of its [kind in] France, to Mr. FRANÇOIS-PONCET, and was sent to every French Senator and Deputy," Provincial Union for the Defense of Amusement Enterprises, Bordeaux, June 7th, 1929, USEF.

[49] Alfred D. Cameron, "Motion Picture Reparation Deliveries," Paris, July 29, 1929, USEF.

[50] A contract was signed on Aug. 8, 1930, which was prolonged for the period July 1, 1931 to June 30, 1932. Copy of an undated agreement in the archive of the USEF, 1931.

[51] "Foreign Office states that local American companies have received instructions from head organizations in the United States looking toward the closing of their establishments and discharging their personnel, thereby giving the impression that they consider the negotiations terminated unfavorably to themselves, which is not the case. However, Foreign Office states that such action on part of company cannot but give the impression of endeavoring to bring pressure to bear on the French Government which may have adverse results if taken up by the press. The Foreign Office hopes that Hays can be persuaded to withdraw such instructions if issued at least until such time as a definite decision has been reached." Telegram no. 266 from Norman Armour, U.S. Embassy France, Paris, June 7, 1929, USDS.

[52] "The offices of the Paris representatives of American picture companies have not closed down, as has been stated in a good many cases. They are carrying on the distribution of pictures which had been sold under the present contingent regulations to exhibitors in France. These offices felt, however, that they could not legitimately sell the 1929–30 products, which would have to be delivered after the first of Oct. when the present contin

gent runs out, without knowing whether or not they would be able to deliver their pictures under the new law or the restrictions of which they are entirely in the dark at the present time. You may be assured that they are most anxious to start selling this new product just as soon as it is at all possible for them to do so...." F.L. Herron, MPPDA, to Assistant Secretary of State William R. Castle Jr., New York, July 30, 1929, USDS.

[53] "M. François-Poncet took this occasion again to assert his dissatisfaction with the contingent system and his intention to continue to study the possibility of substituting increased customs duty. He stated however that even if this principle of tariff protection were approved its application would require new legislation and consequently involve further delay whereas some immediate action is clearly necessary at the present moment. He explained that in view of the insistence by the Chambre Syndicale not only upon the maintenance of the contingent system but of its application in the most severe form and the fact that the Chambre Syndicale is largely under the influence of Sapène who, as the Department is aware, has considerable power both politically and with the press, it would be extremely difficult for the government flatly to reject the proposals of the Chambre." Telegram from Commercial Attaché Armour, USEF, Paris, May 29, 1929, USDS.

[54] "Franco-American Film Accord," telegram from Hays to Stimson, Secretary of State, New York, Sept. 19, 1929, USDS.

[55] Alfred D. Cameron," French Motion Picture Quota Virtually Abolished," Paris, Oct. 8, 1929, USDS.

[56] "History of the French Film Contingent Regulations," undated, post Sept. 19, 1929, USDS.

7

The French Situation, 1930–1933

During the 1930s the political situation and the film policy of France were in constant flux. When Sapène abandoned film production in July 1929, the execution of French film policy fell into the hands of politicians who often were not favorably inclined toward the industry. It lurched from one economic crisis to the next under the constant threat of total disintegration, and there was at first little political will to redress the situation. It did not seem to be the depression, which affected France from late in 1931 to 1935, that caused the bankruptcy of the old French film companies in the mid-1930s, but rather the unstable political situation.

Political instability troubled France throughout the 1930s. At first, there was some stability under a Republican Union government. When the Republican-Democratic Poincaré resigned as premier because of ill health in July 1929, the Left Republican Tardieu followed him. André François-Poncet was undersecretary of fine arts, but in February 1931 he was succeeded in office by Maurice Petsche, who was much more positively disposed towards American film interests. However, when the Republican Union lost the election on May 1, 1932, the Cartel des Gauches took power. There then followed a period of serious political instability which saw a succession of six cabinets in the period June 1932 to February 1934, when the Stavisky scandal brought down the Daladier government. The instability was a result of differences in policy between the Radicals and the Socialists, who advocated nationalization of major industries, including film production. In 1934–35 a National Union cabinet under Gaston Doumergue temporarily stabilized the public crisis. After two more governments, the situation stabilized somewhat more under Pierre Laval, who was premier from June 1935 through January 1936. By that time the old French film companies had ceased to exist. On December 1, 1935, the Pathé-Natan Company was declared bankrupt and the Bernard Natan scandal erupted, in which monetary losses were twice as big as in the Stavisky affair. In June 1936 the Socialist Léon Blum formed the Front Populaire government, a coalition of Radical Socialists and Socialists. Finally, in 1939 the Radical Daladier government took power.[1]

It is ironic that the mid-1930s both initiated one of the richest periods in French cinema and also brought the downfall of the major studios, the GFFA and the Pathé-Natan companies. In this period the directors Jean Renoir, Marcel Carné, Jean Grémillon, and Duvivier emerged, and actors learned to work with sound film. Talented screenwriters such as Jacques Prévert, Charles Spaak, and Henri Jeanson further liberated film from the theater. Production increased rapidly to an average of 130 films per year, but small companies created them. Lacking organization, the French film industry had difficulty fighting Hollywood's competition and enforcing its political demands. Despite successful productions such as *Le crime de Monsieur Lange* (1936), *La Grande Illusion* (1937), *Quai des brumes* (1938), and *La règle du jeu* (1939),[2] French film production did not have the necessary political power to improve its position in the confrontation with the film industry of the United States.

The lack of collaboration between the different parts of the industry continued, and individual producers pursued their own interests. Bernard Natan, who became the director of the Pathé-Cinéromans Company after Sapène, was not politically powerful, and he was unable to unite the producers. Charles Delac, the director of the Chambre Syndicale de la Cinématographie Française, followed a policy that aimed at finding a way to collaborate with the German film industry for his personal benefit. The exhibitors continued to favor free import of American films, but they also demanded—unsuccessfully—a ban on block-booking. The demands of the exhibitors were supported by the dubbing industry, thereby providing the American film industry strong support within France. It was therefore difficult for the politicians to determine which policy to adopt.

In the spring of 1933 the Nazi persecution of Jews in the German industry caused them to flee to France and work in French film. *La Cinématographie Française* reported that for three months a storm had passed over Germany, as the Nazi regime tore down an industry that had appeared to be strong firmly rooted.[3] The influx into France was sudden, occurring over just a few weeks. German assistants, cameramen, technicians, singers, dancers, and composers were suddenly waiting at French studio doors for a chance to work. But the French film producers, already hit by the general business crisis and lack of finances, could not employ the foreigners without the risk of putting their own countrymen out of work. France had already received foreign producers such as Alexandre Korda, Tourjansky and Volkoff, and then came Kurt Bernhard, Max Ophuls, Frederich Feher, Robert Siodmak, Richard Oswald, Robert Liebman, Joe May, and Litwak. They had been received with sympathy, and the actors contributed much talent, but the journal complained that the French industry was in crisis and would have to demand justice and protection for itself.

The new immigrants also invested in film production. In 1933, 136 new film companies emerged. Only 9 of the companies had a working capital larger than 100,000 francs; 36 had a capital between 50,000 and 100,000 francs, while 88 had less than 50,000 francs.[4] Most of the new companies went bankrupt and the competition produced hardships for the existing film production companies. In 1935 a newly formed interministerial commission suggested that to produce a film it should be required to file a certificate that a banking credit of at least sixty percent of the estimated cost of production of a contemplated film had been established.[5]

The situation of French cinema was completely altered after 1934. The French film industry changed its character because the large production companies were liquidated, and film production continued only on a small scale. In 1934, Gaumont liquidated, and in 1935 the Pathé-Natan company went bankrupt, for which Bernard Natan, "the Jew," was scapegoated.

There are several hypotheses about the origins of the Natan affair, which was, in terms of the money involved, twice as big as the better-known Stavisky affair. Bernhard Natan, a Rumanian Jew, was manipulated into serving as a vehicle for pillaging the Pathé company when, after Jean Sapène sold him his business, all debtors were refunded with considerable profits. Neither Sapène nor Charles Pathé seem to have been involved in the affair.[6] The end of the Natan history is also known: Bernhard Natan, being deprived of his French citizenship, left on convoy number 37 from the concentration camp in Drancy, north of Paris, on September 25, 1942, for Auschwitz. He never returned.

The Natan affair gave a tremendous impetus to French anti-Semitism, which already increased after the publication of the film history by Bardèche and Brasillach.[7] Already in 1936 anti-Semitic articles appeared. Even in the respectable *Ciné-Comædia*, an article stated that the cinema, the art of the future, having become a Jewish art, was debased to the roots of civilization. The Jews were called the "obligatory mediator" of the future because they had experience of internationalism and were free from hindrances that impeded the French, such as religious practice, the idea of the fatherland, and the memories of territorial conquests.[8]

Even though the failure of the French film industry and Hollywood's success were not the result of an international Jewish conspiracy, the idea persisted. In 1937 Henry Coston stated that the film industry was totally in the clutches of Israel.[9] His list of Jews was, however, disappointingly brief, including Nathan, Godehaux, Osso, Braunberger, Haïk, Souhami (Paramount), Romains Pinès (Films R.P.), Abel Gance, Diamant-Berger, and Nathanson. Lucien Rebatet elaborated on the involvement of Jews in theater and cinema during the German occupation of France.[10]

Control of film distribution guaranteed control of film business. Hollywood's strong position in France was secured by the control of the distribution network. After GFFA and Pathé-Natan had vanished by 1935, of the thirteen remaining national distributors operating, seven were affiliated with American companies, which distributed 181 American films, 14 French films, and a few from other countries. Two German affiliations distributed 3 American films, 11 French-version films, and 10 German films. The four French distributors distributed only 22 French films, 2 American, and 2 English.[11] There was little space left for the small independent competitors, who distributed the majority of French films but were limited to the regional level. If exhibitors turned to independent European or American producers, the American distributors boycotted these theaters and deprived them of American films. American film companies exerted further control by forcing exhibitors to enter block-booking arrangements.[12]

German-French Film Trade Agreements, 1930–1931

At first the French film producers tried to continue to collaborate with the German film industry, and the Americans continued to oppose the collaboration. George Canty reported that it came as a "bombshell" to American exchange managers that Delac and Dr. Plugge had entered a Franco-German trade agreement on August 8, 1930, a continuation of the Franco-German mutual cooperative trade movement. The German dialogue films made in France would have the same rights in Germany as a German film, and vice versa in the case of French-dialogue films made in Germany. The agreement would terminate at the end of June 1931.[13]

Canty pointed out that such favoritism, given to the Germans and not to the Americans, would violate the French Film Decree Regulations, which clearly specified what constituted a French film. The American exchange managers demanded that the American films should have a similar status in France as the German films, and they wanted to know if Paramount's films produced in France would be included in the Franco-German agreement. Canty feared that the publication of the Franco-German agreement would whet the appetites of the Italian, Austrian, Czechoslovak, Swedish, and British producers for similar agreements.

The State Department informed the American ambassador in Paris of the MPPDA's opinion that if the French authorities approved the Franco-German agreement it would result in direct discrimination against American motion picture interests, in violation of the agreement between the American and the French industry which maintained the status quo until October 1931.[14] The embassy was therefore authorized to discuss the question informally with the French authorities, expressing the hope that the American motion picture industry would be accorded the same favorable treatment as the Germans. The MPPDA was anxious for diplomacy to fore-stall the conclusion of the agreement with Germany and to reap the benefits which the German film industry would derive from it.[15]

It is not possible to determine whether the French and German govern-ments actually installed the regulations recommended by the film industry, because of a lacuna in the available documents between October 1930 and March 1931. It seems, however, that the authorities accommodated the film industries, because the film *Westfront 1918* (*Quatre de l'Infanterie*) and sev-eral other films produced in Germany but dubbed in French were on the list to be classified as French films. In contrast, the American films pro-duced in France, *Spectre Vert* and *Si l'Empereur Savait Ça*, had not yet been classified as French films, and the latter, which had a cast of only French-men, including some of the best French artists, had not been granted this privilege by the cinema commission.[16] Paramount also wanted the films *Morocco* and *Renegades* classified as French, but Harold Smith thought that might be difficult because the films dealt with the Foreign Legion, a touchy topic.

In April 1931 Delac was negotiating a new contract with the Germans, and informed Harold L. Smith about the results.[17] The Germans, Delac said, had proposed a seven-to-one exchange instead of a two-to-one. He'd then had a conference with the minister of the interior, Wirth, and Plugge and Volger from the German "Spitzenorganization," during which the "Spitzenorganization" had offered the French twenty-five contingents, but they refused to allow the American companies operating in France (i.e., Paramount) to participate in the benefits of the accord. The Germans in-sisted that they themselves would make any accords necessary directly with the American companies. Delac thought that this clause in the accord would have to be eliminated for Petsche, the undersecretary of fine arts, to accept it. But Smith did not think that the Paramount Company could be sepa-rated from the other French companies in relation to the accord that Delac proposed. Petsche stated clearly that he wanted the free circulation of films. If the Germans had not instituted a contingent he would have dropped the French contingent immediately. Petsche wanted to make certain that the French industry could get into Germany, but he did not want to negotiate with the Germans without advising the American film industry, nor did he want to do anything to harm the Paramount company in France. According to Smith, the French producers would not be averse to Paramount leaving France, not only because it would result in reduced product competition but primarily because Paramount's presence increased the costs of produc-tion due to competition for artists, stories, etc.

Petsche, obviously unaware of how delicate the negotiations were, stated that he would present this problem to the meeting of the ministers, and he asked Delac for a copy of the German proposal, which Delac was rather reluctant to provide, as he thought it was unnecessary to bring it to the attention of the entire cabinet. Petsche, however, insisted that everything he did should be brought to the attention of his colleagues. Petsche also asked Smith when the commercial attaché Dan Reagan would be back so that he could have a talk with him, as he wanted to keep him informed. After the meeting Delac angrily called him an "idiot" and complained that he had to attend another meeting of "idiots" with Ginisty and the new sub-commission. The minister afterwards called Smith stating that he had told Delac that he quite strongly supported the American point of view.[18]

Petsche's open-minded friendship towards Hollywood made life easy for the American film diplomats. Smith hoped that the Germans would refuse to eliminate the paragraph that excluded American films made in France from the proposal, because he did not believe the minister would approve it. He even thought that the MPPDA should, if possible, kill the accord by indirect means, for example by having the American embassy make tactful inquiries at the Foreign Office. Then the French would be forced to take some other measure to retaliate against the Germans. The problem was complicated because Delac was in close contact with the Germans, doing most of his business with them and planning to make twelve German-dialogue films in the following year. The other French producers took little interest in anything and let Delac run the whole show. In Smith's opinion some of the government functionaries, such as Ginisty, had been far too easy with Delac and allowed him to get away with things that he should not have, for example classifying films made in Germany (like *Westfront 1918*) as French.

The collaboration attempt with the German film industry proved to be an impasse. When Hitler took power in Germany, the Nazis also took control of the film industry, and the propaganda films turned out were of a mediocre quality. Furthermore, many German film producers were of Jewish descent, so the French film industry suddenly became flooded with skillful émigré German and east-European directors and actors.

Film Quotas in the 1930s

With Sapène no longer in film production, the American diplomats had difficulties influencing French film policy, which was increasingly handled by the French state. The undersecretaries of beaux arts continued to uphold quota restrictions on the import of American films. For example, the Herriot-

Hays agreement, which determined that seven American films could be imported for every film produced in France, was further prolonged by François-Poncet for a year to October 1, 1930, and again to October 1, 1931.[19]

When François-Poncet was appointed ambassador to Germany in the beginning of 1931, Maurice Petsche became undersecretary of beaux arts. His friendly attitude towards Hollywood and lack of understanding of the French film situation was expressed in the cinema control regulations, which gave American films free entry into France for the quota year July 1931 to June 1932. The liberal policy did not cause an increase in the number of imported films, but as a result almost all dubbing into French took place in Hollywood. The overly friendly policy towards Hollywood may have contributed to the downfall of the major French film studios in 1934 and 1935.

The dubbing quota policy, 1931–1938

After a year of free importation of American films, the Chambre Syndicale recommended to the Superior Cinema Council that it institute a new form for limiting the import of American films in April 1932. The idea was to prohibit the import of films dubbed into French and to limit the number of import visas for dubbing films in France to two hundred, one hundred each for producers and distributors.[20]

In June 1932, Will Hays asked Undersecretary of State William R. Castle to have the embassy contact the French authorities.[21] He complained that French producers wanted their government to require that Americans hire their studios for dubbing. If French producers obtained a hundred permits, the American representatives would have to buy them from their competitors in order to carry on business in France. Hays thought that such a situation was a return to the subsidy idea which the MPPDA had fought three years earlier. He asserted that French producers had not suffered during the previous year from the competition with Hollywood, since the French exhibitors needed movies from the United States in order to keep their doors open. Hays deliberately avoided mentioning how the competition affected the producers. He also stated that the proposal would result in a film shortage, since the exhibitors needed four to five hundred movies, and the French producers would make only sixty at most. The exhibitors had always opposed film quotas, but the group was not well organized and their influence was not in proportion to their importance in the industry.

But the American protests were not taken into consideration when the proposal of the Chambre Syndicale was adopted on July 21, 1932. Besides the measures originally requested by the Chambre Syndicale, the decree also pronounced that films in the original foreign language could be shown only in five theaters in Paris and five in the provinces.[22] The minister of education and fine arts, A. de Monzie, issued a communiqué explaining

that certain foreign regulations had made it necessary for France to establish a compensating, or retaliatory system, and that the precautions envis-
aged were aimed especially at "dubbing." But ambassador Walter E. Edge
thought it was undesirable to place a theoretical and general prohibition,
even though it justified eventual measures of safeguard for the French industry.[23]

The dubbing quota policy was clearly conceived and introduced to promote the interests of the French film industry, not to protect French culture
or French language. Correspondingly, the minister of fine arts did not introduce dubbing regulation as a reaction to popular pressure in defense of
French language and culture. Instead, the measure served to satisfy lobby-
ists of the production industry, and was used as an object of bargaining by
the French state. Once installed, the American film industry found the dubbing quota more valuable than an increase of the number of movie houses
allowed to show films in the original language, as offered by the French
Foreign Office.[24] The legislation came into being as a result of the pressure
by members of the Chambre Syndicale in the Superior Cinema Council. If
the aim of the decree were merely to protect the French language it would
not have been necessary to limit the number of films entering France and to
stipulate that the dubbing should take place at French studios.

---

[1] David Crowe, *The Essentials of European History 1914 to 1935* (Piscataway, NJ, 1997), pp. 77–
80; Frederick L. Schurman, *War and Diplomacy in the French Republic* (New York, 1969), p.
430–31.

[2] "France," in *The Oxford Companion to Film,* ed., Liz-Anne Bawden (Oxford, 1976), p. 264–
65.

[3] Lucie Derain, "The Foreign Invasion," *La Cinématographie française* (June 24, 1933): 114.
Article in English.

[4] "Le credit du cinéma française menacé par le nombre trop important des sociétés à capital
infime," *La Cinématographie française* (1934), undated clipping, USEF.

[5] Despatch 2162 from Chargé d'Affaires ad interim Theodore Marriner, "French Cinema
Regulations," Paris, Sept. 12, 1935, USDS.

[6] Their names do not occur in the records of the trial in the Archives de Paris; Henrik Fescourt,
La Foi et les Montagnes (Paris, 1959). Marc-Antoine Robert has concluded that "certain
milieux politiques avaient intéret à accabler Natan pour mieux mettre la main sur sa
société... Ces suppositions ne pourront certainement jamais être vérifiées, mais elles
révèlent le trouble des années trente dans lequel s'inscrit, de la même façon que l'affaire
Stavisky, l'épisode Natan." Marc-Antoine Robert, "L'affaire Natan," in Jacques Kermabon
(ed.), *Pathé: Premier empire du cinéma* (Paris, 1994), p. 266.

[7] Maurice Bardeche and Robert Brasillach, *Histoire du cinéma* (Paris, 1935).

[8] Simone Dubreuilh, "Le cinéma, art du futur, plongé des racines dans les passé le plus
lointain, il est l'art juif," *Cine-Comædia* (Aug. 22, 1936).

[9] Henry Coston, *Les juifs contre la France,* (Paris, 1937), p. 11.

[10] Lucien Rebatet, *Les tribus du cinéma et du théâtre* (Paris, 1941).

[11] Paul Leglise, *Histoire de la politique du cinéma Français*, vol. 1 (Paris, 1977), p. 124.

[12] Martine Danan, "From Nationalism to Globalization: France's Challenges to Hollywood's Hegemony," Ph.D. dissertation (Michigan, 1994), p. 101.

[13] G.R. Canty, "Weekly Report No. 7," Paris, Aug. 18, 1930, USDS.

[14] Letter from Undersecretary of State W.R. Castle, Jr., to the American ambassador, Paris, Walter E. Edge, Sept. 17, 1930, USDS. Telegram 234 from the Department of State to the USEF, Sept. 25, 1930, USDS.

[15] "Memorandum of Conversation" between the acting economic advisor, Frederick Livesey and Walter E. Edge, Division of Western European Affairs Sept. 26, 1930, USDS.

[16] Copy to Reagan of a letter from Harold L. Smith to Herron. Paris, Feb. 2, 1931. USEF.

[17] Letter from Smith to Herron, Paris, April 29, 1931, USEF.

[18] Ibid.

[19] Canty's cablegrams to North of Aug. 12 and 14, 1930 are cited in a letter from the Economic Adviser, EA, to Castle, Sept. 17, 1930, USDS.

[20] "Plan for Contingent Regulations from July 1, 1932 to June 30, 1933," [from Chambre Syndicale] Plan no. 1. Meeting to Discuss this Plan, April 4th. Translation made by the MPPDA (New York, April 27, 1932); enclosure with letter from Will Hays to Undersecretary of State, William R. Castle, Jr. New York, June 6, 1932, USDS.

[21] Letter from Hays to Castle, New York, June 6, 1932, USDS.

[22] "Reglementation de la production cinematographique," *Journal Officiel* (July 2, 1932): 8300. Enclosure to despatch no. 2799, Aug. 1, 1932, USDS.

[23] Walter E. Edge, "Import and Exhibition of Films in France," despatch no. 2799 to the Secretary of State, Paris, Aug. 1, 1932, USDS.

[24] On April 27, 1937, the French Foreign Office offered to increase the number of movie houses showing films in the original version in exchange for reduction of the dubbing quota. Harold Smith refused the offer. Letter from the Ministère des Affaires Étrangères to Ministère de Commerce, and Education Nationale, April, 28, 1937, Archive of the Ministère des Affaires Étrangères. The archival documents demonstrate that the objective French ministries pursued was commercial protectionism, not cultural protection. In contrast, Martine Danan argues that dubbing policies emanated from public pressure."Hollywood's Hegemonic Strategies Overcoming French Nationalism with the Advent of Sound," in Higson & Maltby's *"Film Europe" and "Film America"* (Exeter, 1999), p. 225–48.

8

The New Deal and Hollywood

Cordell Hull's Reciprocal Trade Agreement with France, 1936

The Great Depression opened the eyes of American politicians to the fact that trade was a "two-way street" and that exports were bound to decline unless imports increased. When Franklin D. Roosevelt and the Democrats took over government in 1933, his main policy focus involved recovering from the depression through the "New Deal" legislation. The New Deal in foreign policy, arranged by Roosevelt's Secretary of State, Cordell Hull, included the passing of the Reciprocal Trade Agreement bill, which went into effect on June 12, 1933. This represented something of a personal victory for Hull since for long years he had fought for a reciprocal trade policy and the lowering of trade barriers.

The reciprocal trade agreements proved to be a sophisticated and efficient strategy to promote exports, ensuring that American products would be exported at the lowest tariffs possible, and providing the State Department with a tool to remove the troublesome French quota restrictions. The law authorized the president to enter into trade agreements with other countries, and in negotiations he was authorized to increase or decrease any of the Smoot-Hawley tariff rates by as much as fifty percent in return for adequate trade concessions from another country on the most-favored-nation (MFN) basis. The State Department considered quota restrictions and exchange controls to discriminate against U.S. exports and Hull did his best to eliminate them. Quota restrictions would not disappear, however, through the lowering of tariffs.[1]

In the negotiations of the Franco-American Trade Agreement, the American reciprocity policy was on a collision course with the newly established French dubbing quota policy. A State Department directive asserted that foreign governments had to guarantee to the United States equality of treatment in tariff rates and in the administration of customs regulations. In order to obtain benefits for French exporters, the U.S. trade agreement legislation called for France to give concessions to American exporters, among which were the American film producers. In signing the Franco-American Trade Agreement in 1936, the French were forced to accept so as not to worsen the position of American film exports to France in comparison with exports from other countries. American trade agreements provided for a proportional allocation of quotas, so when maintaining exchange allotment systems and quota regimes, foreign governments had to secure for American traders a fair share based on a representative trade period. Thus, it would be possible for a country to offer increases in export quotas to another country only if American exporters were offered a proportional increase too.[2]

Before entering the Franco-American trade agreement, France tried to reduce the number of American films dubbed into French and distributed in the French market. When establishing the dubbing quota for the film year July 1933 to June 1934, dubbing of the Ministry of Commerce was suddenly made responsible for carrying out the decree of July 22, 1933. The Embassy considered that the French had transferred authority to the Ministry of Commerce without informing the American embassy in order to deceive American negotiators.[3] The decree prohibited importation of dubbed films, but allowed dubbing of seventy foreign films twice each year in France. Films in foreign languages could be shown only in five movie houses in Paris and five (later ten) in the provinces. Once passed, the embassy was unsuccessful in its attempts to have it altered.

The decision to limit importation to seventy dubbed films for the second half of 1933 was, in fact, made under pressure from French producers. They wanted the importation suspended for three months. But according to the exhibitors France produced only 120 films a year, to which 140 foreign films should be added, totaling 260 new films as a minimum of films required, even though the exhibitors needed 400 films per year. The Ministry of Commerce found it impossible to prohibit importation of film because it would provoke retaliatory measures from the United States.

The interministerial committee was responsible for French film policy throughout the 1930s. Chairman of the committee was Mr. Louyriac, Directeur-adjoint des Accords Commerciaux. The committee repeatedly discussed how to improve the conditions for French films by reducing the import from Hollywood, but it was paralyzed from fear that the United States might retaliate against the major French products that benefited from conventional reductions, such as wines, liqueurs, perfume, cigarette paper, and lace. The United States might even be inclined to repeal the trade agreement, which, the Foreign Office warned, would lead to a rupture of the economic relation between the two countries, with consequences in the political sphere.[4]

The embassy was much more vigilant when the quota arrangements for the quota year 1934–35 were passed. Having secured a copy of the plan which the Chambre Syndicale supposedly had presented to the government, the embassy promptly telegraphed it to the secretary of state with Harold L. Smith's comments.[5] In the first of its six points, the plan called for the prohibition of foreign film importation for three months; Harold Smith immediately saw that the government would never pass this point. Second, the Chambre Syndicale requested a substitution of the quota for a requirement for exhibitors to show a certain percentage of French films. This requirement would oblige American companies operating in France to buy and present French films. Third, dubbing was to be done in French studios. Fourth and fifth, the customs duties were to be increased, and the resulting extra revenues would be used to subsidize theaters that promoted the showing of French films. Finally, the proposal called for a prohibition of blind selling and block-booking.

The ambassador reported that Harold Smith was endeavoring to crystallize opposition to the plan among French exhibitors, whose opposition to the projects of the Chambre Syndicale had been successfully employed in the past. The exhibitors would not be favorably inclined towards the plan except for certain features, such as the prohibition of blind selling and block-booking.

Colonel Herron, who had also received news of the proposal, immediately telephoned to discuss the situation with the State Department on Friday May 18, 1934.[6] He was anxious that the American ambassador Jesse Isidor Straus be instructed to take the matter up with the French government since in the past the French government had followed rather closely the recommendations of the Chambre Syndicale. Herron stated that the proposal would be prohibitive and an absolute block to the distribution of American films in France if the French government accepted the recommendations of the Chambre Syndicale.[7]

The following morning Herron consulted with the State Department, but he did not see anything more that could be done.[8] In the afternoon the French Commercial attaché Garreau-Dombasle dropped in and said that he would address the matter when he returned to France on June 9. The main purpose of his trip was to study the French commercial situation in light of possible negotiations with the United States with regard to establishing a most-favored-nation trade agreement between the two countries.

When the quota regulations were published on June 26, 1934, the ambassador stated that the new regulations were infinitely better than the original proposal of the Chambre Syndicale.[9] The text was practically identical to that of the previous year's decree, but it was applicable for only six months, from July 1 to December 31, 1934. The ambassador had made every effort to obtain a twelve-month period, to which the Foreign Office had agreed, but the interests of other ministries prevailed. The decree stipulated that a total of ninety-four dubbing visas would be issued each six-months (instead of the previous period's seventy), and unofficially seventy-five of them were reserved for Hollywood films. The Foreign Office informed the embassy in November 1934 that the regulations would continue in effect for the first half of 1935, and on May 27, 1935, the decree was extended unaltered for the period July 1, 1935 to June 30, 1936. [10] The number of dubbing visas continued to be ninety-four (of which 75 were reserved for Hollywood) per six-month period during the quota years 1936/37[11] to 1938/39.[12]

The French government also contemplated other protective measures. In December 1934 a bill was under consideration in parliament aimed at a reduction of the tax on movie houses as well as the prohibition of blind selling and block-booking.[13] An amendment to the original project had been introduced in the bill by deputy Lafont which would detax cinemas that exhibited a certain percentage of French films. The embassy considered the amendment, if passed, to represent serious discrimination against American films. It thought the block-booking provision would also inconvenience American film interests, even though the restrictions aimed at impeding the activities of French producers. The detaxation decree was passed on July 26, 1935,[14] but due to the efforts of the American embassy the Lafont amendment was suppressed. French exhibitors obtained some protection against block-booking in article 4 of the decree, which stated that rental contracts were valid only if entered into later than three days after the first projection of the film.

The French film regulations subsequently became a part of the reciprocal trade agreement between France and the United States, which entered into force provisionally on June 15, 1936.[15] The Franco-American trade agreement stipulated that:

> The number of dubbed films permitted to be shown in France shall not be less than 94 films per semester.
>
> The American original version films authorized to be shown in France may be shown in five theaters in the Department of the Seine and ten theaters in the other French departments, but in a maximum of two theaters in any one of these other departments, although exceptions may be granted by the Minister of National Education.
>
> The French government will take no new measures which would have the effect of placing American films in a position, in comparison with French films, or with those of any other foreign country, less favorable than that which they now enjoy.[16]

The last point was the most ominous, because it froze the position of Hollywood films at an advantageously high level. Article 6, section 3 of the agreement stipulated that supplementary quotas should be subject to revision on the first of July 1937 and the first of July the following years during the life of the agreement. The French film industry did not request any changes in the agreement, which limited only the position of other European producers.[17] Harold Smith reported that in 1937 the French had no reason for changing the regulations because the French film industry was in a better position in its home market than it had ever been since World War I, whereas the American film industry was in a worse position. The American industry was handicapped by the language difficulty, which made it necessary to dub films, the cost of which was a tremendous burden, ranging from $6,000 to $10,000 to adapt an American film for release in France. The situation was more difficult because there had been no increased revenue; on the contrary, receipts had been falling off during the past three or four years.

Smith demonstrated to the embassy that the French film industry was enjoying increasing success at the expense of American films, citing a poll taken from two hundred exhibitors operating the best cinemas in France that pointed out the most successful films in 1936.[18] Of the first twenty successful films, eighteen were French and only two American. Of these one was *Modern Times*, which was sixth on the list due to the popularity of Charlie Chaplin. The other was a normal American production, *The Trail of the Lonesome Pine*, and it was only nineteenth on the list. Of the seventy-five successful films on the list, only fifteen were American. The American films included *Mr. Deeds Goes to Town*, *Mutiny on the Bounty*, *Desire*, *Anna Karenina* with Marlene Dietrich and Greta Garbo, and *Captain Blood*. But the list was deceptive since it lacked information from small and provincial movie houses, which were the best customers of Hollywood films.

In the beginning of 1938, the French dubbing quota arrangement became problematic when the number of visas was exhausted. At the same time, dubbed films from other European countries increased in number. The Germans planned to release at least twenty dubbed films per year, and Russian, Italian, and English films were dubbed and released so that there would be an increasing number of non-American dubbed films available in France. These films would either upset the Franco-American Trade Agreement, which was based on a dubbing quota of 188, of which 150 visas were reserved for American films, or their release would be prohibited.

In May 1938, Cordell Hull insisted that a solution of the problem acceptable to the Americans had to be in conformity with the provisions of the trade agreement, according to which American film interests were entitled to a minimum of 147 visas per year, which was the number of visas accorded them for dubbing in the film year 1935/36.[19] In defiance of the agreement with the Americans, France entered an accord with Italy which gave them a dubbing quota of thirty-two visas, although in no year since 1934 had Italy presented more than four dubbed films for visaing.[20] The French authorities agreed that the Franco-Italian film accord was embarrassing to them, and the American Embassy stated that the accord might be interpreted as discrimination against Hollywood films. After intense negotiations, the French continued to allocate 150 visas to Hollywood, but the problem of too few dubbing visas was not specifically resolved.

The *Front populaire* and Jean Zay's Film Policies, 1936–1938

In June 1936 the Popular Front government, consisting of socialist, communist and radical parties, carried out social reforms but cared little about the industrial sector. The railways were nationalized but the film industry was not.

The secretary of the Ministry of Education and Fine Arts, Jean Zay, immediately encountered serious resistance in trying to solve the problems of the film industry. The French film industry was in a state of "quasi-general collapse" with no large production company left in France. In fact, there were only two companies of any size, and both were foreign. French films came from small companies, created specifically for the production of individual films. Zay realized that it was necessary for the state to intervene on behalf of private business when he stated, "I don't think anyone can expect [that] the classic principles of a liberal market can continue to operate pure and simply, or that the state can continue to preserve a totally noninterventionist stance."[21] Zay's proposed legislative framework for the protection of the industry was, however, not carried out.

Instead of trying to alleviate the conditions of the cinema, the French Senate accepted an amendment to the budget bill for 1938 which reduced the amusement taxes by twenty-five percent for movie houses that offered music hall and orchestral attractions for more than forty-five minutes. Furthermore, movie houses that had a net profit over 200,000 francs per month were subject to a twenty-five percent increase in taxes if they had no orchestra. The proposal came from two communist members of the Chamber of Deputies, Berlioz and Pillot, who wanted to create work for the considerable number of unemployed musicians.[22]

The aim of the movie reforms seems also to have been to reduce the influence of American films, as the state was not merely anxious to protect live performances at the expense of film screening, as claimed by Colin

Crisp.[23] The American embassy regarded the amendment, which also proposed a seven percent tax on movie theaters that showed only foreign films, to be a flagrant violation of Paragraph 3 of Article 11 of the Franco-American Trade Agreement, which it communicated to the Ministère des Affaires Étrangères on December 23, 1937. Harold Smith had stated that the forced introduction of music hall and orchestral numbers in cinema programs would have the logical effect of eliminating the double-feature programs; if one film was to be dropped from the double-feature programs it would be the American rather than a French production.

The embassy's informal representation led to modification of the amendment, but it was not successful in discouraging the submission of another measure also considered detrimental to American interests. The attitude of the Foreign Office was passively defensive, stating that the modification was intended only to alleviate the situation for French music hall artists and musicians, and not to create an atmosphere unfavorable to American films; the French government was within its rights in sanctioning the legislation. The embassy was still invited to explore every possible way to protect the interests of American film producers from the technical discrimination thought to be inherent in the legislation. However, the embassy would just have to wait and see if the measure proved truly detrimental to the showing of American films in France.[24]

The reaction to the law came promptly from the cinema owners, and all Paris cinemas closed on January 4, 1938. Colin Crisp describes how the strike resulted in a state-appointed commission, which ruled in favor of the film industry. The commission concluded that the progressive nature of the state tax hit large cinemas more severely than medium-size ones, and that cinemas generally were more severely hit by the taxation than other categories of spectacles. The imposition of the municipal tax exacerbated this inequality, and the discriminatory regime favored provincial movie houses over the Parisian ones. In February 1939, the tax system was totally reformed, to the satisfaction of the industry. Still, throughout the 1930s the movie houses were systematically hurt by tax laws designed to penalize them disproportionately in comparison to other "superior" forms of entertainment.[25]

Abolition of the Dubbing Quota, 1939

The State Department continued to object to France's increasing the number of dubbing visas allotted to Britain, Italy, and Germany without giving the American film industry a proportional increase. There were only two ways to solve the visa problem—increasing the number of visas, or canceling the dubbing quota regulation; to ignore the trade agreement would undoubtedly result in retaliation against French exports, for example French wine exports to the United States.

The dubbing quota allotment ran into problems when the British government demanded more visas for British motion picture companies, adding that if they did not obtain they them they would boycott the Cannes Film Festival.[26] When the French asked the United States for permission to increase the number of dubbing visas for European films, the State Department obstinately demanded a proportional increase of their market share. Cordell Hull maintained that the State Department would as a matter of principle allow the number of dubbing visas to increase from 188 to 200 only if the allotment to the United States increased from 150 to 160 visas. Hull explained that

> All our trade agreements provide for proportional allocation of quotas, and the State Department considered that principle of outstanding importance in the French agreement. The principal problem involved in the French proposal was not the fixed allocation of 150 films per year, but the fact that the French wished to have a supplementary quota over and above the global quota of 188; no provision was made for the automatic extension to the United States of its proportional share of these additional films. If the total amount of foreign version films permitted entry into France did not exceed 188, then 150 visas for the United States did represent the proportional share. The State Department would not object to the country allocations so long as the allocation to the United States represented its proportional share of the total number of films permitted importation. In other words, if the French proposed a supplementary quota of 12 films, making the global quota 200, then the allocation to the United States should be about 160.[27]

The French government was not willing to give Hollywood more visas as requested by the State Department. Instead, on July 22, 1928, the Foreign Office informed the embassy that the French authorities wanted to suspend all quota limitations on dubbed films. The French government stated that it wanted to suppress the quota because the French industry had developed to the point where the protection was no longer needed; but the American film companies believed that the real reason was that the French producers wanted to have access to a larger number of foreign dubbed films in order to be able to offer more double feature programs. The real reason was probably that the authorities had experienced difficulties in reaching satisfactory adjustment of allocations for other countries, especially Britain, owing to the predominant position of American films.[28]

France repealed the dubbing quota restrictions limiting the number of dubbed foreign films by decree on August 7, 1939, just a few weeks before World War II broke out, on September 1, 1939, after which new restrictions were introduced on international film trade.[29]

---

[1] Hull explains the MFN clause thus: "I won't treat you any worse than the person I treat the best of all, provided you don't treat me any worse than the person you treat the best of all." *The Memoirs of Cordell Hull* (New York, 1948), vol. I, p. 357–59, 369.

[2] Cordell Hull, memorandum to Diplomatic and Consular Officers, June 6, 1935, *U.S. Foreign Relations* (1935) I:156; Arthur W. Schatz, "Cordell Hull and the Struggle for the Reciprocal Trade Agreements Program, 1932–1940,"Ph.D. dissertation, University of Oregon, 1958, p. 203–5; telegram from Hull to the USEF, Paris, June 17, 1939, USDS.

[3] Paul Leglise, *Histoire de la politique du cinéma français* (Paris, 1970), p. 265.

[4] "Étude de l'accord commercial franco-américain. Possibilités d'élargissement de l'accord. Reclamations de l'industrie française du cinématographe," Note, April 9, 1937, Archive of the Ministère des Affaires Étrangères, Paris.

[5] Telegram no. 376 from Ambassador Straus, USEF, Paris, May 19, 1934, USDS.

[6] John Hickerson, Assistant Chief of the Division of Western European Affairs, "Memorandum," Washington, DC, May 18, 1934, USDS.

[7] Letter from Fredrick L. Herron to Hickerson, New York, May 18, 1934, USDS.

[8] "Memorandum of Conversation with Colonel Frederick L. Herron, Foreign Manager of MPPDA," Washington, DC, May 22, 1934, USDS.

[9] Telegrams 469 and 471 from Ambassador Straus, USEF, to the secretary of state, Paris, June 26, 1934, USDS.

[10] Ibid., May 29, 1935.

[11] Text of the quota decree effective from July 1, 1936 to June 30, 1937, published in *Le Journal Officiel* on May 30, 1936, translation by the USEF, Paris, June 8, 1936, USDS.

[12] Despatch no. 2612 from First Secretary Maynard B. Barnes, USEF, "Transmitting French Film Decree and Other Documents," Paris, July 11, 1938, USDS.

[13] Projet de Loi, number 4249, Paris, Dec. 10, 1934, USDS. Also mentioned in a letter from Pierrepont Moffat, Chief, Division of Western European Affairs to F.L. Herron, MPPDA, Washington, DC, Dec. 28, 1934, USDS.

[14] "Modification du régime fiscal des spectacles," *Journal Officiel* (July 26, 1935), USDS.

[15] "Reciprocal Trade Agreement," signed in Washington, D.C., May 6, 1936; entered into force provisionally, June 15, 1936, in Charles I. Bevans, *Treaties and Other International Agreements of the United States of America 1776–1949*, vol. 7 (Washington, 1971), pp. 997–1011.

[16] Description of Articles, p. III–2 of the Reciprocal Trade Agreement, excerpted for the negotiation of the supplementary quotas, 1937, USDS.

[17] Letter no. 582 from the Counsel of Embassy, Edwin C. Wilson, Paris, April 22, 1937, USDS.

[18] Marcel Colin-Reval, "The most successful films of 1936: 75 successful films, *Cesar, Appel du Silence, Le Roi, Mayerling, Veille d'Armes* (all French), Head the List," translation by Harold L. Smith, MPPDA, of extracts of an article in *La Cinématographie française* March 26, 1937, USDS. Accompanying letter from Harold L. Smith to Lewis Clark, Second Secretary, USEF, Paris, April 16, 1937, USDS.

[19] Telegram no. 275 from Cordell Hull to the USEF, Washington, DC, May 10, 1938, USDS.

[20] Letter no. 2612 from First Secretary of Embassy Maynard B. Barnes to the Secretary of State, Paris, July 11, 1938, USDS.

[21] Colin Crisp, *The Classic French Cinema, 1930–1960* (Bloomington, IN, 1993), p. 38; Leglise, *Histoire de la politique du cinéma français*, p. 180.

[22] "French Legislation May Indirectly Affect Market for American Films in France," Letter no. 1439 from First Secretary of Embassy H. Merle Cochran, Paris, January 4, 1938, USDS.

[23] Crisp, *The Classic French Cinema*, p. 19.

[24] Letter no. 2612 from First Secretary of Embassy Maynard B. Barnes to the Secretary of State, Paris, July 11, 1938, USDS.

[25] Crisp, *The Classic French Cinema*, p. 19.

[26] Report no. 4616, "Country Allotment for Foreign Dubbed Films in France," from Robert D. Murphy, Counselor of Embassy, Paris, July 10, 1939, USDS.

[27] Telegram from Secretary of State Cordell Hull to the American Embassy, France, Washington, DC, June 17, 1939, USDS.

[28] Telegram 1354 from Bullitt, USEF, Paris, July 22, 1939, USDS.

[29] "Abrogation des dispositions des articles 3 et 4 du décret du 19 juin 1939 sur l'importation et la représentation des films impressionnés étrangers en France..." Aug. 7, 1939, *Journal Officiel* (Aug. 10, 1939), p. 10113, USDS.

9

The Post-World War II Period

In the postwar period new protective measures had to be introduced because the numerical quota would not provide sufficient protection for French films. The Vichy government had prohibited the importation of American films during the German occupation (May 1940 to August 1944), and as a result Hollywood had a backlog of more than two thousand films. If released freely together with recent American productions, these films would flood the market, squeeze out French films, and wipe French film production out of existence. As a replacement for the numerical quota the French producers demanded a new method of regulation, the screen quota (described below). This demand started a conflict over the size of American exports, because French producers were determined to restrict Hollywood's access to the French market by reserving seven weeks in a quarter of the year for the exhibition of French films. The Americans were equally determined to do away with French restrictions by invoking the advantageous dubbing quota of the Franco-American Trade Agreement from 1936, which continued to be in force. The outcome of the conflict was that the screen quota was introduced with the so-called Blum-Byrnes Agreement on May 28, 1946.

The provisional French government did not revoke the Franco-American Trade Agreement even though it announced the abrogation of all existing commercial agreements on October 1, 1944. The trade agreement provided for a formal six months' notice to be given before it could be revoked, a feature which Herron's successor, Carl E. Milliken, pointed out to the State Department while expressing the grievances of the MPPDA against the French in preparation for a possible renegotiation in case the trade agreement should be abrogated. In his view there should be no restriction on the release in France of American films more than two years old; there should be no limitations on remittances in payment for American films, and the industry's funds should be unfrozen; the restrictions of the release of original versions of American films to fifteen movie houses in France should be eliminated; the dubbing-quota restriction to 150 films should be lifted, and there should be no restriction of the number of feature films that may be included in each program; and finally, the requirement that dubbing must be done in France should be removed.[1]

The embargo on American films continued in the immediate postwar period, however, and the situation became further complicated with the lack of raw films. The only American films entering France were those brought in by the U.S. Army. The films had been brought in by the Office of War Information (OWI) under The Supreme Headquarters Allied Expeditionary Forces (SHAEF). The OWI had ordered five films from each of the major Hollywood producers for the entertainment of the GIs as well as for the French population, and they were handed over to Hollywood's local agents for general distribution in France—in violation of French cinema regulations.

The Emergence of the Screen Quota

The numerical quota restrictions of the Franco-American Trade Agreement of 1936, which continued to be in force after the war, restricted film imports only. By contrast, the screen quota would oblige exhibitors to reserve a certain amount of screen time for the showing of French films.

Charles Pathé had already suggested the introduction of a screen quota after World War I, but it was not presented officially until Pierre Chéret brought it up at a conference of film producers in January 1945.[2] Chéret presented a large statistical report on the economy of French cinema between 1942 and 1944. His intention was to demonstrate that the producers were able to recoup only a part of their investments in productions due to increased expenses. As a remedy, Chéret suggested the lowering of taxes on French cinema, the promotion of film production through a subsidy fund derived from a seven percent tax on box office receipts, and the introduction of a screen quota. French film production, he believed, would need no other method of protection.

The president of the French film producers organization, Jean Séfert, immediately adopted Chéret's protectionist concepts, though he waited half a year before publicizing the producers' request for a protective screen quota.[3] At first the producers requested a screen quota in the proportion of 8 French to 5 foreign films, which would result in a restriction of imports to 60 to 65 films. Séfert estimated that the French film market would be saturated with the release of 160 films per year. Therefore, he must have visualized France producing 100 films a year, even though in 1945 he estimated she could produce only around 65. (Actually France produced 58 feature films in 1945, 95 in 1946, and 94 in 1947). However, the French government negotiated with the United States on the assumption that France would not be able to produce more than 60 films a year, which had to be guaranteed showing on French screens.

The question of quota protection once again resulted in a rupture of the French film industry. The distributors sided with the producers in promoting the screen quota, whereas the exhibitors allied with Hollywood's local representatives in fighting protectionism. The exhibitors regarded the planned support fund providing aid to French film production as yet another encroachment on their box-office receipts, and detrimental to their existence. Their suspicion that the support fund proposal was a disguised general tax increase was confirmed when the Ministry of Finance refused to reduce the amusement taxation by seven percent, which was the amount intended for the support fund.

The French representatives of the Hollywood film companies united in the Syndicat Franco-Américain de la Cinématographie (SFAC) in order to defend their interests, and they sought the assistance of the American Embassy in Paris. At first, the commercial attaché complained that the individual companies did collaborate with each other to the extent desirable in a period of emergency, and recommended that "jockeying for position" should be held in abeyance until the problems were solved. The leadership problem of the organization was temporarily solved when Harold L. Smith returned to Paris of in July 1945.[4] Later, the Motion Picture Association placed its continental headquarter in Paris.

The alliance between French exhibitors and Hollywood's representatives began at a confidential meeting between the SFAC directors and representatives of French exhibitor unions headed by Raymond Lussiez on June 13, 1945. Lussiez stated the exhibitors' opposition to the seven percent tax and the screen quota. He requested that the conversations should remain confidential, and declared himself ready to work with the American representatives in all loyalty and clearness. They should share the study of all the special points of the problem and carry on a concerted action. Henri Klarsfeld (Columbia) declared that the American representatives were in complete agreement with Lussiez, and promised to take action through the distributors and exhibitors organizations.

The exhibitors' "betrayal" of the French cinema, however, should be judged on the basis of the offensive behavior of the producers. The exhibitors were furious of being informed less than twenty-four hours ahead of time of a meeting of the Joint Commission of the industry on June 2, 1945; the short notice made it impossible for provincial exhibitors to attend.[5] The screen quota policy was considered at another meeting of the Joint Commission on June 21, 1945, during which Gentel (RKO) raised an outcry by invoking the Franco-American Commercial Treaty of 1936. Lussiez then made an extremely energetic protest, and it was in part due to his systematic obstruction that no decision was taken. Lussiez concluded saying:

"Gentlemen, if you wish to stab the Americans in the back, you shall not do it in our cinemas."[6]

It was therefore up to the government to introduce the screen quota policy, since the antagonism between producers and exhibitors prevented the French industry from reaching an agreement on which policy to follow. The government, however, already sided with the producers and was favorably inclined towards the screen-quota policy. At a dinner given by the director of the U.S. Information Service (USIS) on June 4, 1945, Pierre-Henri Teitgen, former Minister of Information and newly appointed Minister of Justice by Charles de Gaulle, talked favorably about the screen quota. He stated that France could produce a maximum of sixty films a year at present, which had to be guaranteed showing on French screens. He hesitated to prescribe import quotas for each supplying country, but believed the solution was to enact legislation compelling exhibitors to grant French productions a certain percentage of playing time by establishing a screen quota.[7]

The American Embassy followed the development of the French film situation closely. At another meeting on June 7, 1945, Teitgen informed Robert Schless (Paramount) that nothing definite had been decided yet either about the numerical quota or the screen quota. At the same meeting Michel Fourré-Cormeray, who on May 16, 1945 had replaced Jean Painlevé as General Director of the Cinema, estimated that France could supply sixty of the 180 films he thought she would need. From this Schless deduced that the French government intended to reserve a thirty percent market share for French films.[8]

A crucial point in the quota policy was the number of films Hollywood needed to be able to carry on business in France. In late June, Hollywood's local agents told the embassy that they must have 135, but a month later the number was reduced to 108. In fact the American industry could get along satisfactorily on 90 films the first year, the United Artists foreign manager, Walter Gould, told the commercial attaché Malige in strictest confidentiality.[9]

Actually the numerical quota is a deceptive concept because it is based on the false assumption that spectators go to see *any* movie and not a specific film, so that all films are considered to have equal attendance. Recent films such as *ET* and *Titanic* have demonstrated that even single films may be able to saturate the market.

The conflict between the French and American film companies over the quota policy reached a climax in July 1945. The SFAC stated that the Americans did not intend to flood the French market, and offered to adhere to a self-imposed limitation of imports into France by a gentleman's agreement. They would restrict the release of films dubbed into French to 108 films (12 from each of the nine companies), a reduction from the 150 films granted in

the Franco-American Trade Agreement. If the French government established a screen quota the Americans threatened to withdraw from the French
market.[10]

The French producers, however, demanded that the import of American films be reduced to 72 dubbed films. George Canty, by then employed
in the State Department's Telecommunication Division, explained that the
French proposal would violate the Franco-American Trade Agreement. It
would be unfair to Hollywood to allow an increase of the French market
share. The American industry might be willing to consider an arrangement in which American films would be assured a specified percentage of
the proposed "screen quota," provided that this quota corresponded to the
actual prewar American share of screen-time.[11]

The French screen quota request resulted in furious reactions from Carl
E. Milliken, who became the director of MPPDA's foreign department during the war. He demanded that the State Department contemplate using
"dollar diplomacy" to break the resistance to Hollywood exports: "Why
should our Government be expected to continue supplying prodigious
amounts of fuel, food, clothing and money to these reconstituted countries
unless they in turn accord fair treatment to American business? This question arises first and foremost, in our opinion, with reference to the interests
of the American motion picture industry, not only because the motion picture is the spearhead for all business, and is the vehicle of information
regarding the American way of life, but because it is in the nature of the
case usually the first American business to return to the re-established country on a commercial basis."[12]

The first diplomatic clash over screen quota system occurred at a meeting in the State Department on August 17, 1945. The French negotiator de
Fouchier, Assistant Director of the Bureau of Foreign Economic Relations
of the Ministry of National Economy, complained that it had not been possible to reach a satisfactory agreement; in fact, the American representatives insisted that they would withdraw from the French market if their
proposal of a gentleman's agreement limiting the exhibition to 128 American films was not accepted. The American negotiator, George Canty, explained that the French proposal would worsen the position of American
films in France substantially, by reducing the U.S. share of total imports,
and as a result of increased competition, especially from British and Russian films. Furthermore, the proposal was a direct contravention of the
concession on films contained in the trade agreement of 1936. Canty's col-
league, Vernon Phelps, seconded this argument, stating that the U.S. would
expect that any solution would be worked out within the framework of the
trade agreement.[13]

De Fouchier found it irrelevant that the State Department officers referred to the trade agreement, since conditions had changed substantially since the signing of the agreement in 1936. The French government considered it essential to assist the French film industry in resuming production. Moreover, the dollar position would not permit large foreign exchange allocations for imported films. To this Canty responded that the foreign exchange transfers were relatively small because the American film industry spent a substantial part of its earnings in France.

Canty then reproached the French that their intention was not only to assist their film industry to recover but to expand its market share to the detriment of Hollywood. The French proposal would increase the minimum share for French films to fifty-five percent, whereas the American industry would have to compete with British, Russian and other imported films for the remaining forty-five percent playing time. Canty regarded the film statistics on which the French based their arguments to be unfair, since it did not take into account the effect of a new regulation that reduced the exhibition of American films by prohibiting "double feature" shows, in which one film was American and the other French.

Canty thought that the American industry might be willing to consider an arrangement that would assure American films a specified percentage of the proposed "screen quota," provided that the quota corresponded with the actual prewar share of American films. The State Department considered that the American industry had shown sufficient willingness to assist the French recovery by offering a voluntary reduction of the annual import quota from 188 to 108 films. The screen quota was a new type of restriction to which Hollywood objected in principle.

As it was impossible to reach an accord they agreed to continue discussions in Paris. At first the embassy was instructed by the State Department to accept the screen quota, providing the French would agree to uphold the American share of playing time it had in 1936. But after further consideration, the secretary of state, James Byrnes, decided to uphold the film regulations of the Franco-American Trade Agreement. He thought that the American industry might approve a reduction of the film quota to ninety to one hundred films for the next year in return for abandoning the screen quota.[14]

The Paris talks began on September 6, 1945. The French negotiator Hervé Alphand opened the talks on the basis of the screen quota, but to the great displeasure of the French, the embassy, on James Byrnes's instructions, ruled out the screen quota. Nevertheless, Alphand declared that the Foreign Office would consult with the Ministry of Information in order to find a form of screen quota that they felt would respect the Franco-American Trade Agreement.[15]

French producers had firmly established the screen quota idea with the government as the only solution to the difficulties of the film industry, the embassy noted during the subsequent talks with the Foreign Office in September 1945. The Foreign Office proposed a quota on the following basis: "For each period of thirteen weeks, six weeks would be left in each theater for the showing of films of foreign origin." The proposed percentage corresponded to the statistics for the reference years 1937 and 1938 and ensured American films a percentage of total cinema receipts that would not be inferior to that which they produced under the regime of 1936, so the French claimed. Even though the embassy was unable to do away with the screen quota proposal, it had dissuaded the Foreign Office from including a provision requiring the American producers to show French films in the United States.[16]

On October 2, 1945 the undersecretary of state, Dean Acheson, telegraphed the embassy stating that the department, after having considered the note from the Foreign Office carefully, was unable to approve the French screen quota proposal. He insisted that American feature films held approximately fifty percent of the total number of feature films shown in France in 1937, and that of the ninety-four dubbing permits issued per semester by France, the United States was entitled to eighty percent under the trade agreement. He claimed that Hollywood had made very substantial concessions in agreeing to a temporary reduction in the global quota from 188 foreign dubbed films to 135 films and reducing the American share from 150 films to 108 films, leaving 27 films as the dubbing quota allotment for all other countries for the period July 1, 1945 to June 30, 1946.[17]

At a meeting of the Motion Picture Export Association of America (MPEAA) in New York, the representatives of the eight major American companies requested that the department stand firm on the basis of the trade agreement. Their final offer was a reduction in the number of films to 72, so that each of the eight companies would supply eight dubbed feature pictures each for the film year ending June 30, 1947. They violently opposed the French quota proposal which they regarded as the worst proposition that had yet come from the French government, because it completely ignored the trade agreement obligation guaranteeing American films a proportion of foreign imports.[18]

The French officials, however, were incapable of upholding the dubbing quota arrangement for political reasons. They were under pressure from Russian, British, Czechoslovakian, and other governments whose share could not be reduced to less than 50 films. If the United States insisted on having eighty percent, a global quota would have to be 250 foreign dubbed films! The Foreign Office also stated that the French attitude was dictated by the strength of Communists, who favored greater French and Russian participation at expense of American films. Moreover the countries in question had agreed to reciprocate by buying about 40 French films in all, compared to two films purchased by American companies thus far.[19]

As the French would not give up the introduction of a screen quota, the discussions ended in deadlock even though the Minister of Foreign Affairs, Georges Bidault, confirmed the adherence to the trade agreement of 1936. French producers had firmly established within the government the idea that the only solution to the difficulties of the film industry was a screen quota, which reserved six weeks out of thirteen in each theater for the showing of films of French origin.[20] A telegram from Undersecretary of State Dean Acheson confirmed the American rejection of the screen quota even though this stance meant that American film companies lost a substantial part of the market share. He felt strongly that the United States had already made very substantial concessions.[21]

Even when the French minister of foreign affairs, George Bidault, personally communicated to the secretary of state on November 29, 1945, his plea did not alter Dean Acheson's opposition to the screen quota. Bidault stated that the 1936 trade agreement contained no provision reserving to American production eighty percent of foreign film import quota. Acheson replied that that was technically correct but the State Department consistently maintained the position that "the object of pertinent provisions of the agreement, particularly note (C) to Item 469 quarter in Schedule III, was to consolidate and protect the established position of American films in French market at time of signature." Dean Acheson retorted that "we must insist upon our rights ..., namely, that American films be not placed in a position in comparison with those of any other foreign country less favorable than that which they enjoyed upon signature of agreement. Consequently, our acceptance of reduction in global quota to 90 foreign dubbed films for current year (no new American dubbed films have been admitted thus far this year to our knowledge) is on condition that our position or proportionate share at time of agreement, namely 80 percent of global quota, be protected, and thus that 72 American films be admitted." Acheson also asked the embassy to find in its records more positive evidence that the American share of the global quota was eighty percent.[22]

When searching the embassy files, Ambassador Jefferson Caffery saw from the records of conversations and correspondence a consistent French resistance to permitting formal raising of the percentage issue. Only once did the French government reveal an acceptance that eighty percent of the quota was assured the United States by the trade agreement, namely in a Quai d'Orsay note of June 23, 1939. The Ambassador recommended that the "Department may wish to reconsider insistence that French officially acknowledge that trade agreement confers on U.S. a perpetual privilege of receiving eighty percent of any quota set under any and all circumstances."[23]

In December 1945 James Byrnes was about to propose the initiation of negotiations of a new trade agreement. In this connection he would be willing to review the French concession on American films with the view of working out a mutually satisfactory long-run solution of the problem. The embassy then for the first time got in touch with Pierre Baraduc, of the Direction of Economic affairs in the Foreign Ministry, who was in charge of negotiating the film quota. He agreed to assume discussions of what he called "a generous" numerical quota for the present film year, within which the Americans would be assured their proportional share.[24]

On January 7, 1946, the Commercial Attaché saw Baraduc, who seemed to despair of producing any settlement within the limits of the American position. Dollar shortage was the primary difficulty, Baraduc stated. He alleged the illogic of seeking a dollar loan from the United States if millions were to be spent on a luxury import such as movies.[25] Once again the Franco-American film discussions had been deadlocked; until an agreement could be found there would be no import of American movies to France.

The Blum-Byrnes Agreement, 1946

With the Paris discussions deadlocked, the talks returned to Washington. In order to settle a wide range of economic problems with the United States such as economic recovery loans and military cooperation, France sent a delegation to Washington in April 1946 to hold talks with the State Department, led by the Secretary of State, James Byrnes. The French delegation was headed by Léon Blum.[26]

The motion picture problems were handled in informal conversations between Pierre Baraduc, a member of the French delegation, and Clair Wilcox, director of the Office of International Trade Policy of the State Department, rather than in the Commercial Policy Committee. Gordon from the Office of Commercial Policy took also part in these informal discussions.

Already in the first talk, on April 15, 1946, Baraduc was certain that it would be possible to work out a solution. He thought that the motion picture problem presented two aspects: the question of foreign exchange, which was not an insuperable obstacle, and the question of protection for the French motion picture industry. The French government did not want to continue the quota system because the pressure for increased quotas had become very strong, particularly from the Soviet Union and Czechoslovakia. Consequently it proposed the "screen quota" as a method of protection. Baraduc thought that a period of six weeks out of each quarter might be reserved for the exhibition of French films. After Wilcox demonstrated that six weeks would give the French industry more protection than the prewar import quota, Baraduc claimed that he had used the figure simply for illustrative purposes, and then came down to a screen quota of five weeks. Later Baraduc mentioned that four weeks as an outside possibility.[27]

The following week Clair Wilcox discussed Baraduc's proposal with Governor Milliken from the MPAA. Wilcox explained that the French government was unwilling to reestablish import quotas and desired to protect the domestic producers by instituting a screen quota, which would be the only limitation placed upon the industry. Wilcox thought that the French might be persuaded to cut the quota from seven weeks per quarter to four weeks per quarter, and it might be possible to get other concessions.[28]

Milliken first took the position that the United States should stand on the terms of the trade agreement and that the industry was opposed in principle to the screen quota. But in the course of discussion his stance shifted from the screen quota principle to the question of the size of the quota. A four-week quota, he thought, would give the French industry a guarantee of thirty percent of the business, which was too high. The comparable arrangements with Italy gave domestic producers two weeks out of twelve, or seventeen percent. The Spanish figure was one out of five, or twenty percent, and in Great Britain it was twenty-two percent. Possibly the industry would be willing to accept a French screen quota of three weeks per quarter, or twenty-three percent of the feature playing time. Milliken would consult major companies in his association and inform Wilcox of the Hollywood companies' attitude to the screening quota proposal.[29]

Wilcox explained to Milliken that the only alternative to a screen quota agreement would be a firm determination on the part of the American negotiators to hold up the whole group of financial and economic agreements until the French agreed to the industry's import quota proposal. He was, however, in doubt whether the principals of the United States would be willing to give the motion picture this large a place in the financial settlement.

The same day the MPAA companies accepted the screen quota at a meeting in New York. They found two solutions acceptable: Either a screen quota tapering from four weeks per quarter to three, two, one, and zero; or a flat three-week screen quota. The Hollywood companies would prefer the tapering quota.[30]

In his next meeting with Baraduc, on April 25, Wilcox suggested the tapering quota, under which France would establish a screen quota of four weeks per quarter the first year, three weeks in the second year, tapering down to no protection the fifth year. Baraduc was personally attracted to the idea of a declining screen quota, but he found the initial screen quota of four weeks too low. An initial quota of five weeks would be in accordance with the thinking of his government.[31]

Nevertheless, Baraduc accepted a screen quota of four weeks a quarter—to run until the end of 1947, followed by a quota of three weeks—to run until the French industry was back on its feet. Wilcox convinced Baraduc by recalling his statement at their first meeting that "the French market could probably absorb about 156 feature films per annum, based on the assumption that each theater would have to have three new films a week. Wilcox said that their experts had estimated the capacity of the French film market at about 260 films per annum, since there were several large French cities with five first-run houses, each of which would have to have a different feature film at the same time, to run for a week. Assuming a market for 260 films and taking Baraduc's estimate that the French industry would produce about 60 films per annum, a screen quota of four weeks a quarter would provide an assured market for the entire French output." It would be impossible, said Wilson, to obtain the agreement of all interested parties on the American side to any screen quota figure in excess of four weeks per quarter. Baraduc would consult the French government on Wilcox's proposal and report back.[32]

Having consulted with Paris, Baraduc called again three weeks later with a counterproposal: "the screen quota [would] be set at five weeks per quarter for the first eighteen months, and…the two governments would confer again at the end of that period, with the understanding that the quota after the first eighteen months would be not more than four weeks per quarter."[33]

Wilcox was extremely disappointed by the French unwillingness to accept the American proposal, and he could not conscientiously recommend the acceptance of the French proposal. "A screen quota of five weeks would give the French industry a minimum of forty percent of the playing time, plus whatever additional playing time it could pick up during the competitive period. This screen quota…would be twice as high as any screen quota in effect elsewhere in the world, and would constitute an invitation to other countries to adopt the same figure….The U.S. film industry had already been deprived of half of its market in France as a result of the compulsory single feature law, and… the French proposal would narrow the market for U.S. films even further."[34]

As a result of the French neglect of their film industry and the efficient American diplomacy, the Blum-Byrnes agreement of May 28, 1946 (named after the heads of the delegations) contained only a four-week screen quota requirement, which was all Hollywood would agree to. The text of the agreement stated that:

> Effective July 1, 1946, all previous provisions concerning the number of dubbed films permitted to be shown in France will be abandoned. On the same date, a 'sreen quota' system will be instituted, as a temporary protective measure, to assist the French motion picture industry to recover from the disorganization caused by enemy occupation in France. Under this system, motion picture exhibitors in France will be required to exhibit French films for a certain number of weeks per quarter. During the remaining weeks, French exhibitors will be allowed free choice of films, foreign or domestic.
>
> Beginning July 1, 1946, the screen quota reserved for French films will be not more than four (4) weeks per quarter. The screen quota shall continue at the level of four (4) weeks per quarter unless reduced to three (3) weeks per quarter [depending on the operation of a specific automatic formula].[35]

The Blum-Byrnes Film Agreement was ratified by Georges Bidault on August 17, 1946.[36]

The Communists immediately began to criticize the motion picture accord of the Blum-Byrnes Agreement, and they tried to use it to raise a storm of protest against the French government. Protests against the agreement culminated on the night of June 15 at meeting in Paris of representatives of French movie writers, directors, producers, actors, union representatives, and technicians. They urged unanimously a revision of the film agreement to prevent the death of the French film industry.[37] Léon Blum tried to calm the protests while concealing the lapse; he stated that "if I had to sacrifice the interests of the film corporations for the general good, I would not hesitate to do so."[38]

The American Embassy monitored the comments appearing in the French press, and concluded that objections consisted of five major points. First, four weeks guaranteed playing time did not represent the market share previously held by French films, and would have the effect of reducing French production to forty-eight to sixty films a year. Second, the French film industry had capacity to double its production, but would not be able to expand in competition with two thousand American films already produced and amortized. Third, the agreement would lead to substantial unemployment in the movie industry. Fourth, it did not provide a reciprocal assurance for the export of French films to the United States. Fifth, the damage of the accord to France was not simply commercial, but also cultural and educational.

Hollywood had voluntarily agreed to limit exports to 124 feature films for the quota year commencing on July 1, 1946, but quickly forgot this verbal agreement. The result was that France was flooded with American films, creating a serious currency imbalance for the French franc. Already in June 1946, France contemplated introducing a three million dollar yearly limitation of the transfer of currency to the United States.[39] In 1946, France imported 105 feature films, but the number increased to 228 in 1947. But nothing could be done as long as the Blum-Byrnes Agreement was valid.

The Caffery-Schuman Agreement of September 26, 1948

The Blum-Byrnes film agreement continued to be an embarrassment to the French government as a result of continued Communist attacks. The agreement was, however, in force until July 1, 1948. The Communist deputy, Georges Sadoul, was the first officially to demand a renegotiation of the Blum-Byrnes Agreement in January 1948. He argued that the French film studios worked at only thirty to forty percent of their capacity as a result of the agreement. The French industry had supplied about fifty percent of the films shown in France in 1944, but now the agreement limited the French proportion to thirty-one percent. The American companies had agreed to limit imports to 124 films per year, but in the first six months of 1947, they exported 328 films, which were already amortized in the U.S., and Sadoul described this practice as "dumping."[40]

The French government had, however, already started negotiations with the Americans in December 1947 on the basis of a plan originating from Monnet. The aim was both to increase the screen quota protection and to reintroduce the dubbing quota, now called a distribution quota, and thus limit the number of films that could be censored.

The French proposed to reform the distribution quota so that it introduced three categories of censorship licenses according to the country of origin of the films: American films, films from foreign countries other than the U.S., and French films. The number of distribution licenses would be calculated on the basis of a six-month reference period, Oct. 1, 1946, through March 1947. Based on that period, the total yearly number of censorship permits would be 289 licenses, of which distributors of American films would receive 145 licenses; distributors of other foreign films, 54; and distributors of French films, 90.[41] The Embassy was also aware of another censorship statistic for the period Oct. 1, 1946, to Sept. 30, 1947, during which 934 permits had been issued. Of these, French films obtained 93 permits; American films, 647; and films of other origin, 194.[42]

The French also contemplated prohibiting the showing of all films that had been released during the period 1940–1945. Ambassador Caffery claimed that this would prevent the release of the backlogged American films, and would greatly inconvenience the MPAA companies, since their release schedules contained substantial numbers of films first released during that period.[43]

American diplomacy did not succeed in preventing France from demanding a renegotiation of the Blum-Byrnes film agreement. On February 5, 1948, the press and cinema committee of the National Assembly adopted a resolution that called for opening negotiations to modify the Blum-Byrnes Agreement. The committee also requested an increased screen quota protection, so that seven weeks per quarter would be reserved for exhibition of French films. It would also empower the director of the Centre National de la Cinématographie to limit the exhibition in France of dubbed films.[44]

In a letter from Georges Bidault of February 12, 1948, France officially demanded a renegotiation of the Blum-Byrnes Agreement. Caffery was convinced that official pressure and a press campaign were diverting attention away from domestic solutions and conditions that were mainly responsible for the critical situation in French film production. The original Monnet plan from 1946 called for an analysis of the situation, but no such comprehensive report appeared. Caffery concluded that until such a study had been carried out, it was difficult to understand how the Blum-Byrnes understanding contributed to the current film crisis.[45]

Negotiations lingered on in the spring and summer of 1948. On July 20, 1948, French negotiator Baumgartner stated that GATT Article XII justified the film distribution quota system as it was a means of safeguarding the French balance of payments. He then suggested that censorship permits be issued annually for 108 American films, and that imports from other foreign countries would be limited to 65 annually. If the Americans accepted the film distribution quota system, it would be possible to reduce the screen quota to five weeks per quarter for the film year 1948–49, and four weeks thereafter. The French were also anxious to have MPAA members distribute French films in the U.S., but when MPAA negotiators Gerald Mayer and John G. McCarthy explained the difficulties, the French reluctantly withdrew their proposal. Nevertheless, the MPAA would try to promote the distribution of French films in the U.S. The Embassy suggested that for "psychological reasons" the MPAA ought to explore what assistance they might provide for the distribution of French films in the U.S.[46]

Baumgartner presented the final French offer on August 2, 1948, which became the foundation of the Caffery-Schuman Agreement. The proposal was advantageous to the MPAA companies and to French producers, whereas it was a great disadvantage to the importation of European films and the independent American film producers (SIMPP).[47] The American film industry would receive 121 distribution permits annually, 110 for the MPAA companies and only 11 for the SIMPP members; films from other countries were limited to 65 permits. French productions could obtain an unlimited number of permits. The screen quota was raised to five weeks per quarter for the duration of the accord.[48]

The agreement appeared as a joint declaration of September 16, 1948, and regulated the import of films retroactively from July 1, 1948. The agreement was justified with reference to the special financial conditions facing France, which allowed the government to use GATT Article IV of October 30, 1947, to increase the period reserved for the exhibition of French films to five weeks per quarter. GATT Articles XII and XIII also entitled the French government to limit the distribution of dubbed films to 121 films originating in the United States and to 65 for films originating in other foreign countries. The government also decided to limit the transfer of receipts to the United States.[49] With the establishment of GATT, the film trade conflict between the United States and France ceased to be merely a bilateral phenomenon.

In the 1950s the United States government began to refuse to take part in commodity agreements, but handed over the responsibility for concluding commercial treaties to the individual trade associations. The Blum-Byrnes Accord was a government-to-government agreement permitting the entry into France of 121 dubbed feature films each year and limiting the showing of original version films to 15 movie houses, with specific dollar ceilings on remittance of earnings. This agreement was renewed as a government-to-government agreement until the early 1950s, when it became purely an agreement between the MPEAA and the French government. The shift came about for two major reasons: as a matter of policy the State Department preferred to get the U.S. government out of the position of being party to a specific commodity agreement of this character; and the Department felt that compensation arrangements and "merit" import licenses were inappropriate conditions in agreements to which the U.S. government was a party. Also, the State Department wished to avoid the embarrassment of being party to a quota arrangement that violated the Webb-Pomerene Act and possibly the Sherman Antitrust Act, as was the case with the French film treaties, in which the MPAA initially excluded SIMPP and later reduced their export to France to ten films per year.

But even when the U.S. government was no longer directly involved in the film diplomacy, the French government continued to favor the importation of Hollywood films. As a result of pressures from the Communist Party, the French government was forced to limit the importation of American films to 90 per quota year in 1950, but the Americans were unwilling to accommodate this demand. To circumvent embarrassing problems, the French government announced publicly that Hollywood had been accorded 90 dubbing permits, but secretly awarded the MPAA an additional 20 permits from the next year's quota.[50]

The deceptive tactics continued in 1953, when France announced that 90 dubbing visas would be given to MPAA companies, which was the proportionate share of the 138 dubbing permits per year stipulated by decree to be accorded to all foreign films. However, the government made fifteen additional visas to Hollywood available by secret "under the table" arrangements, and another five would be made available under the guise of being "merit" licenses. The "merit" Hollywood was credited for was in assisting the French film industry by donating money to set up a sales office for French films in New York 1954.[51] Such assistance was extremely problematic because it endangered MPAA's status as a Webb-Pomerene organization. The Webb-Pomerene Law specifically exempted exporters from adhering to the Sherman Antitrust Act only if their activities did not affect trade in the United States.

In 1959, France reduced the allocation of dubbing visas to seventy permits, but allocated another forty according to "merit" principle, so that Hollywood still had 110 visas. In negotiations for the quota year 1959/60 in November 1959, the director of the CNC, Michel Fourré-Comeray, suddenly gave in and allocated a total of 116 permits all to MPEAA, exclusive of "merit permits" and "hors quota" permits granted to films exhibited at the Cannes Festival. Triumphantly MPEAA's negotiator Frederick Gronich crowed that "the 'sound barrier' of 110 is broken, as well as the Government's interference in the choice of films." Gronich confided that 116 permits would satisfy the MPAA companies' needs, sufficing for the really solid, marketable product, and that additional imports, for the most part, would be relatively marginal films. Even with total liberalization, Gronich thought that U.S. film imports would not exceed 130 to 135 films due to the high processing and distribution costs.[52]

The screen-time quotas continue to be upheld in the 1960s by France and Italy, even though they had little significance. A State Department policy paper eplained that the quotas were consequently not a serious impediment to Hollywood exports. Screen quotas were specifically permitted by GATT (Article IV). It did not mean that the U.S. found them desirable, bu they were preferable to other internal quantitative controls over imported films, which GATT ruled out. The quota would restrict quantitatively the use of the imported films only if the percentage was set higher than the proportion of time which domestic films would gain under competitive conditions. Since the percentage had been set very close to what the supply and demand conditions would determine, in practice these quotas were not a serious direct impediment. The percentage of the quota for domestic films was thirty-one to thirty-eight percent in France and thirty-seven percent in Italy. But even though the screen-time quotas were set at "reasonable" levels, they introduced an element of rigidity into the plans of exhibitors.[53]

The State Department, however, instructed U.S. representatives to be alert for any evidence that the idea of a common EEC screen quota was being revived, since that would have restrictive potential. An EEC screen quota might result in a higher European percentage than present national quotas, since films could enter freely from other EEC countries. There were four countries which, lacking extensive production of their own, were taking a higher percentage of American films than did the Community as a whole. The State Department also pointed out that the argument of "cultural preservation" might be persuasive in the case of a thirty-percent national quota, but surely would be far less valid for a sixty-percent Community quota, in which case the motive would most likely be protectionism.[54]

The EEC did not, however, instantly introduce a motion picture screen quota, but after television became more popular, the European Union introduced a television quota, *Television without Frontiers* (1989, 1997-), modeled after the French screen quota. The European Union policy is, however, outside the scope of this book.

For the American film industry, the Blum-Byrnes Agreement has been the single most significant trade arrangement since 1946. The pure beauty of it from Hollywood's perspective is that with the signing of a bilateral trade agreement, American film dominance was reestablished in France at the expense not only of the French film industry, but of the remaining European film producers as well. The crippling of intra-European film trade virtually guaranteed that Hollywood would be able to maintain its uneven competitive edge because the European companies would be forced into a strategy of fighting amongst each other for the small pieces of market share not swallowed up by the Americans. Of course, this effect would be amplified by the difficulty for European film companies in meeting production costs (often increased by heavy taxation) in their domestic markets alone, a problem that Hollywood did not have to face. At the same time, the American market remained only minimally permeable to the flow of foreign films.

Certainly the Blum-Byrnes Agreement worked out so well for the American film industry in large measure because of the unfailing U.S. government support for the negotiations with the French government. From the other side, however, in looking at the French film censorship statistics, it is very difficult to discern many clearly positive protective effects of the highly acclaimed quota system. If anything, the number suggests that the way the quotas were applied, Hollywood was a much greater beneficiary than the French film industry—both before and after World War II.

---

[1] Letter from Carl E. Milliken, MPPDA, to Francis Colt de Wolf, Chief, Telecommunications Division, Department of State, New York, Oct. 6, 1944, USDS.

[2] Pierre Chéret, Exposé sur la situation financière du cinéma français. Conférence donnée à l'IDHEC le 30 janvier, 1945, S.l., s.d. [1945]; Chéret was the accounting specialist of the Vichy film organization COIC. Jean-Jacques Meusy, *Cinquante ans d'industrie cinématographique (1906–1956)* (Lyon, 1996), p. 328.

[3] Jean Séfert, "Défense du film français" *Le Film français*, 2 année, no. 38 (Aug. 24, 1945): 1–2.

[4] Marcel Malige, Economic Counselor, USEF, introduced Harold L. Smith to the group of local Hollywood representatives on July 16, 1945. Telegram no. 4392 from Caffery USEF, to USDS, Paris, July 21, 1945.

[5] Minutes of the meeting of the American Companies, Paris, June 13, 1945, USEF. Lussiez opposed the seven percent subvention fund because the exhibitors had not been consulted. Paul Leglise, *Histoire de la politique du cinéma français* 2 (1977): 150.

[6] Minutes of the meeting of the American Companies, Paris, June 21, 1945, USEF.

[7] Despatch no. 738 from Ambassador Caffery, USEF, to USDS, Paris, June 8, 1946, USEF.

[8] Minutes of the Meeting of the American Companies, Paris, June 7, 1945, USEF.

[9] Telegram 5149 from Fullerton, USEF to USDS, Paris, Aug. 25, 1945, USDS.

[10] Telegram no. 4392 from Ambassador Caffery to USDS, Paris, July 21, 1945, USEF.

[11] Memorandum of Conversation, Assistant Secretary of State Clayton, Subject: "Treatment of American Films in France," Aug. 17, 1945, USDS, Confidential file.

[12] Letter from Milliken to de Wolf, New York, Aug. 1, 1945, USEF.

[13] Memorandum of Conversation, Clayton, in "Treatment of American Films in France," Aug. 17, 1945, USDS, Confidential file. Participants in the meeting: de Fouchier, Assistant Director, Bureau of Foreign Economic Relations, French Ministry of National Economy, Paris; Treuil, French Commercial Councelor, New York; Turner C. Cameron, Jr., USEF; George R. Canty, Telecommunications Department; Winthrop G. Brown, Chief, Division of Commercial Policy; and Vernon L. Phelps, Advisor, European Branch, Division of Commercial Policy.

[14] Telegram 3971 from James Byrnes, USDS, to USEF, Washington, D.C., Aug. 18, 1945, USDS, confidential.

[15] Telegram 5338 from Caffery, USEF, to USDS, Paris, Sept. 6, 1945, USDS, confidential.

[16] Telegram 5545 from Caffery, USEF, to USDS, Paris, Sept. 18, 1945, USDS, confidential.

[17] Urgent Telegram, number unreadable, from Acheson, USDS, to USEF, Washington, D.C., Oct. 2, 1945, USDS.

[18] Letter from Carl Milliken, MPAA, to Canty, Asst. Chief, Telecommunications Division, USDS, New York, Nov. 2, 1945, USDS.

[19] Telegram no. 6658 from Caffery, USEF, to USDS, Paris, Nov. 17, 1945, USDS, confidential.

[20] Ibid., Sept. 18, 1945, USDS, confidential.

[21] Telegram no. 4636 from Acheson, USDS, to USEF, Washington DC, Oct. 2, 1945, USDS.

[22] The letter from Georges Bidault is not to be found in the State Department archive, but is mentioned in telegram no. 5896 from Acheson, USDS, to USEF, Washington, DC, Dec. 17, 1945, USDS, USEF.

[23] Telegram no. 7410 from Caffery, USEF, to USDS, Paris, Dec. 29, 1945, USDS, confidential.

[24] Ibid., and Telegram no. 5683 from Byrnes USDS to USEF, Washington, DC, Dec. 5, 1945, USDS.

[25] Telegram no. 137 from Caffery, USEF, to USDS, Paris, Jan. 10, 1946, USDS, USEF, confidential.

[26] A list of French delegates and advisers from April 1946 mentions: *From Paris*: Léon Blum, Ambassador Extraordinary; Jean Monnet, Commissaire General au Plan; Emmanuel Monick, Governor of the Bank of France; Pierre Baraduc, Deputy Director, Direction of Economic Affairs, the Foreign Office; Guillaume Guindey, Deputy Director, Direction of the Treasury, Ministry of Finance; Pierre M. Viaud, Assistant Chief of Division, Direction of the Treasury, Commissariat for Planning; Leon Kaplan, Special Assistant to the Commissaire General; Michel G. Denis, Special Assistant; Felix Le Norcy, Jean Martial, Special Assistants to the Governor, Bank of France; Robert Blum, Michel Debre, Special Advisors. *From the French Embassy, Washington*: Henri Bonnet, Ambassador; Christian Valensi, Financial Counselor; Raymond Dreux, Commercial Counselor; Rene Siraud, Counselor. From *French Supply Council*: I. Leviant, Acting President; George Ball, General Counsel; Lucien Lelievre, P. Lazard, Advisors.

[27] Memorandum of Conversation. Subject: American Motion Pictures in France. Participants: Baraduc, French Foreign Office, Wilcox, ITP; Gordon, CP; Washington DC, April 15, 1946, USEF. Telegram no. 1956 from Acheson, USDS, to USEF, Washington DC, April 29, 1946, USDS, confidential.

[28] Memorandum of conversation, Subject: French Motion Pictures, participants: Milliken, MPAA; Wilcox, ITP; Washington, DC, April 22, 1946, USDS.

[29] Ibid.

[30] Memorandum of telephone conversation, Subject: French Motion pictures, participants: Milliken, MPAA; Wilcox, ITP; Washington, DC, April 23, 1946, USDS.

[31] Memorandum of conversation, Subject: American Motion Pictures in France, participants: Baraduc, French Foreign Office; Wilcox, ITP; Gordon, CP; Washington, DC, April 25, 1945, USDS, confidential.

[32] Ibid., and Telegram no. 1956 from Dean Acheson to USEF, Washington, DC, April 29, 1946, USDS, confidential.

[33] Memorandum of conversation, Subject: American Motion Pictures in France, participants: Baraduc, French Foreign Office; Wilcox, ITP; Gordon, CP, Washington DC, May 15, 1946, USDS.

[34] Ibid.

[35] Agreement between U.S. and France, May 28, 1946: Understanding between the Government of the USA and the Provisional Government of the French Republic with Respect to the Exhibition of American Motion Pictures in France, *United States Statutes at Large... 1947*, vol. 61, part 4 (Washington, DC, 1948), p. 4213–14.

[36] Decree no. 46–1812 of Aug. 17, 1946, relating to the exhibition of printed motion picture films in France; in *Journal Officiel* (August 18, 1946), translation in USDS.

[37] Telegram no. 2946 from Caffery, USEF, to USDS, Paris, June 18, 1946, USDS.

[38] "S'il m'avait fallu sacrifier les intérêts de la corporation cinématographique à l'intérêt général, je n'aurais pas hésité à le faire"; cited in Paul Leglise, *Histoire de la politique du cinéma français*, 2:171.

[39] Telegram no. 4077 from Caffery to USDS, Paris, June 20, 1946; no. 3289 from Caffery to USDS, Paris, July 5, 1946, USDS, confidential.

[40] Extract of article by Georges Sadoul in *Le Patriote*, Jan. 4, 1948; cited in letter from American Vice Consul Sheldon B. Vance, American Consulate, Nice, Jan. 20, 1948, USDS.

[41] Telegram no. 5429 from Caffery, USEF, to USDS, Paris, Dec. 18, 1947, USDS.

[42] Airgram no. A-43 from Caffery and A.C. Cameron, USEF, to USDS, Paris, Jan. 14, 1948, USDS, confidential.

[43] Telegram no. 291 from Caffery, USEF, to USDS, Paris, Jan. 17, 1948, USDS, confidential.

[44] Telegram from Caffery, USEF, to USDS, Paris, Feb. 6, 1948, USDS.

[45] Telegram no. 889 from Caffery, USEF, to USDS, Paris, Feb. 18, 1948, USDS, confidential.

[46] Telegram no. 3803 from Caffery, USEF, to USDS, Paris, July 21, 1948, USDS, confidential.

[47] For supplementary information on the position of SIMPP in France, see J. A. Aberdeen, *Hollywood Renegades*, p. 173ff.

[48] Telegram no. 874 from Caffery, USEF, to USDS, Paris, Aug. 3, 1948, USDS, confidential.

[49] "Joint Declaration of the Government of the United States of America and the Government of the French Republic on Motion Pictures," *FRUS*, vol. 62, part 3: International Agreements other than Treaties, 1948 (Washington, DC, 1949), p. 3001–3008.

[50] Despatch no. 1095 from First Secretary Harry Conover, USEF, to USDS, Paris, Nov. 15, 1952, subject: Conclusion of Film Agreement between MPAA and the French Government, USDS, confidential.

[51] Despatch no. 1398 from Conover to USDS, Paris, Nov. 25, 1953, subject: Franco-American Film Negotiations, USDS, confidential.

[52] Memorandum of Conversation, subject: Motion Picture Problems Involving France and Germany, participants Griffith Johnson, Vice President, MPEAA; Hand, OT, Washington, DC, Nov. 24, 1959, USDS. Memorandum of Conversation, participants: Frederick Gronich, European Regional Representative, MPEAA; Herman Walker, Deputy Commercial Attaché, Embassy; Martin A. Dale, Second Secretary of Embassy. Place: American Embassy, Paris, Nov. 30, 1959, USDS.

[53] "Screen-Time Quotas and EEC Films Policy," Enclosure 3 to Airgram CA–3239, Guidance Papers from Secretary of State Dean Rusk to assist USEC, Brussels, and USRO, Paris, in their further discussions with the EEC Commission on Commercial Policies Affecting Motion Pictures, Washington, DC, Sept. 20, 1965, USDS.

[54] Ibid.

Conclusion

Oligopolistic competition and strategic interaction among firms and governments rather than the invisible hand of market forces condition today's competitive advantage and international division of labor in high-technology industries.[1]

In this book we have examined how Hollywood has established a permanent dominance over the French market for motion pictures since the interwar period by using monopolistic trade practices and government support. The history of American film policy towards France can be documented by a wealth of diplomatic correspondence, which reveals that American exports were promoted through close collaboration among the State Department, the U.S. Embassy in France, the Department of Commerce, and the MPPDA. This assertion is mainly based on hitherto unstudied documents from these institutions which are kept at the National Archives, Washington, DC, and the archive of the former president of the MPPDA, Will H. Hays, and on a few microfilms from the MPPDA.

Hollywood obtained a dominant position immediately after the end of World War I. While European film production was at a standstill after the war, Hollywood companies dumped hundreds of films at very low prices on the European market. A commercial war emerged when European film producers resumed business and tried to expand their market share to the detriment of American interests, whereas the American film industry attempted to maintain the market share they had obtained. The American film companies used block-booking when renting films to French exhibitors in order to preserve their market share.

Hollywood's dominant position should not be considered as solely the result of successful collaboration between corporate capitalism and the federal government in Washington, because the French government also failed to provide proper assistance to its film industry. In 1919, when the French film industry began to recover from the war, France increased amusement taxes excessively, thereby draining off funds necessary for the development of film exhibition and production. By keeping in place antiquated regulations designed for temporary amusement forms and applying these to movie theaters, the French state impeded the development of the French exhibition sector. The excessive amusement taxation meant that the cost of producing French films could not be recovered in the domestic market. The lack of unity and collaboration between French producers and exhibitors excluded the possibility of establishing a policy to protect French film production, as the exhibitors invariably opposed any attempt of the producers to achieve such protection. The self-centered policy of the leader of the French film industry, Jean Sapène, the director of the Pathé-Cinéromans company who tried to obtain profitable deals with the Americans for himself, also precluded the establishment of broader French and European protective arrangements. Sapène's policy was to keep the American market open for foreign films, but the MPPDA companies succeeded in monopolizing the American market for motion pictures.

When France attempted to protect its film industry from the American film deluge, the conflict became one between the French and the American governments. The French state promoted French film production by increasing tariffs on American films and imposing quota restrictions limiting the number of foreign films entering France. With the Herriot-Hays agreement of May 1928, the quota policy became the favorite method of France for the protection of its film industry. The quota measure was, however, sabotaged by the French exhibitors, resulting in an arrangement that was so generous that the Americans could have exported almost twice as many films as they actually did. In the mid-1930s France introduced a dubbing quota limiting the number of films released in French. By this rule, the dubbing also had to take place in France. The American film industry negotiated an American allotment of 150 dubbing visas, or seventy-five percent of the total number of visas.

Even after World War II, when the Blum-Byrnes film agreement of 1946 changed the numerical quota to a screen quota of four weeks per quarter of a year, the restrictions were too insignificant to provide the French film industry an effective protection. When the numerical quota was reintroduced in 1952 to supplement the screen quota, the restrictions had little effect, since the administrators tried to match the restrictions closely to what competitive conditions would have prevailed.

Hollywood was able to maintain its dominance of the French market, despite stiff opposition from the French government, owing to massive governmental support from the State Department, the American Embassy in France, and the Department of Commerce for the American film producers' association, the MPPDA. The support was both legal and diplomatic.

The MPPDA was able to break the French measures to protect the national film industry by using the Webb-Pomerene Act, which permitted exporters to operate cartels by exempting them from the Sherman Anti-Trust Act. The close collaboration among American film companies in exports prevented the French from playing one American company off against another. The Webb-Pomerene law enabled the MPPDA and the film companies, backed by the State Department and the embassy, to present a united front against the French industry and its government. By threatening to withdraw collectively, the MPPDA was able to break the protective policies introduced by foreign governments, taking advantage of the French exhibitors' dependence on showing a large quantity of American films. Block-booking arrangements further ensured that the American distributors would dominate the booking of films to French cinemas. The wholehearted support and vigilance of the State Department and the American diplomatic corps for export of Hollywood films was of crucial importance.

Ultimately, in the interwar period France showed little concern for protecting its film industry against Hollywood, and in trade negotiations with the Americans in the 1930s, the interests of the French film industry were traded off to the advantage of other export areas such as wine and alcohol. The support French film producers obtained from their government did not begin to compare with the wholehearted support Hollywood received by the MPPDA.

Today, even though France has used the quota policy for about seventy years with little success, the French government still adheres to its principles and even imposes the policy on the European Union. The central element in the audiovisual policy of the European Union remains television quotas, a policy that has failed since Hollywood today holds an 80 to 90 percent maket share in Europe, whereas foreign films hold 1/4 to 1/2 percent in the U.S.[2] With little research into how the American film industry has been able to dominate the European market, and with little information regarding the ineffectiveness of quota policies or possible alternatives, the appearance of a more enlightened European film policy may be lost in European Union bureaucracy.

In many ways the Blum-Byrnes agreement and the French preoccupation with the quota system as the primary protective trade device have colored the European film landscape of the present. American movies maintain a powerful position in every European Union country, deferring only ceremonially to the native language films of each country, which are in turn restricted in neighboring countries due to the same American dominance. Perhaps it is time to reexamine the heavy role that quota systems have played in preserving Hollywood's film hegemony, even to the extent of recommending alternate foundations for film trade policy.

The only remaining alternative to a radical reconsideration of European film policy is to accept Jack Valenti's implication, however unbelievable, that it is, in fact, all about quality and viewer preference, and Hollywood simply has the only successful formula.

But when considering which element in "Hollywood's formula" enables American films to dominate on a global scale, the answer must be sought within the field of international political economy. It may not, in fact, be that different from the explanation that Clyde V. Prestowitz offers for Japanese commercial success—that it may be a result of fundamental deficiencies in the international trade system:

> The Uruguay Round and the GATT are foundering because their two core principles—national treatment and unconditional most favored nation (MFN) status—ignore the importance of the composition of trade, thus avoiding the most difficult and important issues....
>
> That system is based on the premise that its members pursue similar objectives in a similar way. But what if one country...enforces strict antitrust laws and eschews industrial policy, while another allows or even encourages quasicartels and embraces industry targeting? Over time, the industries that the latter country targets will predominate.[3]

---

[1] Organisation for Economic Co-operation and Development [OECD] report, in Dieter Ernst and David O'Connor, *Competing in the Electronics Industry* (London, 1992) p. 27.

[2] Jean-Michel Baer, ed., *The Audiovisual Policy of the European Union, 1998: The New Era of the Picture Industry: Television without Frontiers: Greater Europe in the Year 2000* (Brussels, 1997). Robert W. McChesney, Rich Media poor Democracy. (Urbana, IL, 1999, 2000), pp. 104-105, 33.

[3] Clyde V. Prestowitz Jr., "Beyond Laissez Faire," in Jeffry A. Frieden and David A. Lake, *International Political Economy: Perspectives on Global Power and Wealth* (New York, 1995), p. 514.

Appendix A

The Regulation of Large Enterprise in the United States

The integration within the American film industry was typical of the development towards large enterprise that occurred in American business at the beginning of the century. The federal government at first opposed integration and monopolies within business, but after World War I, the U.S. government began to collaborate with business, and not least with Hollywood through its trade association, the MPPDA. The American success in film exports may be regarded as one of the first examples of fruitful collaboration between big business and the federal government.

A precondition for the emergence of big business was the development of the railroads, the telecommunication revolution, and the technological advances, all of which facilitated the emergence of large mass markets. The development of big business took place in two periods. The first, which occurred before 1895, was marked by a relatively slow development towards larger enterprises, mainly through vertical integration. Enterprises expanded from production into marketing and retailing, whereby separate activities—such as obtaining raw materials, manufacturing products, and wholesaling and retailing goods—became combined within a single corporation. The big businesses arose through vertical growth usually without significant mergers, and the development followed a common pattern. First, several manufacturers in an industry competed vigorously on prices to keep and enlarge their share of the market. After a period of ruinous price competition, they would create a cartel, which was a loose form of organizational control in which the producers remained independent. Cartel behavior took many shapes, but the most common form was the trade association, which served the purpose of fixing prices, setting output quotas, or dividing the market.

In the early period, the federal government was opposed to cartels. With the Sherman Antitrust Act of 1890, the legality of cartel-like behavior became questionable. The act was very vague, simply outlawing "every contract, combination in the form of trust or otherwise, or conspiracy, in restraint of trade or commerce among the several States, or with foreign nations."[1] The American legal system inherited from English law a strong distaste for cartels, and although cartel behavior became increasingly tolerated in England around the mid-nineteenth century, it remained suspect in the United States. In Great Britain, France, and Germany, the legal systems recognized cartel agreements, but in the United States such arrangements were voluntary and could not be enforced by law, and therefore the agreements worked more satisfactorily there than in America.[2]

The intent of the Sherman law was to halt the spread of big businesses and collusive practices, and to encourage a return to a competitive economy with smaller firms, but the way the law was interpreted by the courts further promoted the integration of corporations. The courts ruled that forms of cartel-like behavior were illegal, whereas unified combinations were in most instances acceptable. The law prohibited collusion by independent firms but did not necessarily outlaw the activities of integrated holding companies created by the legal union of previously separate businesses. The result was that independent companies were led from cartel-like arrangements to combinations in part by legal changes originally designed to prevent the rise of big businesses.[3]

Consequently, the United States proved a more fertile ground for the spread of big businesses than did early twentieth-century Europe. American businesses moved quickly to the formal amalgamation of previously independent companies, because both federal and state law opposed collusive practices in restraint of trade.[4] The general concentration and its patterns have not changed greatly since 1910. The most important factor in the rise and persistence of big business has been the advancement of technology. Advanced industries could sustain economies of scale and were able to link mass production to mass distribution. The modern corporation, rather than Adam Smith's invisible market forces, became the principle that ordered modern economic life.

Another aspect of the rise of big business was the ruthless and unscrupulous use of economic power by men like John D. Rockefeller and James Duke. In order to crush rivals, they used unfair competitive practices, such as secret rebates, waging selective price wars to drive competitors into bankruptcy and forcing them to sell out at bargain prices, refusing to supply wholesalers unless they agreed to market only the supplier's products, and so on. The government tried to pass laws prohibiting the use of unfair economic tactics.

The second period of combination occurred between 1895 and 1905, the years in which the motion picture industry emerged. The characteristic of this period was that the size of big businesses increased through "horizontal growth"—that is, combinations of companies within similar lines of trade. The new combination was usually not engaged in activities on other levels of business. The motivation behind the creation of horizontal combinations was clearly different from those derived from vertical growth, since the primary goal was to gain control over output, prices, and profits. If a market control was reached, the company could gain excessive monopoly profits, but such profits would burden society, and therefore the federal government and the courts opposed monopolies.[5]

John D. Rockefeller's successful combination, Standard Oil (established around 1882), led other businessmen to imitate his behavior. Standard's near-monopoly position ended as late as in 1911 with the Supreme Court's division of the company into a number of firms independent of each other. The appearance of various horizontal combinations in the form of trusts or holding companies helped prepare the way for the rapid spread of big businesses. Around 1910, with most of the well-known giant corporations established, the industrial structure of the modern American business had been formed. The large-scale enterprises depended on advances in science and technology, which improved mass production through the use of more efficient assembly lines and mass distribution. The companies mass-produced new products such as chemicals, electrical products, or automobiles—and motion pictures belong in this category as well. The new giant firms used complex technologies and large production plants, which turned out high volumes of goods at a low cost per unit. The companies embodied larger pools of capital, which could be gathered only through investments from large groups of investors. Typical examples of big businesses that emerged in this period are General Motors, IBM, Exxon, Du Pont, and General Electric. Individuals such as Vanderbilt, Harriman, Rockefeller, Carnegie, Ford, and Morgan dominated these companies. It should be noted that Rockefeller and Carnegie also had large investments in the American film industry.[6]

Often the concentration of production meant that the power over production came to rest in the hands of relatively few large companies, called oligopolies. These came into existence in industries by processes which involved both horizontal and vertical growth. The American film industry is an example of such an oligopoly.

Changes in the legal environment played a contributing role in the development of big business. In Europe the accountability of business enterprises was a matter of concern which led to the demand of compulsory registration of companies by the German and British Commercial laws beginning in 1900, whereas American law relied on punishment after the fact.[7] The result was that corporations became more common in the United States than elsewhere. An important development was the appearance of state general incorporation laws, such as New Jersey's in 1889. The new incorporation laws, designed to attract industry to New Jersey and Delaware, meant that a company could obtain a charter merely by filling out a form and paying a fee. The new company could then operate in other states and acquire subsidiaries without difficulty. These legal changes facilitated the rapid spread of mergers.[8]

At first lawmakers wanted to outlaw monopolistic business practices. Therefore, regulatory agencies were created which had broad general powers to oversee business behavior. Under the administration of Theodore Roosevelt, the U.S. Bureau of Corporations was set up as an agency to investigate and publicize the unethical competitive methods of offending businesses. The idea that publicity about a business's doings would cause it to behave better proved to be overly optimistic. Consequently, Roosevelt proposed a stronger regulatory body.

Discontent with the questionable maneuvers of big business led to the establishment of the Federal Trade Commission (FTC) and the passage of the Clayton Antitrust Act of 1914. The state tried to ensure fair behavior by enabling the FTC to issue cease-and-desist orders to the firms it regulated.[9] The Clayton Act tried to define which activities came within the purview of the Sherman Act and the FTC. Practices endemic to corporate enterprise, such as price discrimination, exclusive dealing and tying contracts, intercorporate stockholding, and interlocking directorates were singled out as actions fostering restraint of trade. Business practices within the film industry, such as block-booking, fell within the definition of what constituted "restraint of trade" and therefore the FTC throughout the silent era scrutinized Hollywood companies. But the film industry merely ignored the FTC's rulings, as the FTC had no power to enforce them.

The reconciliation between the regulatory powers and large enterprise began with the Supreme Court's landmark 1911 decision in the Standard Oil case, which announced the "rule of reason," distinguishing between good and bad trusts. Giant companies that operated fairly and did not use objectionable competitive methods, the court indicated, would not be judged guilty of violating the antitrust legislation. The judiciary would not attack any firm on the basis of its size alone, but rather on the basis of its behavior.

The result of the development was that the national government acquired a new policing role in the economy as watchdog of the private sector. The Justice Department, the FTC, and the courts were supposed to prevent discriminatory use of economic power. Regulation became an ever changing series of political settlements and compromises.

World War I fostered a close relationship between big business and the regulatory infrastructure of the federal government. The war made politicians and corporate leaders realize the advantages of cooperation among private corporations and government in the regulation of the economy. The pro-business stance flourished in the 1920s with the Republican administrations in power, the growing acceptance of corporate consolidation by the courts, and Herbert Hoover's encouragement of business associationalism.[10] Motion picture production and export was a product he especially encouraged.

---

[1] Morton Keller, "The Pluralist State: American Economic Regulation in Comparative Perspective, 1900–1930," in Thomas K. McCraw, *Regulation in Perspective* (Boston, 1981), p. 67.

[2] Glenn Porter, *The Rise of Big Business 1860–1920*, 2nd ed. (Arlington Heights, IL, 1992), p. 38.

[3] Ibid., p. 74, 76–78.

[4] Ibid., p. 78.

[5] Ibid., p. 58ff.

[6] Ibid., p. 7ff.

[7] Morton Keller, *Regulating a New Economy* (Cambridge, MA, 1990), p. 87.

[8] Donald Dewey, *Monopoly in Economics and Law* (1959), cited in Porter, *The Rise of Big Business*, p. 76.

[9] Keller, *Regulating a New Economy*, p. 32.

[10] Keller, "The Pluralist State," p. 74–75.

Appendix B

American Film Export Statistics

The American overseas film hegemony emerged when hundreds of American films were dumped on the European market in the wake of World War I. The statistics seem to indicate that American film began to dominate the French market in 1919–1920. American films dramatically increased the number of films available, as well as the box office receipts of French cinemas by 300%. American films held a uniquely dominant position until the mid-1920s, when the number of American film titles decreased by 2/3, while French and German films improved in number by around 100%. The total amount of film measured in feet exported to France from the US apparently decreased less drastically through the 1920s, but the statistics may not be trustworthy.

The smaller number of American films exported in the 1930s seems to have resulted from fewer American films having been produced with the introduction of sound and perhaps due to the depression as well. The decline seems only minimally related to French quota policies, despite the limitation on the number of American films for dubbing to 150 films per year. This is because the dubbing quota did not constitute a genuine limitation on American film exports to France, the number having been negotiated and approved by the MPPDA.

In the late 1920s and 1930s French and German films matched the number of American films. By cooperating, they would have been able to compete with the American films. Thus, the statistics alone do not explain the bankruptcies of the major French film companies in the mid-1930s. Statistics reveal only the symptoms and do not explain the underlying reasons for the American success in dominating the European market for motion pictures.

The American motion picture statistics indicates that there were two types of development. When looking at the number of feet exported, the statistics indicate that the American film industry had already obtained its dominant position in the United Kingdom and in overseas areas by midway through World War I, whereas the dominance in France and in Scandinavia did not become a reality until late in the war or even just after the war ended.[1] The American exports to France, Denmark, and Sweden began during the war, but became significant only in 1919–1920. It should be noted that no information is available for 1921 and 1922, that data for

1923 and 1924 given in round numbers seem inaccurate, and that the figures for those years concerning France appear to be too small. Exports to France increased immediately after the war, and export to France was much larger than to Scandinavia.

Whereas the imports to Scandinavia remained fairly constant, huge fluctuations occur in the number of feet exported to France before 1931. After 1931 American film exports stabilized at around six to eight million feet per year. This stabilization on a constant lower level was the result both of a reduction in the size of film production with the introduction of sound as well as France's introduction of a dubbing quota limitation on imports. See Figure 1, p. 171.

French Censorship Statistics

The development of American motion picture exports to France can also be observed in the statistics of the number of films passing censorship. Statistics are missing from the beginning of the 1920s, but a steep decline must have occurred from a peak around 1920, similar to the drop observed in other European countries. Some information is available for 1918, when 80% of the new film stock available in France was foreign, mainly American, and in October 1919, 90% of the film titles were foreign.[2] The statistics available for the period 1924–47[3] document a decline in the import of American films, from 589 in 1924 to 211 in 1929, and a stabilization at around 230 American films per year throughout the 1930s. In the interwar period the percentage of American films on the French market fell from 85% in 1924 to around 50% in 1929, and that level was maintained throughout the 1930s. Supplies dropped to zero during World War II, but increased quickly to prewar levels in the postwar period.

Although the stabilization in the 1930s seems to have been the result of a production decrease in Hollywood, the French seem to have regarded the reduction of imports as the result of quota restrictions.

The MPPDA first entered an agreement on August 19, 1929, with Charles Delac (president of the Chambre Syndicale) which maintained the status quo; the agreement was prolonged by one year, and afterwards the French government unilaterally reduced the number of American films that could be imported. The limitations were, however, moderate enough so as not to hurt French cinema owners, who needed a stable supply of new films in order to operate their movie houses. The French film quota policy thus had a limited effect, since twice as many American as French films were shown in France during the 1930s, and the export of French motion pictures to the United States was negligible.[4] See figure 2, p. 172.

A Comparison of French and Swedish Censorship Statistics

The reduction in the import of American films to France was not a result of the quota policy but was caused by a general reduction in the number of films exported by Hollywood. This is reflected by the fact that despite the complete lack of quota restrictions in Sweden, American exports there show a nearly identical reduction to that in France. Trends were similar across Europe, and therefore it is possible to compare the French statistics with the Swedish.[5]

The United States became the largest supplier of films to Sweden in 1915. The import of American films peaked in 1919, when 557 films passed censorship. The number of American films dropped significantly throughout the 1920s to 238 in 1929; in the 1930s it stabilized at a slightly lower level. Roughly 70% of the films passing through censorship in the 1920s and 60% in the 1930s came from the United States. As American film exports increased, the number of European films declined to 50–90% of the 1917 level. American films did not merely supplant European productions, but increased the total number of available films by 200–300%. European films were not available in large numbers before and during World War I, when only a few hundred films, mainly German, Danish, and French appeared in the censorship statistics per year. Only Germany supplied a larger quantity of films to Sweden. See Figure 3, p. 173

French politicians seem to have been convinced that the French quota policy caused both a decline in the number of American films exported and a consequent contraction of the American market share in France between 1924 and 1929. The percentage of American films on the French market dropped from 85% in 1924 to around 50% in 1929. In reality, the decline was due to a general drop in American film exports.

A parallel decline can be observed in exports to Sweden, which had not adopted any policy to restrict the import of American films. Therefore, a comparison of the French censorship statistics with their Swedish equivalents for the period 1929 to 1939 reveals that French quota legislation was largely ineffective. During this period, when French quota policy was at its highest, on average 111 more films were censored per year in France than in Sweden. Of this excess, on average 93 films were European. Only seventeen *more* American films passed censorship per year in France, resulting primarily from fewer European films being exported to Sweden. French films, in particular, were less common in Sweden. In contrast, the distribution of European films was much smaller in Sweden than in France.

The fact that seventeen more American films were censored in France than in Sweden, which did not have any quota restrictions, is surprising, considering the active French policies to reduce film imports from the United States. A possible explanation might be that the AB Svensk Filmindustri monopolized the Swedish market and thereby might have been able to limit the American dominance of the Swedish market. A more reasonable explanation, however, is that the French quota arrangements simply did not work.[6]

Although the actual number of films available in the French market was about one third larger than in the Swedish, the number of American films exported to Sweden was only 8% larger than the number exported to France. The real difference between the French and Swedish film markets was that there were 66% fewer European films available in Sweden than in France. Consequently, it does not make sense to compare the size of the American market share in different countries, because the number of American film exported remained fairly constant from country to country, whereas the number of films from other European countries fluctuated.

What defines the dominant position of the American film industry as hegemonic was not only the size of Hollywood's market share in a given country but also its ability to reduce the market share of European competitors. American film exports prevented European films from being distributed in other European countries. European film companies consequently experienced difficulties recouping their investments in film production when confined to their domestic markets and were therefore forced to reduce production. See Figures 4 and 5, p.174.

French Box-Office Statistics

The statistics on French box-office receipts suggest that the American film hegemony was established between 1918 and 1920, when the receipts increased by three hundred percent. It is likely that the increase was a result of American film imports, but it might also have resulted from increasing admission prices. The receipts of French cinemas have been presented as a graph by Colin Crisp in his *The Classic French Cinema, 1930-1960*, p. 8, which cites Chirat and Leroy's *Le Cinéma française, 1911-1920*, but this book provides neither the actual numbers nor the size of the American share of the receipts, nor the origin of the statistical information. Nevertheless, the information conforms to the statistics from Denmark.

The receipts before World War I were insignificant in comparison to the time after 1920. The growth in receipts was less rapid during the 1920 and the 1930s, when the receipts reached a level ten times higher than the figures before the war. Growth continued in the period 1925 to 1935; Frenc returns increased another 300%, which was probably a result of the establishment of new theaters combined with high inflation. It is not possible to conclude that the increase in receipts was a sign of a prosperous French film industry, when, in fact, the major French film producers went bankrupt in 1935 and 1936.

---

[1] From *Monthly Summary of the Commerce of the United States,* cited in (for years 1918–20)*Wid's Yearbook,* 1920, p. 241, and 1921, p. 377; for years 1913 and 1923–26, *Film Year Book* (New York, 1927), p. 937; for years 1913 and 1923–27, *Film Year Book* (1928), p. 956–57; for years 1927–28, *Film Year Book* (1929), p. 1023.

Statistics for 1932 and 1933: N. D. Golden, "Exports of American Films Increase during 1933," *Motion Pictures Abroad,* T-120 (Feb. 2, 1934) : p. 2.

Statistics for 1938 and 1939: "Decrease in World Exports of American Motion Picture Films and Equipment during 1939," *Press Memorandum, Motion Picture Division,* USDC, U.S. Bureau of Foreign and Domestic Commerce. Feb. 2, 1940. p. 3.

[2] Richard Abel, " Survivre à un novel ordre mondial," in Jacques Kermabon (ed.), *Pathé: Premier Empire du cinéma* (Paris, 1994), p. 163.

[3] Colin Crisp, *The Classic French Cinema, 1930–1960* (Bloomington, IN, 1993), p. 8. Paul Léglise, *Histoire de la politique du cinéma français,* vol. 2 (Paris, 1970), p. 214.

[4] France and Germany were the largest European suppliers of films to French cinemas. The number of French films gradually increased throughout the interwar period, from 68 in 1924 to 122 films censored in 1938. Germany was the second largest supplier of films towards the end of the 1920s; German films peaked in 1929, when 130 films were censored, but in 1924 and 1938 fewer than 30 German films were censored per year.

[5] Swedish film censorship began in 1910 and was the oldest in Europe. The statistics are available in Bertil Wredlund & Rolf Lindfors, *Långfilm i Sverige* (Stockholm, 1991), vol. 1 (1910–1919), p. 224, vol. 2 (1920–1929), vol. 3 (1930–1939).

[6] "Review of Foreign and Domestic Markets," USDC (Washington, DC, 1936), p. 72.

FIGURE 1: AMERICAN FILM EXPORTS IN FEET, 1918-1936

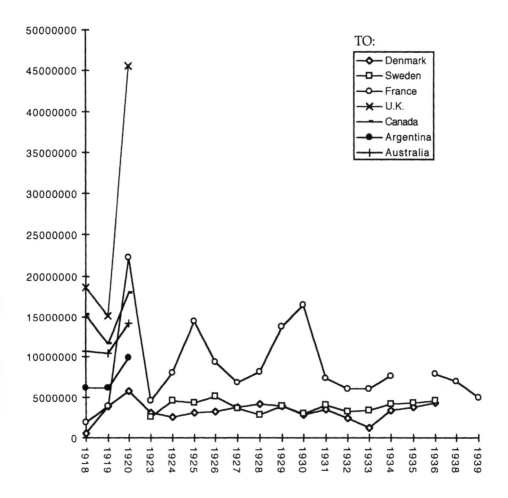

FIGURE 2: FILMS CENSORED IN FRANCE, 1924-1947

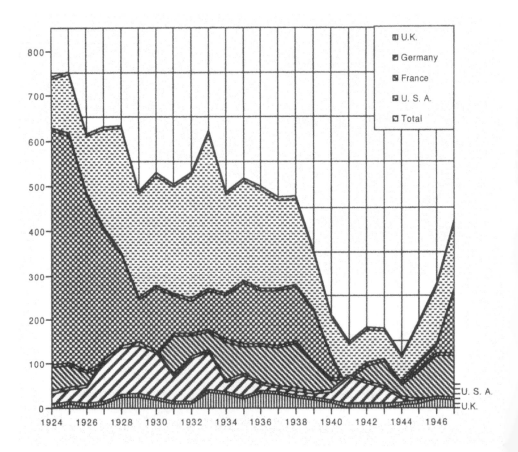

FIGURE 3: NUMBER OF FILMS CENSORED IN SWEDEN, 1910-1939

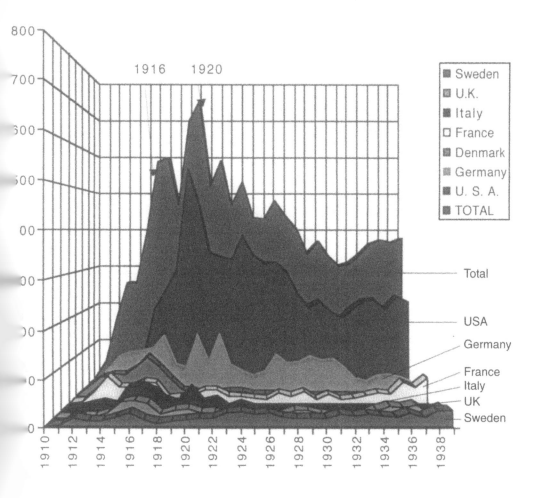

Figure 4: Number of films censored in France, 1929-1939

	1929	1930	1931	1932	1933	1934	1935	1936	1937	1938	1939
Eur.	227	241	233	271	342	216	218	217	194	187	123
US	211	237	220	208	230	220	248	231	230	239	183
Total	438	478	453	479	572	436	466	448	424	426	306
US%	48%	48%	49%	42%	40%	50%	53%	52%	54%	56%	60%

Average number of films per year: 234 European, 227 US, 462 total.

Source: Crisp, *The Classic French Cinema* (Bloomington, IN, 1993), p. 11.

(La Cinematographie française).

Figure 5: Number of films censored in Sweden, 1929-1939

	1929	1930	1931	1932	1933	1934	1935	1936	1937	1938	1939
Eur.	165	134	151	140	126	111	117	139	174	136	160
US	238	204	218	190	177	200	219	222	200	230	217
Total	403	338	369	330	303	311	336	361	374	366	377
US%	59%	60%	59%	58%	58%	64%	65%	62%	54%	63%	58%

Average number of films per year: 141 European, 210 US, 351 total.

Source: Bertil Wredlund and Rolf Lindfors, *Långfilm i Sverige 1910-1919* (Stockholm, 1991), vol
1920-1929, p. 322; vol. 3: 1930-1939.

Appendix C

Diplomatic Service Involved in Film Diplomacy

Archives

I have transcribed the major diplomatic documents from 1922-1935 in my dissertation, part 2. The archival documents of the USDS have to a large extent been microfilmed, whereas the documents from the American embassies are kept in bound ledgers, separated in USEF and USCP.[1] I have not examined the archives of American consulates in the French provinces. While the U.S. Embassy files from France have survived, the archive of the American Embassy in Berlin was lost due to bombing during World War II.

The U.S. Department of State

The film policy of the United States was decided by the State Department. The Secretary of State decided the policy, which he carried out jointly with his Undersecretaries of State, the Assistant Secretaries of state, the Director of Western Affairs, and the Economic Adviser. See table 1.

The U.S. Embassy and Consulate

The film policy of the American Embassy and consulate was carried out by top diplomats. The staff of the American Embassy consisted of fourteen diplomats in 1928. Myron T. Herrick, who was ambassador in the mid-1920s, carried out the film policy. When he died, Walter E. Edge became American Ambassador in 1929. The diplomats Sheldon Whitehouse, chargé d'Affaires, Norman Armour, the Counselor of the Embassy, and George A. Gordon, the First Secretary of the Embassy, were also involved in motion picture policy.

The Commercial Attaché's office was constantly active in carrying out the American film policy. In the 1920s, the major diplomats involved in film diplomacy were Henry C. MacLean, American Commercial Attaché, Daniel J. Reagan, Acting Commercial Attaché, and George R. Canty, Trade Commissioner for Motion Pictures, who gathered information for the Department of Commerce but he was not actively involved in film politics to any large extent. The consul general in Paris, Alphonse Gaulin, also corresponded directly with the officers of the MPPDA. Vice-consul Alfred D. Cameron, who replaced Harold L. Smith when he became head of MPPDA's Paris office in April 1928, was also involved in the film diplomacy efforts.

From around 1928, film diplomacy was handled by higher embassy staff only. After II, ambassador Jefferson Caffery carried out film diplomacy. See table 2.

U.S. Department of Commerce

The Department of Commerce gathered information about the economic situation in foreign markets for a wide range of products, including motion pictures, but the department was not particularly involved in film policy. A Motion Picture Section was established in the department in 1926 by a Special Act of Congress. C. J. North, with N. D. Golden as assistant, headed this section. The section had, furthermore, a special representative at the embassy in Paris, George R. Canty, who (under the title of Trade Commissioner, but not assigned as a diplomat) surveyed markets in Europe. On July 1, 1927 came E. I. Way, whose charge was to promote educational, industrial and other films of a non-entertainment character.[2]

The purpose of the motion picture section was to provide detailed information on important developments in all foreign markets. The information came from fifty-one foreign offices of the department in the chief capitals and commercial centers of the world and also from the more than four hundred consular offices abroad. The reports were distributed to the trade through the newsletters of the section and the trade press. The reports were of great assistance in keeping the industry informed of conditions abroad, concerning both the activities of competitors and also new market possibilities. American businessmen traveling in foreign countries were urged to get in touch with the trade representatives at the American embassies, who rendered assistance on questions of trade and commerce and would place facilities at the disposal of visiting exporters.

MPPDA

Individual companies did not directly handle the foreign relations of the American film industry, but operated through representatives of the MPPDA and American diplomats, who safeguarded the interests of the entire American film industry. In 1921, the American film industry established the MPPDA to protect the interests of the motion picture industry. The MPPDA is mainly known for the censorship code organized under the leader of the organization Will Hays, but the organization had several different functions.

Around 1924–25 the MPPDA created a Foreign Department, headed by Major Fredrick L. Herron. Herron directed the film policy of the MPPDA towards France in almost daily consultations with the State Department or the embassy of the United States in Paris. At first the MPPDA had agents in Europe, such as Edward G. Lowry, but in 1928 the MPPDA opened a Paris office headed by Harold L. Smith, a former diplomat at the Paris embassy. Local agents of American film companies in France were not involved in film policy-making. So even though the global distribution apparatus of the American film industry by the mid-1920s rivaled the United States Foreign Service in the number of employees, it did not rival it in importance.[5] During World War II, the MPPDA is supposed to have created its own diplomatic organization,[6] but it still depended on support from governmental film diplomacy.

The archives of the MPPDA consisted of several different sections. The central archive was disposed of when the New York office was dissolved in the 1980s, except for some selected materials, which were microfilmed.[7] These films contain few documents relevant to French film politics.

The director's archive from the time of Will Hays's directorship (1921–1945) has been published by Douglas Gomery as the _Will Hays Papers_ on seventy-eight microfilms, which contain some documents relevant to French film politics, supplementing the governmental records. Still, it is possible to follow the MPPDA's foreign policy in detail only through its intense correspondence with government institutions.

France

The organization of French film diplomacy was in constant flux. The Ministére des Beaux-Arts was responsible for the film industry, but several other ministries, such as the Ministére de Commerce and the Ministére des Affaires Étrangéres, were also of vital importance for carrying out film policy. The policy was, however, hampered by the constant change of governments. See table 3.

---

[1] RG59 for USDS, and RG 84, USEF, and USCP, Decimal file no. 840.6.

[2] _Film Yearbook_ (New York, 1928), p. 937. RG 151 for USDC.

[5] Herbert I. Schiller, "The Privatization and Transnationalization of Culture," in _Cultural Politics in Contemporary America_, ed. by Ian Angus and Sut Jhally (New York, 1989), p. 327.

[6] Paul Swann, "Little State Department: Hollywood and the State Department in the Postwar World," _American Studies International_, 29: 1 (1991): 3–19. See also Swann, "The Little State Department: Washington and Hollywood's Rhetoric of the Postwar Audience," _Hollywood in Europe_, ed. by David W. Ellwood and Rob Kroes (Amsterdam, 1994), p. 176–95.

[7] The MPPDA microfilms are kept in the Margaret Herrick Library in Los Angeles. Professor Richard Maltby, Flinder's University, has a more complete collection.

Table 1: State Department diplomats involved in film diplomacy

(Source: *Register of the Department of State,* for the years 1918-1939).

PRESIDENT	SECRETARY OF STATE	UNDER-SECRETARY OF STATE	ASSISTANT SECRETARIES OF STATE	OFFICE OF WESTERN EUR. AFFAIRS	OFFICE OF ECONOMIC ADVISER
Harding 1921-23	CE Hughes 1921/3-1925	HP Fletcher 1921/3-1922		WR Castle 1921/3-1927	
Coolidge 1923-1929	FB Kellogg 1925/3-1929	W Phillips 1922/3-1924 N Armour 1922/12-1924/5 ass			AN Young 1922/9-1929
		JC Grew 1924/4-1927	WJ Carr 1924/7-		
		RE Olds 1927/7-1928	WR Castle 1927/4-1931 (3 total)	JT Marriner 1927/4-	
		JR Clark,jr 1928/8-			
Hoover 1929-1933	HL Stimson 1929/3-	JP Cotton 1929/6-			F Livesey 1929/3-1931
		WR Castle 1931/4-			
Roosevelt 1933-45	C Hull 1933/3-1944	S Welles 1933/4-		J Pierrepont Moffat 1932/7-1935 1937/7-?	

Table 2: U.S. Embassy, France, personnel involved in film diplomacy

(Source: *Register of the Department of State*, for the years 1918-1939).

AMBASSADOR/ COUNSELOR	SECRETARIES	COMMERCIAL ATTACHÉS	CONSULS: PARIS
1918: WG Sharp (12 diplomats)	6 secretaries	2 attachés	(8 consuls 1918)
Myron T Herrick 1921/4-1929 (10 diplomats 1922)	4 secretaries 1923/24	Chester L Jones 1922/8-1927	(11 consuls 1922)
S Whitehouse 1921/4-1928/3	Halett Johnson 1924/7- (5 secretaries).	Raymond C Miller, asst. 1925/5-1928/2	RP Skinner CG 1924/8-1926/7 AD Cameron VC 1925/4- 1929/5 Harold L Smith 1925/9-1928/4 VC
(10 diplomats 1928) (9 diplomats 1929) Norman Armour 1928/4-1932	GA Gordon 1927/5-1930 (5 secretaries)	Henry C. MacLean 1927/12-1929 Daniel J Reagan asst. 1927/4-1939? FW Allport 1929/6-1930/12	Alphonse Gaulin CG, 1926/7-1929 (15 consuls 1928) (18 consuls 1929)
Walter E. Edge 1929/11-1933/4 JT Marriner 1931/4- Jesse I Straus 1933/3-1936/8 William C Bullitt 1936/8-39?	WS Howell 1929/2-1934 H Merle Cochran 1932/11-1939/6	William L Finger 1930/5- asst. FW Allport 1931/11-1932? Henry C. MacLean 1933/7-1936?	
Jefferson Caffery 1944/11-49/7			

Note:

George R. Canty, Trade Commissioner for motion pictures, 1926-1939, did not have diplomatic status.

Table 3: French Politicians involved in film diplomacy

(Source: Malcolm W. Davies and Walter H. Mallory, *A Political Handbook of the World* (New York, 1928-1939).

Presidents	Prime Ministers	Ministers of Public Instruction & Fine Arts
1913/2/18-1920 Poincaré, Rep.-Dem.	1917-1920/1 Clemenceau	1919/9/27-1920 Léon Bérard 1
1920/2/18-9/16 Deschanel	1920/1-1920/9 Millerand 1920/9-1921/1, Leygues	1920/1/20-1921 André Honnorat
1920/9/23-1924 Millerand	1921/1-1922/1, Briand 4 1922/1-1924/6 Poincaré	1921/1/16-1924 Léon Bérard 2 Republican-Democratic
	1924/6 François-Marsal	1924/3/29-6/1 Jouvenel
1924/6/13-1931 Doumergue	1924/6-1925/4 Herriot, Radical	1924/6/14-1925 F. Albert
		1925/4/17-10/11 de Monzie 1
		1925/10/11-11/22 Delbos 1, Radical
		1925/11/28-1926 Daladier 1, Radical
		1926/3/9-6/15 Lamoureux, Radical
	1926/7-1929/7 Poincaré, Rep. Union	1926/6/23-7/17 Nogaro
		1926/7/19-21 Daladier 2
		1926/7/23-1928 Herriot, Rad.
	1929/6-1929/11, Briand 1929/11-1930/2 Tardieu 1, Left Republ.	1928/11/11-1930 Marraud 1 (François-Poncet, under-sec. of F.A. to 1931/2)

Table 3: French Politicians involved in film diplomacy

Presidents	Prime Ministers	Ministers of Public Instruction & Fine Arts
	1930/2-3 Chautemps	1930/2/21-25 Durand
	1930/3/12 Tardieu 2 Left Repub.	1930/3/2-12/4 Marraud 2
	1930/12-1931/1 T. Steeg	1930/12/13-1931 Chautemps, Rad.
1931/6-1932/5 Doumer 1932/5-1940/7, Le Brun	1931/1-1932/2 Laval 1932/2-6 Tardieu 3	1931/1/27-1932 Roustan 1 (François-Poncet) (Petsche from 1931/2- ?)
	1932/6-12, Herriot 3 1932/12-1933/1 Paul-Boncour 1933/1-10, Daladier 1 1933/10-11, Sarraut 1 1933/11-1934/1 Chautemps 2	1932/6/3-1934 de Monzie 2, Socialist
	1934/1-2, Daladier, Rad. 1934/2-11, Doumergue 2	1934/1/30-11/8 Berthod, Rad.
	1934/11-1935/6 Flandin	1934/11/8-1935 Mallarmé, Rad. Left
	1935/6 Buisson	1935/6/1-4 Roustan 2
	1935/6-1936/1, Laval 2	1935/6/7-13 Marcombes
		1935/6/17-1936 Roustan 3
	1936/1-6 Sarraut 2	1936/1/24-6/4 Guernut
	1936/6-1937/6 Léon Blum 1937/6-1937/3 Chautemps 3 1938/3-4, Léon Blum 2 1938/4-1940/3, Daladier 3	1936/6/4-1939/9/13 Jean Zay

Appendix D

USIA

Opinion Research *memorandum*

Office of Research, U.S. Information Agency, Washington, DC 20547

January 3, 1994

West Europeans Mixed on Whether American Films Are "Harmful"*

One critical area of international trade left unresolved in the Uruguay round of the Gatt negotiations is the audiovisual sector. The U.S., France and EU agreed to a cultural exception covering television and film products. Recent USIA-commissioned surveys across the region indicate west Europeans have mixed perceptions of the impact of American films on their culture.

- Only in Turkey and France do a majority agree that American films are harmful to their country's culture (Figure 1). Majorities in Germany, Spain, Britain, and Italy disagree with this view, and Belgians are divided. Still, American films are seen as a cultural threat by a third or more in each country surveyed.

Figure 1. West European Views of American Films

Percent who agree/disagree that American films are harmful to their culture

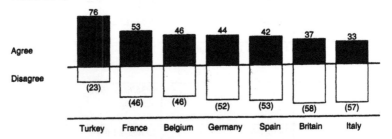

- Those who see American films as threatening are more likely than others to endorse protectionist policies and view the U.S. as uncooperative in resolving economic problems with western Europe. Moreover, these people tends to view the U.S. as a rival rather than a partner.

---

*This report is based on USIA-commissioned surveys conducted in late October-early November in Belgium, Britain, France, Germany, Italy, Spain, and Turkey.

- On issues of national security, those who think American films are a harm to their culture are more negative than others in their views of NATO and the U.S.-European security relationship. These people tend to believe:

  -- the U.S. should not be involved in the defense of western Europe;

  -- NATO is not needed because there is no longer a Soviet threat;

  -- their country's security interests are different from those of the U.S.; and

  -- ties between their country and the U.S. are less important than they were before the end of the Cold War.

- Finally, this group tends to be older, less well-educated, female, working class and describes their financial situation as bad. In some countries (Britain, France, Germany, and Spain) individuals who view American films as a threat to their culture are less likely than others to have had any contact with Americans in or outside their country.

These data show that attitudes toward American films are part of a larger set of beliefs that encompass trade and military security issues. Significantly, contact with America or Americans appears to have a slight moderating effect on some west Europeans' negative view of the impact of U.S. films.

Prepared by: Mary McIntosh and Phillip Riggins (619-5143)   M-1-94
Issued by: Office of Research, USIA

Bibliography

I. American Primary Sources
Federal

Department of State: Record Group 59, National Archives. The materials relating to motion pictures is to some extent published on microfilms:
Microfilm Publication M560, Records *of the Department of State Relating to Internal Affairs of France 1910–1929*. Roll 46–47.
Microfilm Publication M1442. Records *of the Department of State Relating to Internal Affairs of France 1930–1939*. Roll 22.
Microfilm Publication M336. Records *of the Department of State Relating to Internal Affairs of Germany 1910–1929*. Roll 79.
Embassy Files: Record Group 89. U.S. Embassy, France and U.S. Consulate, Paris.
Department of Commerce: Record Group 151. Bureau of Foreign and Domestic Commerce. Index file 281.
Department of Justice: Record Group 60. Anti-trust file 60-6.

MPPDA

Gomery, Douglas. The *Will Hays Papers*. 78 microfilms. Part I: December 1921–March 1929, 43 reels. Part II: April 1929–September 1945, 34 reels. Frederick, MD, 1986.
MPPDA microfilms in the Margaret Herrick Library, Los Angeles, and in the private archive of Richard Maltby.

II. French Primary Sources

Ministère de l'Instruction Publique et des Beaux Arts. 5 boxes in the Archives Nationales, Paris.
Ministère des Affaires Étrangères. Dossier B40. 13 Boxes in the Ministry Archive, Paris.
Ministère de l'Économie. Archive in Savigny-les-Temples and in Archives Nationales.

III. Secondary Sources

Abel, Richard. "Booming the Film Business: The Historical Specificity of Early French Cinema." *French Cultural Studies* I (1990): 79–94.

———. *The Ciné Goes to Town: French Cinema 1896–1914*. Berkeley: University of California Press, 1994.

———. *French Cinema: The First Wave 1915–1929*. Princeton, NJ: Princeton University Press, 1984.

———. *French Film Theory and Criticism: A History /Anthology 1907–1939*. 2 vols. Princeton, NJ: Princeton University Press, 1988.

———. "French Silent Cinema." In Geoffrey Nowell-Smith, *The Oxford History of World Cinema*. Oxford: Oxford University Press, 1996, pp. 112–23.

———. " Survivre à un novel ordre mondial." In Jacques, ed., *Pathé: Premier Empire du cinéma*. Paris, 1994, pp. 158–89.

Aberdeen, J. A. *Hollywood Renegades: The Society of Independent Motion Picture Producers*. Los Angeles, CA: Cobblestone Entertainment, 2000.

Acheson, Dean. *Present at the Creation: My Years in the State Department*. New York: Norton, 1969.

Armes, Roy. *French Cinema*. New York: Oxford University Press, 1985.

Bächlin, Peter. *Der Film als Ware*. Basel, 1953.

Balio, Tino. *The American Film Industry*. Madison: University of Wisconsin Press, 1976. Rev. ed., 1985.

Bancal, Jean. *La censure cinématographique: son histoire, son but, son perfectionnement*. Paris, 1934.

Bardéche, Maurice and Robert Brasillach. *The History of Motion Pietures*. Trans. Iris Barry. New York: W. W. Norton, 1938.

———. *Histoire du cinéma*. Paris, 1935. 2nd ed. Paris: Denoel, 1943.

Barnet, Richard J. *Global Dreams: Imperial Corporations and the New World Order*. New York: Simon & Schuster, 1994.

Barsamian, David. "Monopolies, NPR & PBS: An Interview with Robert McChesney," in Z Magazine (feb. 2000):41-45.

Bawden, Liz-Anne, ed. *The Oxford Companion to Film*. Oxford: Oxford University Press, 1976.

Benghozi, Pierre-Jean. *Le cinéma: entre l'art et l'argent*. Paris: Harmattan, 1989.

Bertrand, Daniel. *The Motion Picture Industry: A Pattern of Control*. Washington, DC, 1941. Investigation of concentration of economic power: Temporary National Economic Committee; monograph no. 43 (76th Congress, 3d session.) "A study made for the Temporary National

Economic Committee, Seventy-sixth Congress, third session, pursuant to Public Resolution no. 113 (Seventy-fifth Congress) authorizing and directing a select committee to make a full and complete study and investigation with respect to the concentration of economic power in and financial control over, production and distribution of goods and services."

Billard, Pierre. *L'Âge classique du cinéma Français: Du cinéma parlant à la Nouvelle Vague.* Paris: Flammarion, 1995.

Billecocq, Georges. *Le régime fiscal de l'industrie cinématographique en France.* Paris: Occitania, 1925. Thèse pour le doctorat, l'Ecole des Sciences Politiques, Toulouse.

Blumenthal, Henry. *Illusion and Reality in Franco-American Diplomacy 1914–1945.* Baton Rouge: Louisiana State University Press, 1986.

Bordwell, David, Janet Staiger, and Kristin Thompson. *The Classical Hollywood Cinema: Film Style & Mode of Production to 1960.* New York: Columbia University Press, 1985.

Brogan, D. W. *The Development of Modern France, 1870–1939,* Vol. 2. New York: Harper & Row, 1966.

Chandler, Alfred. *The Visible Hand: The Managerial Revolution in American Business.* Cambridge, MA: Belknap, 1977.

Caron, François. *An Economic History of Modern France.* Trans. Barbara Bray. New York: Columbia University Press, 1979.

Carter, Edward C., Robert Forster, and Joseph Moody, eds. *Enterprise and Entrepreneurs in Nineteenth- and Twentieth-Century France.* Baltimore: The Johns Hopkins University Press, 1976.

Chastenet, Jacques. *Histoire de la Troisième Republique: les années d'illlusions, 1918–1931.* Paris: Hachette, 1960.

Chevanne, Andre. *L'Industrie du cinéma: le cinéma sonore.* Bordeaux: Delmas, 1933.

Chirat, Raymond. *Catalogue des films français de long métrage: Films sonores de fiction 1929–1939.* 2nd ed. Brussels: Cinématheque Royale de Belgique, 1981.

———. *Catalogue des films français de long métrage: Films de fiction 1940–1950.* Luxembourg: Imprimerie Saint-Paul, 1981.

Chirat, Raymond, and Eric LeRoy, ed. *Le Cinéma française, 1911–1920.* Paris: Cinématheque française, 1993.

Chirat, Raymond, and Roger Icart. *Catalogue des film français de long métrage: Films de fiction 1919–1929.* Toulouse: Cinématheque de Toulouse, 1984.

La Cinématographie française. Paris.

Ciné-Comædia. Paris.

Clair, René. *Cinema Yesterday and Today*. Trans. Stanley Appelbaum. New York: Dover, 1972.

Cobban, Alfred. *A History of Modern France*. Vol. 3 (1871–1962). London: Penguin, 1965.

Coissac, G.-Michel. *Histoire du cinématographe: des ses origines jusqu'à nos jours*. Paris: Cinéopse, 1925.

Comes, Philippe de, and Michel Marmin, eds. *Le Cinéma français: 1930–1960*. Paris: Atlas, 1984.

Conant, Michael. *Antitrust in the Motion Picture Industry*. Berkeley: University of California Press, 1960.

Cook, David A. *A History of Narrative Film*. New York: Norton, 1981.

Costigliola, Frank. *Awkward Dominion: American Political, Economic, and Cultural Relations with Europe, 1919–1933*. Ithaca, NY: Cornell University Press, 1988.

Coston, Henry. *Les juifs contre la France*. Paris: Office de Propagande Nationale, 1937.

Courtade, Francis. *Les Maledictions du cinéma français: une histoire du cinéma français parlant (1928–1978)*. Paris: Alain Moreau, 1978.

Crisp, Colin.*The Classic French Cinema, 1930–1960*. Bloomington: Indiana University Press, 1993.

Dallek, Robert. *The American Style of Foreign Policy: Cultural Politics and Foreign Affairs*. New York: Knopf, 1983.

———. *Franklin D. Roosevelt and United States Foreign Policy, 1933–1945* . New York: Oxford University Press, 1979.

Davies, Philip and Brian Neve, eds. *Cinema, Politics and Society in America*. Manchester: Manchester University Press, 1981.

de Grazia, Victoria. "Mass Culture and Sovereignty: The American Challenge to European Cinemas, 1920–1960." *Journal of Modern History* 61 (1989): 53–87.

Demichel, André. "Les pouvoirs du maire en matière de police du cinéma." *Annales de l'Université de Lyon, troisième série, droit, fascicule 20: Études économiques et politiques* (ca. 1960): 7–28.

Deslandes, Jacques. *Histoire comparee du cinéma*. Vol. I. Tournai, Belgium: Casterman,1966.

Deslandes, Jacques and Jacques Richard. *Histoire Comparée du cinéma*. Vol. 2 (1896–1906). Paris: Casterman, 1968.

Ellis, L. Ethan. *Republican Foreign Policy, 1921–1933*. New Brunswick, NJ: Rutgers University Press, 1968.

Ellwood, David and Rob Kroes. *Hollywood in Europe: Experiences of Cultural Hegemony*. Amsterdam: VU University Press, 1994.

Feis, Herbert. *The Diplomacy of the Dollar: The First Era, 1919–1933*. Baltimore: Johns Hopkins Press, 1950.

Fescourt, Henri. *La Foi et les montagnes*. Paris: Paul Montel, 1959.

Fielding, Raymond. *A Technological History of Motion Pictures and Television*. Berkeley: University of California Press, 1967.

Film Year-Book. New York, 1921-. (Succeeded *Wid's Almanac*).

Filmen, Copenhagen.

Ford, Charles. *Histoire populaire du cinéma*. Paris: Mame, 1955.

Frieden, Jeffry A. and David A. Lake. *International Political Economy: Perspectives on Global Power and Wealth*. New York: St. Martin's Press, 1995.

Fugate, Wilbur L. *Foreign Commerce and the Antitrust Laws*. Vols. 1–2. 3rd ed. Boston, MA: Little, Brown, 1982, supplement, 1983.

Garçon, Francois. *De Blum à Petain: Cinéma et Société française (1936–1944)*. Paris: Cerf, 1984.

Garnier, Jacques. "Cinémas. " In *Forains d 'hier et d'aujourd'hui*. Orleans: Jacques Garnier, 1968, pp. 318–38.

Gill, Stephen and David Law: *The Global Political Economy: Perspectives, Problems, and Policies*. New York: Harvester, 1988.

Girard, Jean. *Le Lexique français du cinéma, des origines à 1930*. Paris: Centre national de la recherche scientifique, 1958.

Gomery, Douglas. "Economic Struggle and Hollywood Imperialism: Europe Converts to Sound." *Yale French Studies* 60 (1980): 80–93.

————. *The Will Hays Papers: a Guide to the Microfilm Edition of the Will Hays Papers*. Frederick, MD: University Microfilm, 1986.

————. *The Will Hays Papers*. Frederick, MD: University Microfilm, 1986. 78 microfilms. Part I: December 1921–March 1929, 43 reels. Part II: April 1929–September 1945, 34 reels.

Grantham, Bill. *"Some Big Bourgeois Brothel": Contexts for France's Culture Wars with Hollywood*. Luton: University of Luton Press, 2000.

Guback, Thomas H. "Cultural Identity and Film in the European Economic Community." *Cinema Journal*, 14: 1 (Fall, 1974): 2–17.

————. *The International Film Industry: Western Europe and America since 1945*. Bloomington: Indiana University Press, 1969.

————. "Hollywood's International Market." In Tino Balio, ed.,*The American Film Industry*. Madison: University of Wisconsin Press, 1976, pp. 387–409. Rev. ed., 1985, pp. 463–86.

————. "Theatrical Film." In Benjamin M. Compaine, et al., *Who Owns the Media? Concentration of Ownership in the Mass Communications Industry*. White Plains, NY: Knowledge Industry Publications, 1979, pp. 179–241. 2nd ed. 1982.

————. "Non-Market Factors in the International Distribution of American Films." In Bruce A. Austin, ed., *Current Research in Film*, 1 (1985): 111–26.

Guibbert, Pierre, ed. *Les Premiers Ans du cinéma français*. Perpignan: Institut Jean Vigo, 1985.

Guillaume-Grimaud, Geneviève. *Le cinéma du Front Populaire*. Paris: Lherminier, 1986.

Haight, Frank Arnold. *French Import Quotas: A New Instrument of Commercial Policy*. New York: Macmillan. Kraus Repr. 1970.

———. *A History of French Commercial Policies*. New York, 1941.

Hampton, Benjamin B. *History of the American Film Industry*. New York, 1931. Arno Press, 1970.

Harpole, Charles. *History of the American Cinema*. Berkeley, University of California Press. Vol. 1–5:

Charles Musser. *The Emergence of Cinema: The American Screen to 1907*. 1990.

Eileen Bowser. *The Transformation of Cinema 1907–1915*. 1990, 1994.

Richard Koszarski. *An Evening's Entertainment: The Age of the Silent Feature Picture 1915–1928*. c1990, 1994.

Tino Balio. *Grand Design: Hollywood as a Modern Business Enterprise 1930–1939*. c1993, 1995.

Hawley, Ellis W. *The New Deal and the Problem of Monopoly: A Study in Economic Ambivalence*. Princeton: Princeton University Press, 1966. 2nd ed. New York: Fordham University Press, 1995.

———. "Three Facets of Hooverian Associationalism: Lumber, Aviation, and Movies, 1921–1930." In Thomas K. McCraw, ed., *Regulation in Perspective: Historical Essays*. Cambridge, MA: Harvard University Press, 1981, pp. 95–123.

Hayes, Carlton J. H. *A Nation of Patriots*. New York: Columbia University Press, 1930.

Hays, Will H. *The Memoirs of Will H. Hays*. Garden City, NY: Doubleday, 1955.

"The Hays Office." *Fortune*, 18 (December, 1939): 69–72. Reprinted in Tino Balio, ed. *The American Film Industry*. Madison: University of Wisconsin Press, 1976, pp. 295–314.

Hayward, Susan. *French National Cinema*. New York: Rouledge, 1993.

Herriot, Édouard. *Europe*. Paris: Rieder, 1930. In English: *The United States of Europe*. New York: Viking Press, 1930.

Higson, Andrew and Richard Maltby. *"Film Europe" and "Film America": Cinema, Commerce, and Cultural Exchange 1920–1939*. Exeter: University of Exeter Press, 1999.

Huettig, Mae D. *Economic Control of the Motion Picture Industry: A Study in Industrial Organization*. Philadelphia, University of Pennsylvania Press, 1944. Jerome S. Ozer, 1971.

Hugin, Adolph Charles. *Private International Trade: Regulatory Arrangements and the Antittrust Law*. Washington, DC, Catholic University of America, 1949.

Hull, Cordell. *The Memoirs of Cordell Hull*. Vols 1–2. New York: Macmillan 1948.

Hull, David Stewart. *Film in the Third Reich*. New York: Simon and Schuster, 1973.

Hunnings, Neville March. "France." In *Film Censors and the Law*. London: George Allen and Unwin, 1967, pp. 332–60.

Icart, Roger. "L'Avènement du film parlant." *Cahiers de la cinématheque* 13–14–15 (1974): 25–218.

Ilchman, Warren Frederick. *Professional Diplomacy in the United States, 1789–1939: A Study in Administrative History*. Chicago: University of Chicago Press, 1961.

Jacobs, Lewis. *The Rise of the American Film: A Critical History*. New York: Teachers College Press, 1939, 1978.

Jarvie, Ian. "Dollars and Ideology: Will Hays' Economic Foreign Policy 1922–1945. *Film History* 2 (1988): 207–21.

———. *Hollywood's Overseas Campaign: The North Atlantic Movie Trade, 1920–1950*. Cambridge: Cambridge University Press, 1992.

———. "The Postwar Economic Foreign Policy of the American Film Industry: Europe 1945–1950." In *Hollywood in Europe: Experiences of a Cultural Hegemony*, ed. by David W. Ellwood and Rob Kroes. Amsterdam: VU University Press, 1994, pp. 155–75.

Jeancolas, Jean-Pierre. *Quinze ans d'annees trente: Le Cinéma des français 1929–1944*. Paris: Stock, 1983.

———. "L'arrangement: Blum-Byrnes `a l'épreuve des faits..." In *1895*, no. 13 Paris: AFRHC, 1992: 3-49.

Jeanne, Rene. *Cinéma 1900*. Paris: Flammarion, 1965.

Jeanne, Rene and Charles Ford. *Le Cinéma et la presse, 1895–1960*. Paris: Armand Colin, 1961.

———. *Histoire encyclopédique du cinéma*. Vol. I: *Le Cinéma français, 1895–1929*. Paris: Laffont, 1947. Vol. IV: *Le Cinéma parlant (1929–1945, sauf U.S.A.)*. Paris: S.E.D.E., 1958.

Jenks, Jeremiah Wipple. *The Trust Problem*. Garden City, NY: Doubleday, 1929.

Kaplan, Alice Yeager. *Reproductions of Banality: Fascism, Literature, and French Intellectual Life*. Minneapolis: University of Minnesota Press, 1986.

Katz, Ephraim. *The Film Encyclopedia*. New York: G. P. Putnam's Sons, 1982.

Keller, Morton. "The Pluralist State: American Economic Regulation in Comparative Perspective, 1900–1930." In Thomas K. McCraw, ed., *Regulation in perspective*. Cambridge, MA: Harvard, 1981.

———. *Regulating a New Economy: Public Policy and Economic Change in America, 1900–1933*. Cambridge, MA: Harvard, 1990.

———. *Regulating a New Society: Public Policy and Social Change in America, 1900–1933*. Cambridge, MA: Harvard, 1994.

Kennedy, Joseph. *The Story of the Films*. Chicago, 1927.

Kent, Nicolas. *Naked Hollywood: Money and Power in the Movies Today*. New York: St. Martin's Press, 1991.

Kermabon, Jacques, ed. *Pathé: Premier empire du cinéma*. Paris: Centre Pompidou, 1994.

Kindleberger, Charles P. *The World in Depression, 1929–1930*. Berkeley: University of California Press, 1986.

Kirsh, Benjamin S. "Foreign Trade Functions of Trade Associations: The Legal Aspects." *University of Pennsylvania Law Review*, 76 (June 1928): 1–35.

Klingender, F.D. & Stuart Legg, *Money Behind the Screen*. London, 1937.

Kuisel, Richard F. *Capitalism and the State in Modern France*. Cambridge: Cambridge University Press, 1981.

———. *Seducing the French*. Berkeley: University of California Press, 1992.

———."The Fernandel Factor: The Rivalry between the French and American Cinema in the 1950's." In *Yale French Studies* (New Haven, 2000):119-134.

Lake, David A. *Power, Protection, and Free Trade: International Sources of U.S. Commercial Strategy, 1887–1939*. Ithaca, NY: Cornell University Press, 1988.

League of Nations. *Abolition of Import and Export Prohibitions and Restrictions: Convention and Protocol between the United States and Other Powers* (Washington, DC, 1930), Treaty Series No. 811. International Convention for the Abolition of Import and Export Prohibitions and Restrictions, League of Nations.

Ledoux, Jacques and Raymond Chirat. *Catalogue des films français de long métrage: films sonores de fiction, 1929–1939*. Brussels: Royal Film Archive of Belgium, 1975.

Leffler, Melvyn P. *The Elusive Quest: America's Pursuit of European Stability and French Security, 1919–1933*. Chapel Hill: University of North Carolina Press, 1979.

Leglise, Paul. *Histoire de la politique du cinéma français: le cinéma et la IIIe Republique*. Paris: Pierre Lherminier, 1970.

———. *Histoire de la politique du cinéma français*. Vol. 2: *Le Cinéma entre deux républiques (1940–1946)*. Paris: Pierre Lherminier, 1977.

————. "Les Institutions cinématographiques des années vingt." *Cahiers de la cinématheque*, 33–34 (Autumn, 1981): 46–56.

Leprohon, Pierre. *Cinquante ans du cinéma français*. Paris: Editions du Cerf, 1954.

————. *Histoire du cinéma: Vie et mort du cinématographe (1895–1930)*. Paris: Editions du Cerf, 1961.

Lewis, Howard T. *The Motion Picture Industry*. New York: Van Nostrand, 1933.

Lyon-Caen, G. & P. Lavigne. *Traité théorique et pratique de droit du cinéma français et comparé*. Paris: Librarie Générale de Droit et de Jurisprudence, 1957.

McChesney, Robert W. *Rich Media, Poor Democracy*. Urbana, IL, University of Illinois Press, 1999, 2000.

Machlup, Fritz.*The Political Economy of Monopoly: Business, Labor and Government Policies*. Baltimore: John Hopkins Press, 1952.

Maltby, Richard. *Hollywood Cinema: An Introduction*. Oxford: Blackwell, 1995.

————. "The Political Economy of Hollywood: The Studio System." In Philip Davies and Brian Neve, *Cinema, Politics and Society in America*. Manchester: Manchester University Press, 1981, pp. 42–58.

————. "Made for each other: The Melodrama of Hollywood and the House Committee on Un-American Activities, 1947." In Philip Davies and Brian Neve, *Cinema, Politics and Society in America*. Manchester: Manchester University Press, 1981, pp. 76–96

Mathy, Jean-Philippe. *Extrême-Occident: French Intellectuals and America*. Chicago: University of Chicago Press, 1993.

Mattelart, Armand. "European Film Policy and the Response to Hollywood." In John Hill and Pamela Church Gibson, *World Cinema: Critical Approaches*. Oxford: Oxford University Press, 2000, pp. 94–101.

May, Lary. *Screening Out the Past: The Birth of Mass Culture and the Motion Picture Industry*. New York: Oxford University Press, 1980.

Mazdon, Lucy. *Encore Hollywood: Remaking French Cinema*. London: BFI, 2000.

Meignen, E. *Le code du cinéma*. Paris, 1921.

Meusy, Jean-Jacques. *Cinquante ans d'industrie cinématographique (1906–1956): Archives économiques du Crédit Lyonnais*. Paris: Le Monde-Éditions, 1996.

Mikesell, Raymond F. *United States Economic Policy and International Relations*. New York: McGraw Hill, 1952.

Mirow, Karl Rudolf. *Webs of Power: International Cartels and the World Economy*. Boston: Houghton Mifflin, 1982.

Mitry, Jean. *Histoire du cinéma*. Vols. 1–3, Paris: Editions Universitaires, 1967–73. Vols. 4–5, Paris: Jean-Pierre Delarge, 1975–80.

Moley, Raymond. *The Hays Office*. Indianapolis, IN: Bobbs-Merill, 1945.

Moving Picture World. New York.

Monaco, Paul. *Cinema and Society: France and Germany During the Twenties*. New York: Elsevier, 1976.

Muscio, Giuliana. *Hollywood's New Deal*. Philadelphia: Temple University Press, 1996.

Nester, William R. *A Short History of American Industrial Policies*. London: Macmillan; New York: St. Martin's Press, 1998.

The New York Times

The New York Times Encyclopedia of Film

Norden, Martin. "The Pathé Frères Company During the Trust Era." *Journal of the University Film Association*, 33 (Summer 1981):15–32.

Notz, William F. and Richard S. Harvey. *American Foreign Trade: As Promoted by the Webb-Pomerene and Edge Acts: Historical References to the Origin and Enforcemnet of Anti-Trust Laws*. Indianapolis, IN: Bobbs-Merill, 1921.

Nowell-Smith, Geoffrey. *The Oxford History of World Cinema*. Oxford: Oxford University Press, 1996.

Nussy, Marcel. *Le cinématographe et la censure*. Montpellier: Imprimerie Emmanuel Montane, 1929. Thèse, Facultet de Droit, Université de Montpellier.

Parrini, Carl P. *Heir to Empire: United States Economic Diplomacy*. Pittsburgh, PA: University of Pittsburgh Press, 1969.

Pastor, Robert A. *Congress and the Politics of U.S. Foreign Economic Policy 1929–1976*. Berkeley: University of California Press, 1980.

Pathé, Charles. "De Pathé Frères à Pathé Cinéma." In *Premier Plan 55*. Lyon: SERDOC, 1970.

Porter, Glenn.*The Rise of Big Business 1860–1920*. 2nd ed. Arlington Heights, IL: Harlan Davidson, 1992.

Portes, Jacques. *l'Amerique comme modèle, l'Amerique sans modèle* Villeneuve d'Ascq: Presses Universitaires de Lille, 1993.

———. *De la scène à l'écran: Naissance de la culture de masse aux États-Unis*. Paris: Belin, 1997.

———. "Les origines de la légende noire des accords Blum-Byrnes sur le cinéma." *Révue d'histoire moderne et contemporaine*, 33 (1986): 314–29.

Prindle, David F. *Risky Business: The Political Economy of Hollywood*. Boulder, CO: Westview, 1993.

Puttnam, David.*The Undeclared War: The Struggle for Control of the World's Film Industry*. London: Harper-Collins, 1997.

Rebatet, Lucien. *Les tribus du cinéma et du théatre*. Paris, 1941.

Rossel-Kirschen et Gilles Willems. "En marge du centenaire du cinéma: Bernard Natan à la direction de Pathé-cinéma." In *1895: Revue de l'association française de recherche sur l'histoire du cinéma*, no. 21. Paris: AFRHC, 1996, p. 163.

Roziers, Laurent Burin de. *Du cinéma au multimedia: Une bréve histoire de l'exception culturelle.* Paris: IFRI, 1998. WWW.ifri.org/f/publications/notes

Sadoul, Georges. *Histoire générale du cinéma.* Vols. 1–6. 3rd ed. (Bernard Eisenschitz, ed.). Paris: Denoel, 1977.

———. *Histoire générale du cinéma.* Vol. 2, *Les Pionniers du cinéma, 1897–1909.* Paris: Denoel, 1947. Vol. 3, *Le Cinéma devient un art, 1909–1920 (L'Avant-guerre).* Paris: Denoel, 1951. Vol. 4, *Le Cinéma devient un art, 1909–1920 (La Premiere Guerre mondiale).* Paris: Denoel, 1974. Vol. 5, *L'Art muet (1919–1929).* Paris: Denoel, 1975. Vol. 6, *L'Art muet (1919–1929).* Paris: Denoel, 1975.

———. *Le Cinéma français.* Paris: Flammarion, 1962.

———. *The French Cinema.* London: Falcon Press, 1952.

Schatz, Arthur W. "Cordell Hull and the Struggle for the Reciprocal Trade Agreements Program, 1932–1940." Ph.D. dissertation. University of Oregon, 1958.

Schiller, Herbert I. "The Privatization and Transnationalization of Culture." In Ian Angus and Sut Jhally, eds., *Cultural Politics in Contemporarary America.* New York, 1989, p. 327.

Schramm, Wilbur. *Mass Communicationse.* Urbana, IL, 1949.

Schulzinger, Robert D. *U.S. Diplomacy Since 1900.* New York: Oxford, 1998.

Schuman, Frederick L. *War and Diplomacy in the French Republic.* New York: Howard Fertig, 1969.

Seabury, William Marston. *Motion Picture Problems: The Cinema and the League of Nations.* New York, 1929.

———. *The Public and the Motion Picture Industry.* New York, 1926.

Seager, Henry R. and Charles A. Gulick Jr. *Trust and Corporation Problems.* New York, 1929.

Segrave, Kerry. *American Films Abroad: Hollywood's Domination of the World's Movie Screens from the 1890's to the Present.* Jefferson, NC: McFarland, 1997

Shaffer, Butler. *In Restraint of Trade: The Business Campaign Against Competition, 1918–1938.* Lewisburg, PA: Bucknell University Press; London: Associated University Presses, 1997.

Shindler, Colin. *Hollywood in Crisis: Cinema and American Society 1929–1939.* London: Routledge, 1996.

Sklar, Robert. *Movie-Made America: A Cultural History of American Movies.* New York: Vintage, 1975. Rev. ed., 1994.

Sorlin, Pierre. *European Cinemas, European Societies 1939–1990.* London: Rouledge, 1991.

Staiger, Janet. "Combination and Litigation: Structures of US Film Distribution, 1896–1917." In Thomas Elsaesser and Adam Barker, eds., *Early Cinema: Space-Frame-Narrative.* London: BFI, 1990, pp. 189–210.

Stanley, Robert H. *The Celluloid Empire: A History of the American Movie Industry.* New York: Hastings House, 1978.

Stocking, George W. and Myron W. Watkins. *Monopoly and Free Enterprise.* New York, 1951.

Strauss, William Victor. "Foreign Distribution of American Motion Pictures." *Harvard Business Review,* 8 (1929): 307–15.

Swann, Paul. "Little State Department: Hollywood and the State Department in the Postwar World." *American Studies International,* 29: 1 (1991): 3–19.

———. "The Little State Department: Washington and Hollywood's Rhetoric of the Postwar Audience." In David W. Ellwood and Rob Kroes, eds., *Hollywood in Europe.* . Amsterdam: VU University Press, 1994, pp. 176–95.

Sørensen, Knud Rønn. *Den danske filmindustri (prod., distr., konsumption) indtil tonefilmens Gennembrud.* Copenhagen: Institut for Filmvidenskab, Københavns Universitet, 1976.

Thompson, Kristin. *Exporting Entertainment: America in the World Film Market 1907–1934.* London: British Film Institute, 1985.

Thomson, David, ed. *France: Empire and Republic, 1850–1940.* New York: Walker, 1968.

Tiersky, Ronald. *French Communism 1920–1972.* New York: Columbia University Press, 1974.

Tomlinson, John. *Cultural Imperialism.* Baltimore: Johns Hopkins University Press, 1991.

Ulff-Møller, Jens. "The "Film Wars" between France and the United States: Film-Trade Diplomacy, and the Emergence of the Film Quota System in France, 1920–1939." Ph.D. diss., Brandeis University. Ann Arbor, MI: UMI, 1998.

———. "Hollywood's 'Foreign War': The Effect of National Commercial Policy on the Emergence of the American Film Hegemony in France, 1920–1929." In Andrew Higson and Richard Maltby, eds., *"Film Europe" and "Film America": Cinema, Commerce and Cultural Exchange 1920–1939.* Exeter: University of Exeter Press, 1999, pp. 181–206.

———. "The Origin of the French Film Quota Policy Controlling the Import of American Films." *Historical Journal of Film, Radio and Television,* 18: 2. (1998): 167–182.

United States Congress. *Proposed Investigation of the Motion-Picture Industry: Hearings before a Subcommittee of the Committee on the Judiciary.* Sixty-seventh Congress pursuant to S. Res. 142 Directing an investigation of the alleged political activities of the motion-picture industry. Washington: GPO, 1922.

———. S 3012. Report no. 2378, Calendar no. 2506. 74th Congress, 2d Session. Washington, DC, 1936. ("Neely bill").

———. 74th Congress, 1st Session. H.R. 4757. Washington, DC, 1936. ("Pettengill bill").

———. *Motion Picture Distribution Trade Practices, hearings before a subcommittee of the Select Committee on Small Business,* U.S. Senate, 83rd Congress, 1st Session. Washington, DC, 1953.

———. *Motion-Picture Distribution Trade Practices—1956.* Hearings before a subcommittee of the Select Committee on Small Business, U.S. Senate, 84th Congress, 2nd Session. Washington, 1956.

United States Department of Commerce. *Motion Pictures Abroad.* U.S. Department of Commerce, Bureau of Foreign and Domestic Commerce, Specialties Division, the Motion Picture Section. Washington, DC 1926.

———. *Commerce Reports.* Washington, DC.

———. *Daily Consular and Trade Reports.* Washington, DC.

———. *Trade Information Bulletin.* Washington, DC.

———. *Review of Foreign and Domestic Markets.* Washington, DC.

United States Department of State. *Trade Agreement between the United States and France: Analysis of the General Provisions and Reciprocal Concessions.* Washington, DC, 1936.

———. *Reciprocal Trade: Agreement and Protocol of Signature Between the United States of America and France.* Executive Agreement Series, No. 136. Washington, DC, 1939.

United States Federal Trade Commission. *Federal Trade Commission v. Famous Players-Lasky, et al..* Washington, DC, 1921. Complaint no. 835.

———. "Motion Picture Industry." *Trade Practice Conferences.* Washington, DC, 1928 and 1929.

———. *Webb-Pomerene Associations: A 50-Year Review.* Washington, DC, 1967.

United States National Archives and Record Administration. *Diplomatic Records: A Select Catalog of National Archives Microfilm Publications.* Washington, DC, 1986.

United States Temporary National Economic Committee. *The Motion Picture Industry: A Pattern of Control.* A Study made for the Temporary National Economic Committee, Seventy-Sixth Congress, Third Session, Pursuant to Public Resolution No. 113 (Seventy-Fifth Congress) Authorizing and Directing a Select Committee to Make a Full and Complete Study and Investigation with Respect to the Concentration of Economic Power in, and Financial Control over, Production and Distribution of Goods and Services. 76th Congress, 3rd Session. Washington, DC, 1941.

Valenti, Jack. *International Communications and Information.* Hearings before the Subcommittee on International Operations, Committee on Foreign Relations, United States Senate, 95th Congress, 1st Session, 1977. Washington: GPO, 1977, pp. 211–12.

———. "Webb-Pomerene: The Great U.S. Ally in the Battle for World Trade: Delivered before the First National Conference on Export Trading Companies, Sponsored by U.S. Chamber of Commerce, Washington, DC September 30, 1980." *Vital Speeches of the Day,* 47: 1 Oct. 15, 1980): 26–28.

Vasey, Ruth. *The World According to Hollywood.* Exeter: University of Exeter Press, 1997.

———. "The World-Wide Spread of Cinema." In Geoffrey Nowell-Smith, *The Oxford History of World Cinema.* Oxford: Oxford University Press, 1996, pp. 53–62.

Verdier, Daniel. *Democracy and International Trade: Britain, France, and the United States, 1860–1990.* Princeton, NJ: Princeton Uinversity Press, 1994.

Vincendeau, Ginette. "The Popular Art of French Cinema." In Geoffrey Nowell-Smith, *The Oxford History of World Cinema.* Oxford: Oxford University Press, 1996, pp. 344–53.

Wasko, Janet. *Movies and Money.* Norwood, NJ: Ablex Publishing Corporation, 1982.

Werking, Richard Hume. *The Master Architects Building the United States Foreign Service, 1890–1913.* Lexington: University of Kentucky Press 1977.

Williams, William A. *Tragedy of American Diplomacy.* New York: Dell, 1962.

Whittlesey, Charles R. *National Interest and International Cartels.* New York, 1946.

Wilcox, Clair. *Public Policies Toward Business.* Rev. ed. Homewood, IL: Richard D. Irvin, 1960.

Williams, Alan. *The Republic of Images: A History of French Filmmaking.* Cambridge: Harvard University Press, 1992.

Wredlund, Bertil & Rolf Lindfors. *Långfilm i Sverige.* Stockholm, 1991. Vol. 1: 1910–1919. Vol. 2: 1920–1929. Vol. 3: 1930–1939. (Index of motion pictures censored in Sweden.)

INDEX